China Insights

This book series collects and presents cutting-edge studies on various issues that have emerged during the process of China's social and economic transformation, and promotes a comprehensive understanding of the economic, political, cultural and religious aspects of contemporary China. It brings together academic endeavors by contemporary Chinese researchers in various social science and related fields that record, interpret and analyze social phenomena that are unique to Chinese society, its reforms and rapid transition. This series offers a key English-language resource for researchers and students in China studies and related subjects, as well as for general interest readers looking to better grasp today's China. The book series is a cooperation project between Springer and China Social Sciences Press.

More information about this series at http://www.springer.com/series/13591

Yuyan Zhang · Weijiang Feng

Peaceful Development Path in China

中国社会科学出版社
CHINA SOCIAL SCIENCES PRESS

Springer

Yuyan Zhang
Institute of World Economics and Politics
Chinese Academy of Social Science
Beijing, China

Weijiang Feng
Institute of World Economics and Politics
Chinese Academy of Social Sciences
Beijing, China

Translated by Hao Xu, Linlin Xie

Sponsored by Chinese Fund for the Humanities and Social Sciences

ISSN 2363-7579 ISSN 2363-7587 (electronic)
China Insights
ISBN 978-981-13-1437-7 ISBN 978-981-13-1439-1 (eBook)
https://doi.org/10.1007/978-981-13-1439-1

Jointly published with China Social Sciences Press, Beijing, China

The print edition is not for sale in China Mainland. Customers from China Mainland please order the print book from: China Social Sciences Press.

Library of Congress Control Number: 2018947468

This Springer imprint is published by the registered company Springer Nature Singapore Pte Ltd.
The registered company address is: 152 Beach Road, #21-01/04 Gateway East, Singapore 189721, Singapore

Series Foreword

Since the Opium War, modern China has come under attack and been bullied for its backwardness; this cultural circumstance has given many Chinese people a psychological inferiority complex, as China has lagged behind other countries technologically, institutionally, and culturally. Efforts to change the situation in which Western countries were strong but China was weak and to revitalize China needed to start with cultural criticism and culture renovation. Therefore, the Chinese people turned their eyes to the outside world and learned from Japan, Europe, the USA, and even Soviet Russia. We have always been overwhelmed by stress and anxiety and have had a burning desire to reverse the state of being bullied as a result of underdevelopment, poverty, and weakness and to catch up with and surpass the Western powers. In pursuing the more than one-hundred-year-old dream of building a powerful country and reviving China, we have focused on understanding and learning from others, but seldom, if ever, have others learned from and understood us. This has not greatly changed in the course of modernization since China's reform and opening-up in 1978. The translation and introduction of many Western works in the 1980 and 1990s is a very good example. This is the history of the Chinese people's understanding of the relationship between China and the rest of the world since the beginning of modern times.

At the same time, in pursuing the dream of turning China into a powerful country and rejuvenating it through material (technological) criticism, institutional criticism, and cultural criticism, the Chinese people have struggled to find a path that would make the country prosperous and the people strong while preventing the country from being ruined and the race from being destroyed. This path first represents a thought, a banner, and a soul. The key issue has been what kind of thought, banner, and soul can save the country, making it prosperous and the people strong. For more than one hundred years, the Chinese people have constantly carried out experiments and attempts amidst humiliation, failure, and anxiety. They have experienced failure in adopting advanced Western technology and thought on the basis of safeguarding China's feudal system and practicing a constitutional monarchy after the collapse of the Western capitalist political path and a great setback in worldwide socialism in the early 1990s. The Chinese people ultimately embarked on a path toward a successful revolution with national independence and liberation; in particular, they have adopted a path leading to the socialist modernization of China—a road toward socialism with Chinese characteristics—by combining the theoretical logic of scientific socialism with the historical logic of China's social development. After more than 30 years of reform and opening-up, China's socialist market economy has rapidly developed; tremendous achievements have been made in economic, political, cultural, and social constructions; comprehensive national strength, cultural soft power, and international influence have substantially improved; and a great success has been achieved in socialism with Chinese characteristics. Although the latter project has not yet become full-fledged, its systems and institutions have basically taken shape. After more than one hundred years of pursuing dreams, China is rising among the nations of the world with a greater degree of confidence in the path it has chosen, the theory it has adopted, and the institutions it has created.

Meanwhile, we should be aware that given the long-standing cognition and cultural psychology of learning from Western countries; we seldom take the initiative in showcasing ourselves—historical China and current China in reality—to the world, though China has emerged as a great world power. Due to a deeply rooted view that "Western countries are strong and China is weak," developed through Western-Chinese cultural exchanges, Western people and nations seldom have a sense of Chinese history or the current developments in China, let alone an understanding of China's developmental path and such in-depth issues as the scientificity and effectiveness of China's theory and institutions or their unique value for and contributions to human civilization. As self-recognition is not displayed, the "China Collapse Theory," "China Threat Theory," "China State Capitalism," and other so-called theories coined by certain people with ulterior motives and differing political views have been widely spread.

During our development, based on "crossing the river by feeling the stones," we have paid attention to learning from Western countries, understanding the world and learning to know ourselves through Western experience and discourse but have neglected self-recognition and efforts to let others know us. When we strive to become part of the world in a more tolerant and friendly way, we are not objectively, truly understood. Therefore, we should describe the path to the success of socialism with Chinese characteristics, tell Chinese stories, disseminate Chinese experiences, use international expressions to show a real China to the world, and help people around the world realize that the Western manner of modernization is not the endpoint of human historical evolution and that socialism with Chinese characteristics is also a valuable treasure of human thought. This is undoubtedly a very important task for an academic cultural researcher with a sense of justice and responsibility.

In this connection, the Chinese Academy of Social Sciences organized its top-notch experts and scholars and several external experts to write the China Insights series. This series not only provides an overview of China's path, theories, and institutions but also objectively describes China's current development in the areas of political institutions, human rights, the rule of law, the economic system, finance, social governance, social security, population policies, values, religious faith, ethnic policies, rural issues, urbanization, industrialization, ecology, ancient civilization, literature, art, etc., thus depicting China in a way that helps readers visualize these topics.

We hope that this series will help domestic readers more correctly understand the course of the more than 100 years of China's modernization and more rationally look at current difficulties, enhance the urgency for and national confidence in comprehensively intensifying reform, build a consensus on reform and development, and gather strength in this regard, as well as deepen foreign readers' understanding of China, thus fostering a better international environment for China's development.

January 2014 Zhao Jianying

Foreword: The Metaphor of "Long"

What will become of the world with a powerful China? This is a question increasingly occupying those concerned with global affairs in recent years. One way to look at it is to explore the Chinese national intention and act by understanding the Chinese national traits and the characteristics of its culture. Hans Morgenthau, the worldly-renowned realist theorist of international relations, once made an insightful and keen observation of the Russian, the American, the British, and the German. He remarks that the "elementary force and persistence" of the Russians, the individual initiative and inventiveness of the Americans, the undogmatic common sense of the British, and the discipline and thoroughness of the Germans are some of the qualities which will manifest themselves, for better or for worse, in all the individual and collective activities in which the members of a nation may engage.[1] According to Morgenthau, national traits such as these are permanent to the degree that even a thorough change in the social and economic structure, in political leadership and institutions, and in the ways of life and thought cannot be able to affect them.

Call Me "Long"

In Morgenthau's times, China did not attract much attention as it does now, hence we cannot know for sure his idea about the national character of China. But from the perspective of the Chinese people, the totem of dragon may serve to give the spirit of the Chinese civilization a best illustration. The Chinese people see themselves as the descendants of dragon. They have dragon boat racing for the Dragon Boat Festival (the 5th day of the 5th lunar month), and dragon dancing for the Chinese New Year and various opening ceremonies. A credit card issued by China

[1]Morgenthau, H. J. 2006. *Politics Among Nations: The Struggle for Power and Peace*, 6th edition, revised by Kenneth W. Thompson. Peking University Press. p. 181.

Construction Bank, one of the four major banks of China, is justifiably called the Dragon Card. Dragon is an important figure in Chinese mythology. In times of the remote past when the dawn of science has not shone, the Chinese people would pray to the Dragon King for rain when in drought (Dragon King Temples can still be found in many places). Among the 12 animals marking the Chinese Zodiac, only dragon is fictional. The symbol of dragon is deeply entwined with the life of the Chinese throughout the ages. In a manner of speaking, the totem holds the key to uncovering the Chinese national character and to decoding the gene of the Chinese culture.

However, the symbol of dragon tends to convey a culturally misleading message. The Chinese character "龙" is literally translated as *dragon* in English, but what the word stands for differs widely from the Chinese Dragon in both appearance and spirit. A better choice might be to borrow the Chinese pronunciation for "龙", that is "Long". The translation is not that different from understanding China as porcelain material, but China as the ancient Eastern country. Besides sounding alike, "Long" also has an essential property of being long, as shown by the Chinese idiom "you can see the head of a Long but not the tail (the idiom is used to describe one's secretive movement and trace)." Other than that, the image of Long can be diverse. One image shows it as possessing a horse head and a snake tail, while another represents it as possessing "camel-like head, antler-like horns, rabbit-like eyes, bull-like ears, snake-like neck, clam-like belly, carp-like scales, eagle-like claws and tiger-like palms." In a word, the image of Long integrates the features of many animals.

In contrast, *dragon* means a different thing. According to the *Webster Dictionary*, dragon is "a mythical animal usually represented as a monstrous winged and scaly serpent or saurian with a crested head and enormous claws." It may also mean "an ancient serpent", "a violent, combative, or very strict person", and "something or someone formidable or baneful."[2] The *Oxford Dictionary* words it as "a mythical monster like a giant reptile. In European tradition the dragon is typically fire-breathing and tends to symbolize chaos or evil…"[3]

In the Western culture, *dragon* has some well-known connotations. Notably, dragon is related to enormous treasure, and usually serves as its guardian. For instance, in Greek mythology, a hundred-headed dragon, which Heracles kills, guards the Garden of the Hesperides.[4] Vast as the wealth is, the dragon bears no loss. In the English epic *Beowulf*, a dragon will, for the loss of a treasure, mete out cruel punishment to all the people in its vicinity.[5] It reflects the dragon's greediness and cruelty. Besides, dragon also stands for strong power, while the power more often than not involves evil. In mythologies, dragons usually stand against heroes,

---

[2] http://www.merriam-webster.com/.

[3] http://oxforddictionaries.com/.

[4] Ogden, D. 2013. *Dragons, Serpents, and Slayers in the Classical and Early Christian Worlds: A Sourcebook*. Oxford University Press, pp. 57–60.

[5] Gummere, Francis B. 2008. *Beowulf*. Wildside Press LLC., p. 68.

and eventually fall in their hands. As discussed by Kissinger in *On China*, the Western approach treats "history as a process of modernity achieving a series of absolute victories over evil and backwardness…."[6] And dragon embodies such evil and backwardness.

The image and symbolic meaning of Long is an entire different story. Asking a Western kid for his impression of dragon, you are likely to get a more or less similar picture: serpent-looking; emerald in color and could be otherwise sometimes; with metallic hard skin and four legs; winged and fanged; fire-breathing; living in a cave; guarding some treasure; man-eating; always ending up slain by a knight or hero.[7] If the same question is posed to a Chinese kid, the answer will be very different. The images that come into his mind might be dragon boats of the Dragon Boat Festival, the dragon robe sported by emperors in TV dramas, and the Dragon King who can do nothing with Sun Wukong, the Monkey King in Chinese mythology. What is for sure is that he will never come up with anything related to cruelty and evil.

To most Chinese, Long stands for a fully legitimate deity within the god and man order. It is different from dragon or Satan, who goes against God and breaks order. In China, with the dissemination of Buddhism, the Dragon King is believed to rule all oceans and waters. In a way, the Dragon King of East Sea corresponds to Poseidon, the God of the Sea. However, the Dragon King of East Sea does not rule the oceans alone. His brothers have respective control over West Sea, South Sea, and North Sea. Then the Dragon King of East Sea is not the supreme ruler. In the famous fantasy *A Journey to the West*, the Dragon King of Jing River once changed the raining timetable and rainfall set up by the Jade Emperor, which is severely punished by law and cost its life. Another episode narrates that the Dragon King of East Sea stood opposed to the hero Sun Wukong so as to ensure natural order, while Sun Wukong is the rebellious order-breaker. After Sun Wukong turned into a conformist, the Dragon King provided lots of help for his journey to the West for Buddhist scriptures, even to the point of assigning his heir to transform into White Dragon Horse to actually participate in the journey. We can conclude that to the Chinese, the family of dragon gods are upholders of and contributors to the legitimate order.

Second, Long maintains an amiable relation with human leaders and common people. As the legend goes, a winged Long once helped the Yellow Emperor suppress rebellions,[8] and helped Yu the Great, who is the first emperor of Xia Dynasty, to tame the flood.[9] To the common people, the Dragon King is in charge

---

[6]Kissinger, H. 2011. *On China*. New York: the Penguin Press, p. 31.

[7]Ogden, D. 2013. *Dragons, Serpents, and Slayers in the Classical and Early Christian Worlds: A Sourcebook*. Oxford University Press, p. 1.

[8]"Chi You attacked the Yellow Emperor. The Yellow Emperor asked a winged Long to fight it in the battle field of Jizhou." See *North Da Huang* of *Shan Hai Ching*.

[9]In *Heavenly Questions of the Songs of the South*, a question concerning Yu the Great's feat of taming the flood goes like this "what did the winged Long trace on the ground? Where did the seas and rivers flow?" Hong Xingzu adds "When Yu of the Xia Dynasty tamed the flood, a winged Long drew on the land with its tail, and the waters drained." See Hong Xingzu. 1983. *Additions and Annotations to the Songs of the South*. Zhonghua Book Company, p. 91.

of rain and hence controls the weather essential for crops. When in drought, people lead by a local gentleman come to Dragon King Temple to pray for rain. At other times, they will hold activities such as sacrifice, market trade, and entertainment in the vicinity of the temple on a regular basis.

Thirdly, Long is closely related to the royal power. The first biographical history of China, *Shi Ji*, records that ancient emperors (such as the Yellow Emperor and the Yan Emperor) are dragons themselves[10] or share blood relationship with dragons.[11] By the Qin and Han period, Long has started to assume the symbolic role of royal power. Liu Bang, Emperor Gaozu of Han Dynasty, modeling his life story on the mythology of the Yan Emperor, claimed that his mother was possessed by a divine Long when giving birth to him. The claim aimed at heightening his authority and establishing the legitimacy of the new regime with the divine authority of Long. From the early Han Dynasty, emperors of all ages declared themselves to be the "Heir of the Real Long", and Long came to stand for the royal authority and obtain an ever more majestic image. Lastly, the Chinese Long can be infuriated sometimes, especially when its reverse scale is touched, things could be precarious. *Han Feizi* specifies the situation: the one-foot-long reverse scale under the throat of Long shall not be touched by man, or he will bear damages; correspondingly, emperors also have a reverse scale which is said to be touched when they are expostulated by officials, and under such a condition, the officials might face death penalty. Since then, the act of audacious expostulation on the part of officials is called "touching the reverse scale" of Long.

However, some recent articles and books on the development of China confuse the Chinese Long with Western dragons. They wrongly depict and characterize the traits of China in terms of the negative features conveyed by the image of Western dragons. They will say something like this: dragons are greedy, so is China as the country is devouring the raw materials,[12] energies,[13] primary products and

[10]"The Yellow Emperor Xuan Yuan has a body of Long." See *Histories of Celestial Officials* of *Shi Ji*.

[11]"A woman surnamed Wo, as wife of Shao Dian, was possessed by a divine dragon when giving birth to Yan Emperor." See *Histories of the Three Ancient Emperors* of *Shi Ji*.

[12]Laurance, W. 2012. Hungry Dragon. *Australian Geographic*, pp. 118–119.

[13]See Douglas, J. K., M. B. Nelson and K. Schwartz. 2006. *Fueling the Dragon's Flame: How China's Energy Demands Affect Its Relationships in the Middle East*. US-China Economic and Security Review Commission.

Jae-Hyung. 2002. China's Expanding Maritime Ambitions in the Western Pacific and the Indian Ocean. *Contemporary Southeast Asia*, Vol. 24, No. 3, pp. 549–568.

Klare, M. T. 2008. *Rising Powers, Shrinking Planet: The New Geopolitics of Energy*. New York: Metropolitan Books.

Navarro, P. 2011. *Death by China: Confronting the Dragon—A Global Call to Action*. New Jersey: Person Prentice Hall.

Blumenthal, D. and J. Lin. 2006. Oil Obsession: Energy Appetite Fuels Beijing's Plans to Protect Vital Sea Lines. *Armed Forces Journal*, June.

manufacture market[14] of the whole world, and China grows strong at the cost of other regions; dragons are ferocious, so is China as the country continues to enhance its threatening and increasing military power,[15] and adopts more and more aggressive diplomatic policy[16] and cyber power.[17]

Misunderstandings are usually accidentally caused rather than inherent. If unstopped, the seeds of misunderstandings may develop into disputes or even enmity. As one keen observer comments, European and North American newspapers have regularly fostered sentiments that portray China as an insatiable and aggressive.[18] As a matter of fact, the correspondence or equivalence between the Eastern Long and the Western evil-related dragon was recently constructed and disseminated by Western missionaries. The construction and its dissemination were set against a particular background: the mutual non-respect and non-tolerance between the East and the West led to misunderstandings, which in turn were actualized as confrontation. Only with misunderstandings clarified can a reconciliation be achieved, and only based on mutual understanding and empathy can the expediency of peace be eliminated, wars be stopped and the world step towards perpetual peace.

The Origin of Long

The image of Long has already taken shape as early as the late Neolithic Age. The ancients had many descriptions for Long. One had it that Long is a winged snake with no legs, but capable of flying, another differentiated several types of Long: the scaled Long is called *Jiao* Long, horned is *Qiu* Long, hornless *Chi* Long, winged is *Ying* Long.[19] Scholars have proposed various kinds of theories concerning the prototypical animal of Long, such as alligator, whale, lizard, horse, bear, and

---

[14]Gallagher, K. and R. Porzecanski. 2010. *The Dragon in the Room: China and the Future of Latin American Industrialization*. Stanford University Press, p. 1.

[15]Timperlake, E. and W. C. Triplett II. 2002. *Red Dragon Rising: Communist China's Military Threat to America*. Regnery Publishing.

[16]Swaine, M. D. 2010. Perceptions of an assertive China. *China Leadership Monitor*, 32(2).

[17]See Gomez, M. A. 2013. Awaken the Cyber Dragon: China's Cyber Strategy and its Impact on ASEAN (pp. 252–261). Presented at the Second International Conference on Cyber Security, Cyber Peacefare and Digital Forensic (CyberSec2013), The Society of Digital Information and Wireless Communication. Hjortdal, M. 2011. China's Use of Cyber Warfare: Espionage Meets Strategic Deterrence. *Journal of Strategic Security*, 4(2). Clarke, R. 2011. China's cyberassault on America. *Wall Street Journal*, June 15.

[18]Mayer, M. and J. Wübbeke. 2013. Understanding China's International Energy Strategy. *The Chinese Journal of International Politics*, Autumn 6 (3).

[19]Qian, Mingci. 2007. *Mythologies and Legends of Ancient China*. Commercial Press, pp. 37–38.

thunderbolt,[20] and the most widely known is snake.[21] Regardless of the prototypical animal, most scholars agree that Long integrates many totems, and that the integrating and evolving process is also the process of integration and evolution of different clans.

The top priority for the Chinese ancients was food and then plantation. The timing for seeding directly affected the harvest. The ancients, with limited relevant knowledge, had difficulties in grasping the rules of climate, but in practice, they found that everything has its timing. Migrant birds flew to the south and back in a particular period of time of the year, snakes crawled out of holes when it turned warm, fish emerged in the river on a particular day, animals showed up at a particular time. Such coming and going, presence and absence of birds, snakes, fish, and deer provided a specific reference frame for the people to set up a calendar or solar terms, which aimed at guiding the seeding and tilling so as to ensure and enhance agricultural produce. The calendar established in such a manner is termed phenological calendar.[22] These time-marking animals are then called "phonological objects". As they brought good harvest to the people, a certain divinity started to be associated with them, and gradually they assumed the role of clan totem. Long-term exchange and communication among the clans resulted in their ultimate integration. For the sake of social stability or that of the economy of integration, totems for all the clans shall be taken into consideration. That may be why a snake started to sport scales, eagle claws, cattle head, goat horn and lizard tail. Eventually, a mixed totem came into being, the Long, which was nowhere to be found in the real world.

The integration of clans might involve military conquests, but in most cases, was achieved via negotiations, or at least settled via negotiations.[23] The situation can be seen in the relation of the Yellow Emperor and the Yan Emperor, in which both victor, the Yellow Emperor, and the defeated, the Yan Emperor, are considered the ancestors of the Chinese people. Military conquest begets hatred and enmity, no real reconciliation and integrated can grow out of a life-or-death condition. Only with negotiations of a voluntary nature can a redistribution of political power, religious authority and economic interests be achieved, and then sincerely carried out by all the members of the newly integrated clan. In this manner, interests of separate clans are identified with those of the whole tribe, giving rise to Incentive

[20]He Xin holds that the primary prototype of Long is alligator, and the secondary is whale. See He, Xin. 2002. *Long: Mythology and Truth*. Current Affairs Press.

[21]Wen, Yiduo was the first to come up with the theory in a systematic way. See Qian, Mingci. 2007. *Mythologies and Legends of Ancient China*. Commercial Press, p. 38.

[22]China is the first country in the world to establish and apply phenological calendar. *Xia Xiao Zheng*, a book of 3000-year history, is a phenological calendar recording phenological, climatic, astronomic, agricultural and political affairs. The Twenty-Four solar terms and the Seventy-Two Pentads are also phonological calendars. Since the Northern Wei Dynasty, the Seventy-Two Pentads were adopted as a national calendar.

[23]Sheng, Hong. 2000. The birth of Long: a political-economic story. *Du Shu* 12.

Compatibility. On the one hand, separate clans may retain their own totems and ancestor worship. On the other hand, a lord of common domination, who holds the totem of Long, is recognized. In the oldest Chinese political scripture *Shang Shu* (*the Book of History*), the process discussed above is called "to harmonize ("和谐" as in Chinese) all nations". That is what people call *he* ("和" or harmony) later.

In fact, the character "和" in ancient China stands for a wooden instrument, and "谐" means the organic cooperation among different instruments of an orchestra. Four points can be derived from the etymology. First, the word shows respect for diversity. An orchestra consists of various kinds of instruments, or their music would not be colorful and expressive. Second, it values equality. All instruments in an orchestra have their specific role to play. It makes no sense to say that one instrument occupies a position more important than another. Third, it manifests common interest. The performance of an orchestra has everything to do with the reputation of all performers, and even with their rewards. In a manner of speaking, each has a stake in the success of another. Fourth, it reveres cooperation. Without coordinated action based on cooperation or team work, no potential common interest can be achieved.

To sum up, the formative process of Long shows or at least suggests a major feature of the Chinese civilization, that is, inclusiveness in the sense of respect for diversity and dedication to equality. In a word, Long symbolizes the collective aspiration of the Chinese people to "harmonize all nations" or a "harmonious world".

China's "harmonizing all nations" is a special case in the way of expanding civilization. Quite different ways are adopted in Africa as reflected in the development of their totems. A case in point is the kingdom of Foumban, now 370 kilometers north of Yaounde, the capital of Cameroon. The articles contained in the museum of the Foumban Royal Palace provide us an inkling of the way of expansion for African tribes. The two totems of Foumban, double-headed snake and spider, signifying power and wisdom respectively, belong to the Foumban people alone, while totems of those conquered in the founding of a unified kingdom, such as lion, goshawk, and elephant, are trophies on display in the Palace.[24]

"Harmonizing all nations" may not be an accidental choice. It may result from the inability of a single clan to provide necessary public service under the geographical, ecological, and political conditions specific to ancient China. For instance, when preys were ferocious or hunting conditions are hard, cooperation and coordination between clans became necessary to develop more sophisticated ways of organization and more advanced hunting techniques, and to enlarge the scope of hunting. Severe natural conditions also necessitated large-scale cooperation to accomplish public projects aiming at ameliorating the environment or

---

[24] Zhang, Yuyan. 2003. Double-headed snake, spider and dragon. *Du Shu* 8.

preventing natural disasters.[25] It was likely for ancient China to face the latter situation. Deluge legends feature many civilizations. While the Bible story and the Sumerian legends record human ancestors building ark to preserve species under the auspices of God, the Chinese legends have a human hero leading the people of all clans to accomplish flood-taming projects, such as building dams to block off floods or opening channels to drain floods. It can be taken to mean that the people in the ancient oriental world had already learnt to provide public service by "harmonizing all nations". The concept is encoded in the DNA of the Chinese civilization with indelible influence on the latter-day Chinese state politics and world view.

According to Francis Fukuyama, "the chief driver of Chinese state formation was not the need to create grand irrigation projects, nor the rise of a charismatic religious leader, but unrelenting warfare."[26] As his citation of Charles Tilly, "war made the state, and the state made war", is meant to characterize European states, its application to China might be mistaken. Admittedly, before Yu the Great tamed the flood, there were wars, such as that between the Yellow Emperor and Chi You, contributing to a common community, but by no means can the war be viewed as the origin of such a community (and its spirit). According to *Shi Ji*, the war followed as a result of "the decline of the Shennong regime" (i.e., failing to provide sufficient public service). While wars may make states in history, states are never a political unit widely acknowledged in the oriental world. Instead, *tianxia*, or "the land under heaven" is adopted wherein public service and a charismatic leader ("a sacred king") providing the service are the nucleus and the soul of the community. It is usually for the lack of public service or a charismatic leader that wars break out.

In short, the Chinese civilization features a unification between diversity and integration, and this is symbolized by the origin of Long, which means peaceful coexistence of different cultures with each retaining its individuality while being integrated to the totality.

Long: A Renewed View of China's Path

Efforts are made here to tell the concept of the Chinese Long apart from that of dragon, and to explore the anthropological and folklore value of Long to the Chinese people. There are two reasons for the efforts.

[25] Wittfogel distinguishes two types of society, namely, nonhydraulic society as represented by Western Europe and North America and hydraulic society as represented by China. Hydraulic projects require nationwide coordination, which leads to oriental despotism. See Wittfogel, A.K. 1957. *Oriental Despotism*. Yale University Press, p. 44.

[26] Fukuyama, F. 2012. *The Origins of Political Order*. Farrar, Straus and Giroux, p. 107.

In the first place, China holds vast historical and cultural assets, which have a subtle effect on the current international conduct of China. The Chinese Long ranks among the first rate of such assets. However, assets of such a kind never show their influence in a conspicuous or direct way, but in a manner similar to the subconscious in Freud's psychoanalysis. But for a detailed and thorough interpretation, nothing could be known to a conscious mind. Moreover, the confusions between Long and dragon should be eliminated, otherwise, the understanding of the present-day China and its path of development may always run the risk of being twisted.

In the second place, it is an opportune moment to clarify the aforesaid misunderstanding. Generally speaking, we only learn what we want to learn, and what we want to learn is always from those respected by us or beneficial to us, or at least from those considered to be on a par with us. Missionaries such as Matteo Ricci, the self-styled Western Confucian, held respect for the ancient Chinese culture, which provided the basis for equality necessary for in-depth dialogue between East and West. When human history entered the modern era, the Western world has made tremendous achievements, while China became ever more conservative and declined as a result, not only losing its leading position of the world, but also falling into the hard situation of lagging behind and being invaded. Naturally, China of such a condition could not wish to gain understanding and respect for a common Westerner. Since its reform and opening-up, the economy of China grows at a high speed. The country is on the road to return to the center of the world. An increasing number of Westerners start to be willing to understand what China thinks, says and does.

The concept of Long suggests at least three key points of understanding the present-day China and its path.

The first point is that China, as the formative process of Long suggests, tends to adopt cooperation-oriented integration in foreign affairs. Compared with confrontation-oriented or conquest-oriented integration, it is more inclusive and costs less, and an integration proceeding in such a manner will be more acceptable to the parties involved. And it is in sharp contrast with the competition-oriented integrated as familiar to the West. While European economic integration enjoys a high level of cooperation, it essentially "exposes regional or national governments to competition" via a common market, economic policy and administrative organs, and the economic integration of Europe results in "factual or potential increase of competition."[27] Lying behind the cooperation based on an alliance or a principle of subsidiarity is still the age-old principle of free competition first. The vulnerability of the competition-oriented economic cooperation will emerge under external impact. For fear of violating the principle of subsidiarity, the European Union adopted an ambiguous stance during the American subprime crisis, failing to take proactive measures to stem its development, and a global economic crisis ensued.

[27] Jacques Pelkmans. 2001. European Integration: Methods and Economic Analysis. *Financial Times/Prentice Hall*, p. 3.

"When the Greek crisis began to intensify in February 2010, the Greek government was hesitant about adopting further consolidation measures, and European partners dithered over making a loan to Greece and agreeing to IMF involvement. As the crisis intensified, policymakers started to blame 'speculation', or suggest *ad hoc* measures, such as banning certain financial products and setting up a European credit rating agency. When policymakers are busy with these kinds of redundant activities and provide conflicting signals about their intentions, markets are likely to draw the conclusion that policymakers do not have the means to resolve the crisis."[28] Moreover, competition-oriented integration also suffers from hindering a powerful nation from rendering necessary help to the weak. When a crisis breaks out, the powerful, with its obligations fulfilled, will question the necessity of helping another nation and tend to consider such a nation as unsalvageable. For instance, Germany showed their reluctance to make a commitment to provide direct monetary assistance to Greece in the European sovereign debt crisis.[29]

The conduct of Germany contrasts sharply with that of China in the Asian financial crisis of 1997–1998, who took immediate and effective actions to fight it. Immediately upon the crisis, China made a promise not to devalue its currency, RMB, and provided assistance of various kinds to countries like Thailand and Indonesia through bilateral channels within the framework of IMF. The especially disastrous floods of 1998 notwithstanding, China persisted in its commitment and assistance. Quite different from the regional economic cooperation led by the Europe and the United States, which focuses on competition, the economic integration of the East Asian countries clearly assumes cooperation orientation, in which China plays a special and pivotal part. In the framework agreement between China and the Association of Southeastern Asian Nations (ASEAN), there is an early harvest program, which allows both parties to reduce or exempt customs duty on products of certain industries upon their preference, and to adopt policies to obtain direct interests in trade and investment facilitation.[30] To China, the early harvest program is more an expression of good will to cooperation, building up confidence on both sides in the follow-up comprehensive cooperation, than a means to gain benefits. China, at the request of the ASEAN countries, has made great concessions on opening agricultural sections, in which the ASEAN countries enjoy competitive advantages over China.[31]

---

[28] Darvas, Z. Forthcoming. Fiscal federalism in crisis: Lessons for Europe from the US. Bruegel Policy Contribution, June 10, 2010.

[29] Wielaard, R. 2010. Greece Debt Crisis: Germany Holding up European Union Bailout. *The Huffington Post,* March 19, 2010.

[30] Medalla, E. and J. D. Balboa. 2007. The Impact of ASEAN-China FTA Early Harvest Program: the Case of the Philippines with Focus on Short-run Effects on the Agriculture Sector. *Research Paper Series*, available at http://ideas.repec.org/b/phd/rpseri/rps_2007-01.html.

[31] Ko, A. H. Not for Political Domination: China's Foreign Economic Policy towards Vietnam, Singapore, and Malaysia in the Open Era. Available at http://theses.gla.ac.uk/2235/.

The second point, as suggested by the role of Long in Chinese mythologies, is that China does not and will not want to destroy or overturn the world order. Long and its family in the mythologies of ancient China generally perform the role of guardians for the current order, from which they gain enough benefits. In a similar manner, China, as a major beneficiary and shareholder of the current world order, tends to actively safeguard it so as to ensure its own peace and prosperity and that of the world.

In the report of the 18th National Congress of the Communist Party of China (CPC), it is stated that "China will continue to keep in mind both the interests of the Chinese people and the common interests of the people of all countries, get more actively involved in international affairs, play its due role of a major responsible country, and work jointly with other countries to meet global challenges"; that "China upholds the principle of balancing rights with obligations. We will take an active part in global economic governance"; that "we will continue to promote friendship and partnership with our neighbors, consolidate friendly relations and deepen mutually beneficial cooperation with them, and ensure that China's development will bring more benefits to our neighbors"; that "we will actively participate in multilateral affairs, support the United Nations, G20, the Shanghai Cooperation Organization, BRICS and other multilateral organizations in playing an active role in international affairs, and work to make the international order and system more just and equitable." In September 2016, Chinese President Xi Jinping stresses in his keynote speech at the opening ceremony of the Hangzhou B20 Business Summit that "the new mechanisms and initiatives launched by China are not intended to reinvent the wheels or target any other country. Rather, they aim to complement and improve the current international mechanisms to achieve win-win cooperation and common development. China's opening drive is not a one-man show. Rather, it is an invitation open to all. It is a pursuit not to establish China's own sphere of influence, but to support common development of all countries. It is meant to build not China's own backyard garden, but a garden shared by all countries."

These remarks make it clear that China seeks neither to challenge the leading position of the United States in global governance, nor to establish a new international mechanism opposite to the existing one or aiming at substituting it. Rather, China is willing to stick to the current system and shoulder the responsibility suiting its status and capability.[32] The choice of China is a lesson learned from the past: China is a major beneficiary of the public service provided by the current international system. There are "selective incentives" involved, namely, participation in collective activities generates more expected interests than nonparticipation, and nonparticipation brings more opportunity cost.[33] Consequently, China has consistently supported the role of the international system of rules and regulations and put a huge amount of resources in it. A power game, disrupting the mechanism of

---

[32] He, Fan, Feng Weijiang and Xu Jin. 2013. Challenges of global governance and the strategies of China. *World Economics and Politics*, 7.

[33] Zhang, Yuyan. 2013. Global governance: Balance between common interests and conflicting interests. *IPER Observations*, No. 1322.

international community hence reducing the efficiency of international public service, would directly bring to a lower level China's benefits from international public service, and at the same time, would lead to a squander of resources already invested in relevant areas, which could hardly be withdrawn.

The third lesson that can be learned from Long is that, as a Long does not allow its reverse scale to be touched, China has its own bottom line on certain affairs in international cooperation, bearing no tampering. These affairs concern the core interests of China. Some scholars accuse China of being strategically blurry, lacking a negative list of such affairs. And some, from the perspective of the United States, classify the concerns on which the United States may conflict with China. For example, Amitai Etzioni, a professor of international relations in George Washington University, classifies conducts unbearable to China but acceptable to the United States based on a system of traffic lights: "A red light that warns against the use of force by China to change the status quo; a yellow light for tolerating its increased influence in the region, and a green light for China's drive to secure the flow of energy and raw materials it needs."[34] From the perspective of China, it means that to expand influence and obtain energy and raw materials are satisfactory, but to incite war is unacceptable. In fact, since China benefits a lot from the current international system, it does neither want nor need to change the status quo by force. China is a nation with patience and confidence. As its comprehensive power continuously increases, it is natural that China will shoulder more international responsibilities and assume more influence in the region.

The report of the 18th Party Congress makes a clear statement about "reverse scale": "We are firm in our resolve to uphold China's sovereignty, security and development interests and will never yield to any outside pressure." Sovereignty, security and development interests can be considered the three major pillars or factors in foreign affairs with China in the years to come. The three national interests complement each other, and neither of them can be dispensed with. Development interests can hardly be ensured if sovereignty and security are in jeopardy. It should also be pointed out that among the three, to uphold development interests has a more fundamental or decisive significance. Without development, sovereignty and security may only be a carte blanche. As the report says, development provides the fundamental solution to all issues of China. The development interests of China in foreign affairs concentrate on the following three interrelated areas: market, technology, and bulk commodity. International market provides a platform for China to give full play to its absolute and relative advantages, and also an important route to enhance employment and capital accumulation. There is a gap in economic development between China and developed Western countries. China is now facing the bottleneck in its economic transformation and upgrading. The country still occupies the middle or low end on the continuum of international

[34]Etzioni, A. Accommodating China. *Survival: Global Politics and Strategy*, 2013, 2(55), 45–60.

division of labor. All these are concerned with backward technology. In the country's efforts to catch up, one resourceful way is to learn and borrow from developed countries, purchasing their advanced technology. In the process of modernization for China, there is a big supply–demand gap in energy and resources, and importation serves as a basic way to fill the gap. As is often said, China needs the world. It largely points at the above three development interests. The fundamental method to ensure development interests is to safeguard an open and just trade and investment system. If China were isolated by the world, the result would be disastrous to both China and the world.[35]

Beijing, China
August 2016

Yuyan Zhang

[35] Zhang, Yuyan, 2013. Setting up foreign strategies of China based on its national interests. *Contemporary International Relations*, 10.

Contents

List of Figures

List of Tables

List of Charts

Chapter 1
The China Miracle: Facts and Process

Karl Marx and Fredrick Engels write in the *Communist Manifesto*, "the bourgeoisie, during its rule of scare one hundred years, has created more massive and more colossal productive forces than have all preceding generations together." Now in a similar tone a scholar claims that "[t]he country has accomplished in three decades what many developing nations have taken half a century or more to achieve."[1] The statement does make some sense. While the country may still lag behind the United States in comprehensive terms, China is well en route to rejuvenation since its reform and opening-up, as can be seen in its material, monetary, institutional and conceptual development and achievements. The route, however, has its twists and turns, not without setbacks, which cost the whole nation fortunes and lives. Understanding the hard-won route will shed a clear light on why China cherishes so much the present situation of peace and stability.

Surpassing the United States?

The word *rejuvenation* is just right about China. The country's economy is about to restore its usual global position of the past two thousand years. This may shock those lacking a historical insight. They remain ignorant of the fact that from the beginning of the Common Era to the eve of the Opium War, the Gross Domestic Product (GDP) of China consistently accounted for more than 20% of the world.[2]

---

[1] Guthrie (2012).

[2] According to Angus Maddison's estimates adjusted for purchasing power parity (PPP), China accounted for 26.2% of the global economy in 1 A.D., 22.7% in 1000 A.D., 25% in 1500 A.D., 29.2% in 1600 A.D., 22.3% in 1700 A.D., and in 1820 A.D. reached the highest ever of 32.9%, almost a third of the overall GDP of the world. Even in 1870, a year after the Opium War, China still accounted for 17.2% of the global GDP, for all external exploitations of Western countries and internal convulsions of the Taiping Rebellion. Maddison (2006).

Y. Zhang and W. Feng, *Peaceful Development Path in China*, China Insights,
https://doi.org/10.1007/978-981-13-1439-1_1

The share rose from 2.3% only to 17.1% from 1980, a beginning year of China's reform and opening-up, to 2015. For the large part of the past twenty centuries, the current major world economies could not be comparable in volume to China. They have only obtained their current position in the recent two hundred years.

Admittedly, the above data have their limits. For example, the GDP for a long period of time is estimated in terms of purchasing power parity (PPP). As a matter of fact, GDP in preindustrial times mainly comes from materials of livelihood such as grain and textiles, while in industrial times it largely comes from materials of production such as steel and concrete. Then a preindustrial nation may not be considered more powerful than an industrialized nation, even though the GDP for the former is estimated to be higher than the latter. As can be seen from Maddison's historical economic data adopted here, China, up till the early 19th Century, accounted for a larger part of global economy than the United States, the biggest Western economy, but that is no reason to consider China to be the economic power leading all Western countries. Even so, we may still conclude that China ranked among the top economies when the world was largely preindustrial, and that when the world entered the industrial and information era, China lagged behind. Now, the country, with its fast development, is catching up, struggles to restore its usual top position of the past, and presses ahead to national rejuvenation.

It may not be an exaggeration to call the economic achievements of China in the past thirty or so years a China Miracle. The gap in economy between China and the United States continues to narrow down. In 1980, one of the beginning years of China's reform and opening-up, the economy of China, calculated with market exchange rate, only accounted for one-tenth of that of the United States. When China surpassed Japan in GDP calculated with market exchange rate in 2010, the economy of the United States was 2.52 times larger than China. The ratio was lowered to 1.96 two years later, in 2012, to 1.63 in 2015 with China's GDP standing at $10.98 trillion and that for the United Stated at $17.95 trillion. The IMF predicts that the ratio will be further lowered to 1.28 in 2021.[3]

The figure may look even more striking if it is PPP-adjusted. According to IMF World Economic Outlook Database, China's GDP (PPP-adjusted) amounted to $17.6 trillion in 2014, while the United States stood at $17.4 trillion. It indicates that with PPP-adjusted data China has already replaced the United States as the biggest economic power of the world. And it was also the first time for the United States to be overtaken as the world number one economy in more than one and a half century, since the country surpassed the Great Britain in 1872 in terms of PPP. The former Soviet Union and Japan, previous major rivals of the United States, could not match the United States in economy volume even in their prime, not to mention surpassing the country. In the mid and late 1930s, with the United States and European countries bearing the impact of a great economic crisis, the Soviet Union, exploiting the benefits of the socialist system, made a tremendous progress in economic development. Even then, the GDP of the Soviet Union at its ever high point in 1938 only accounted for 50.69% of the United States (in other years of the period, no more than 50%). In the

[3]World Economic Outlook Database, October 2014.

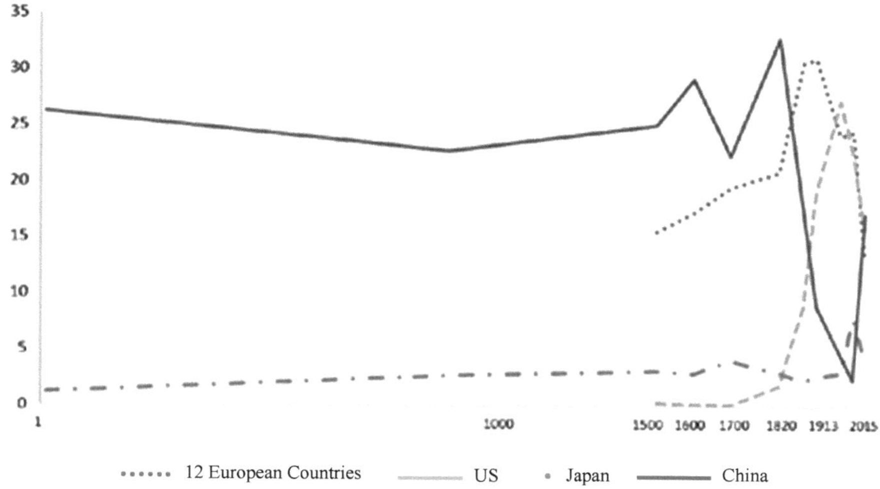

Fig. 1.1 Share of World GDP for Major Economies, 1-2015 A.D. *Note* The 12 European countries refer to Austria, Belgium, Denmark, Finland, France, Germany, Italy, Holland, Norway, Sweden, Switzerland and the Great Britain. For ease of comparison with Maddison's PPP-adjusted data (PPP can be calculated by comparing the prices of an identical good between a country and a benchmark country, that is, calculated in terms of the purchasing power of the currency of the benchmark country. Compared with the normal calculation with exchange rate, PPP can reflect a country's genuine price level of goods and services. However, estimation with exchange rate may be a better indicator for power comparison, especially in international resource mobilization, for when resources, goods and services are purchased in international market, calculations can only be made in terms of market exchange rate rather than the domestic PPP.), the data adopted for years of 1980–2015 are PPP-adjusted. *Sources* 1-1950: Maddison (2006); 1980–2015: IMF Database

1970s, the height of the Cold War era, the percentage only arrived at 44.40% (in the year of 1975). Japan, the long-time runner-up of Western economies, has a wider gap with the United States in economy volume than generally believed, even though it turned into the second largest world economy due to the downfall the Soviet Union. Since the 1980s, the idea of "Japan as No. 1" [4] became popular, and an optimistic view that "there is no need to the play the student to the United States and European countries any more" swept the Japanese economic sector. Nevertheless, the country's GDP (PPP) at its ever high point in 1991 only took up 41.42% of that of the United States, and the economy, after the bubbles of its stock market and housing industry burst, soon came into a long-term standstill (Fig. 1.1).

Some foreign media are keen to the hype about China's surpassing the United States in GDP, while some experts have a truer view of the power gap between the two countries and provide detailed technical analysis on the issue. Scholars such as Derek M. Scissors, senior research at the American Enterprise Institute, and Jeffrey Frankel, professor at John F. Kennedy School of Government, Harvard, and also member of the

[4]In the late 1970s, Harvard Professor Ezra F. Vogel published a book entitled *Japan As No.1: Lessons for America*, which turned out to be a bestseller at the time.

Council of Economic Advisors in the Clinton administration, question the report that China replaces the United States as the world's biggest economy.[5] Such questioning comes down to four points. First, based on the most recent PPP-comparison standard, the GDP of China expands by 21% compared with the old one. The increase results from a different standard, having nothing to do with the economic growth of China. Second, PPP is more appropriate to be applied to measure personal income, since it gives more weight to the prices of non-trade commodities and services, than to compare economic performance across nations. Thirdly, PPP is more suitable to measure purchasing power than economic volume. While GDP includes factors such as governmental expenditure, investment and trade as well as personal expenditure, PPP-adjusted data only take personal consumption into account. It is improper then to calculate factors of GDP other than personal consumption in terms of PPP. Fourthly, GDP is a flow concept which measures annual general product. It is unsuitable to measure economic volume. A more appropriate index would be national wealth.

As a matter of fact, Derek M. Scissors, citing the estimated data by Credit Swiss, points out that in 2013 the total sum of personal wealth of China amounts to $22 trillion, while that the United States stands at $72 trillion. Though personal wealth is by no means a comprehensive indicator, the giant gap of $50 trillion between the two countries renders the statement of China surpassing the United States dubious. He adds that according to the estimation of the Federal Reserve, the total sum of personal wealth of the United States will reach $80 trillion to the end of 2013. With public debt deducted, it will be about $65 trillion to $70 trillion. In contrast, there are many heavily debt-burdened state-owned enterprises in China, whose net wealth is hard to estimate, probably less than $10 trillion. With this in view, the total sum of personal wealth of China will amount to $30 trillion to $35 trillion, $35 trillion behind that of the United States.

Frankel proposes that when measuring the economic volume or power of China, the following questions should be answered. First, how big is the Chinese market viewed from the perspective of multinational corporations? Second, can the currency of China, RMB, challenge the status of the US dollar in international financial system? Third, how much weight does China carry in IMF and other multilateral organizations? Fourth, from the perspective of nations involved in land and sea sovereignty disputes with China, how many arms and weapons can China purchase?

Stephen G. Brooks, assistant professor at Dartmouth College, and professor William C. Wohlforth also hold that China does not have the power to challenge the United States now and for a long time to come. They propose a three-phase argument. First, similar to the idea of Derek M. Scissors, they consider the GDP as an indicator over-valuing the economic power of China. GDP is an indicator established to measure the manufacture-based economy in the mid 20th Century. Against the background of globalization, the more a nation relies on knowledge for power, the more likely GDP will be to underestimate the economic power of that nation.

[5] See Scissors (2014).
Frankel (2014).
Cohen-Setton (2014).

Moreover, GDP as a flow concept is inadequate to reflect the true economic power of a nation. They propose to apply inclusive wealth, an indicator newly released by the United Nations, instead of GDP. The indicator takes an account of three types of stock assets of a nation: manufacturing assets (such as roads, constructions and mechanical equipment), human capital (such as technology, education and health), and natural assets (such as land resources, ecological system and atmosphere). According to the indicator, the total sum of inclusive wealth of the United States amounts to $144 trillion, 4.5 times that of China, which amounts to $32 trillion. Second, there is a big gap in technological development between China and the United States, even though China approximates the United States in terms of economic volume. The situation is quite different from that in history, where a rising power tended to narrow its gap in technology with the current leading power. They adopt the number of triadic patents (i.e., those registered in the United States, Europe, and Japan) as an indicator, and point out that in 2012, nearly 14,000 such patents originated in the United States, compared with just fewer than 2,000 in China. Besides, as for articles in science and engineering-those in the top one percent of citations, the United States accounts for almost half of these articles, more than eight times of China's share. Thirdly, given that China has gained the economic power and technological capacity, the obstacles of "transforming all this latent power into the full range of systems needed for global power projection and learning how to use them" are hard to overcome.[6]

Looked back from 20 years or 30 years later, 2014 might be a year the significance of which has been underestimated. That year, the GDP (PPP-adjusted) of China surpassed that of the United States, but the two countries enjoyed a peaceful relation. This was largely a result of the Chinese government's clear understanding of its own power, and the low-profile adopted accordingly when the surpassing occurred. When the news was made open, Zhu Guangyao, Vice Minister of Finance of China, made a targeted expression on an international occasion that there is still a big gap between China and the United States in terms of the quality of economic growth. He emphasized that China is still a developing country, will continue to improve the quality of economic growth by promoting reform and opening-up and heighten the livelihood of the people.[7] Ma Jiantang, Director of the National Bureau of Statistics, put it directly that the Bureau does not agree with the statement that China surpasses the United States in terms of GDP. The Bureau has participated in the new round of PPP comparison commissioned by the World Bank starting from 2011, but it held that the new calculating method underestimated the level of price of China, and consequently overestimated the GDP as adjusted by PPP. Head of the Bureau also stressed that the increasing overall economic volume notwithstanding, with a large population, the GDP per capita of China still stood at a low level, and China will stay a developing country for a long time to come.[8]

---

[6]Brooks and Wohlforth (2016).

[7]Ministry of Finance: China's GDP surpassing the United States: a big gap in quality. http://news.xinhuanet.com/fortune/2014-10/10/c_127079590.htm.

[8]National Bureau of Statistics: Disagree with the statement "China surpasses the United States in GDP", http://news.xinhuanet.com/fortune/2015-01/20/c_1114063170.htm.

Similar to the official attitude, the major media, scholars and experts generally remained calm to the news of China's surpassing the United States in GDP, and were in no hurry to challenge the questioning coming from foreign researchers. As can be seen in the reports and reviews of the major media of China, most of them adopted a skeptical attitude to the statement of China's surpassing the United States. Among the 18 reports and reviews on the issue retrieved from the research database CNKI.net, only one largely confirms the calculation of the economic volume of China by way of PPP.[9] Some analyses even endorse the idea that China's "passively-gotten No. 1" is a kind of "pengsha", that is, to lavishly praise China with the secret purpose to make the country complacent, rest on its achievements, and overlook risks, or to revoke the status and treatment of China as a developing country, which may put China under more international responsibilities than it can bear (Table 1.1).

Though most ideas deny that China surpasses the United States in economy (not to mention in other fields), a majority of analysts agree that China has made tremendous progress and many adopt a positive view about its prospect of fast development.

In comparison with other countries catching up with the United States in history, the rising of China features comprehensiveness in addition to fast development. For example, in contrast with the Soviet Union, the rising of China lays more emphasis on economy and the livelihood of the people; with Japan, China enjoys an independent security system. As a matter of fact, China's achievements are remarkable in many areas such as materials, currency, institution and conception.

Increasing Material Power

In terms of material power, besides the economic volume discussed above, China's achievements can also be more thoroughly reflected by such economic index as exports and direct investment abroad, and by index of technological power and military power.

Both the structure of exports and that of investment abroad show the process of transforming and upgrading of the Chinese economy. Since 1995, manufacturing products account for more and more percentage in exportation of China (from 85.56% in 1995 up to 95.49% in 2015), while the percentage of primary products lowers continually (form 14.44% in 1995 down to 4.57% in 2015). The percentage in exportation of high technology products, such as biotechnology, life sciences and technology, photoelectric technology, computer and communication, electronics, computer-integrated manufacturing techniques, material technology and aerospace engineering, increases from 14.9% in 2000 up to 28.82% in 2015.

In comparison with exports, direct investment abroad more clearly indicates the outflow of the nation's producing capacity. In terms of areas of China's investment

[9]The author holds that "though PPP calculation is not perfect, it provides a valuable reference in the sense of an estimated order of magnitude." In the meantime, he points out that China is in need of improving the portion of technology in GDP and the GDP per capita. See Liu (2014).

Table 1.1 Reports and reviews of major Chinese newspapers on China's surpassing the United States

	Title	Newspaper	Date (day/month/year)
1	World No. 1 GDP: An undue and harmful title for the Chinese economy?	Chongqing Daily	15/5/2014
2	Chinese official media try to cool the hype of China's GDP surpassing the US	Oriental Morning Post	5/5/2014
3	Overestimation of the Chinese GDP by the World Bank report?	China Business News	6/5/2014
4	Less ranking, more quality	Guangming Daily	22/5/2014
5	How to understand China's economy this year "overtaking the US"?	Guangming Daily	22/5/2014
6	A rational look at China's passively-gotten title as the world No. 1 economy	PLA Daily	14/5/2014
7	Chinese experts say no to the prediction that China will become the world's biggest economy	Entrepreneurs' Daily	19/5/2014
8	China turns into the biggest economy of the world?	Nanfang Daily	6/5/2014
9	China as a developed nation: a long way to go	People's Daily Overseas Edition	7/5/2014
10	A calm reflection on China's passively-gotten title as the world No. 1 economy	Innovative Finance Observation	12/5/2014
11	Where does China lag behind the United States?	China Securities Journal	20/9/2014
12	Don't be tricked by the title "world No. 1"	International Business Daily	8/10/2014
13	China surpassing the United States in GDP: an event sooner or later	Guangming Daily	10/10/2014
14	A reflection on "China's surpassing the United States" from three "non-changes"	Wenhui Daily	15/10/2014
15	Scientifically positioning of China as a "newly rising economic power"	People's Daily	3/11/2014
16	Say no to the non-substantial GDP increase	China Securities Journal	13/10/2014
17	Understanding China's frequently passively-gotten title of "No. 1"	China Business News	10/10/2014
18	China regaining world No. 1: A historical lesson	China Economic Times	16/10/2014

Source CNKI.net

abroad, primary industries such as mining and manufacturing industry take up a large percentage. Both industries showcase the advantageous manufacturing capacity of China. The former industry seeks a stable supply of energy and resources for the manufacturing system of China, and the latter reflects the outflow of its manufacturing efficiency. In view of the tendency in recent years, the percentage of investment in the two areas in the overall investment abroad somewhat decreases, with net investment in mining lowering from 48.3% in 2003 down to 15.4% in 2014, and that in manufacturing industry from 21.9 to 8.9% in the same period of time; in contrast, investments in culture industry (as represented by sports and entertainment business) and high-tech industry (as represented by information, computer and software) are on the rise, with the former increasing from 0.04% up to 0.48%, and the latter from 0.31% up to 2.96%. The change in investment structure reflects the rise of soft power of China. It can be foreseen that China's direct foreign investment abroad in culture and high-tech areas will account for an even higher percentage.

In technological innovation, China is now doing its best to catch up. A case in point is that China has done a great job in integrating its high-tech capacity into its already competitively-advantageous exporting capability. According to the statistical caliber of the World Bank, high-tech exports refer to products involving high intensity of research development, such as aerospace technology, computers, medicines, science equipment and electric machines. The data reported by the World Bank corroborate the above statistics concerning the high-tech exports of China. According to the World Bank calculation, China's high-tech exports in 2014 reach $558.6 billion. It is the largest amount of the world, 2.8 times that of Germany and 3.6 times that of the United States. It should be pointed out that in 2005, the amount based on the same caliber was 1.5 times of Germany and 1.1 times of the United States, while in 2000, it took up only 48% of Germany and 21% of the United States.[10] If the growth continues, China will enjoy a major improvement in high technology and its industrialization. The number of patents provides another indicator of China's fast development and advanced level in the high technology. World Bank data show that the number of patent applications by Chinese residents in 2014 reached 801,135, 2.8 times that of the United States, accounting for 46.8% of the total number of the world. In contrast, that number was only 56,769 in 2003, 15.8% of Japan, the biggest country then, 30% of the United States, the second best, and 6.6% of the total number of the world.[11] Certainly, the gap will still look great between China and the best countries in the world if validity of patents or intellectual property rights is adopted. In 2015, the royalties of intellectual property rights generated from overseas for China were $1.08 billion, ranking No. 20 of the world, and only 0.86% of the world's No. 1, the United States.[12]

China has also made a great progress in military construction. The country has enlarged its investment in national defense by a big margin, and there is still a

---

[10]For relevant data and statistical caliber, see http://data.worldbank.org.cn/indicator/TX.VAL.TECH.CD?order=wbapi_data_value_2012+wbapi_data_value+wbapi_data_value-last&sort=desc.

[11]http://data.worldbank.org.cn/indicator/IP.PAT.RESD.

[12]http://data.worldbank.org.cn/indicator/BX.GSR.ROYL.CD.

potential to further the process of strengthening national defense. According to the National Bureau of Statistics, the defense expenditure of China in 2014 was 828.954 billion RMB, accounting for 5.5% of the overall fiscal expenditure of the country and 1.29% of the GDP of the year. Back in 2007, that number was 355.491 billion RMB, less than half of 2014, and accounting for 7.14% of the overall fiscal expenditure and 1.33% of the GDP of the year, which number is higher than in 2014.[13] While the defense expenditure continues increasing in recent years, its percentage in the overall fiscal expenditure lowers. It means that China, when in need, has enough elbow room in finance to strengthen national defense and increase military investment. The current military investment contributes to improving the equipment of the army and its combating capacity. As a series of high-tech military equipment, such as aircraft-carrier and fourth-generation fighters, comes into service and generates fighting power, China will further enhance its capacity to safeguard its sovereignty, security and development interests. In a report released by the RAND Corporation, *War with China: Thinking Through the Unthinkable*, it is pointed out that "if hostilities [between the United States and China] erupted, both have ample forces, technology, industrial might, and personnel to fight across vast expanses of land, sea, air, space, and cyberspace," that "as the United States and China become more equal in their ability to destroy each other's forces, neither can be confident of winning at an acceptable price", and that "a Sino-U.S. war would be so harmful that both states should place a very high priority on avoiding one."[14] All these remarks reflect that the RAND corporation, which has an important influence on the judgment of the US Department of Defense, has a high evaluation of the military power of China.

Expanding Influence of RMB

The internationalization of RMB, the currency of China, is now accelerating, and thus gaining an expanding influence. Since 2008, the People's Bank of China (PBOC) has signed bilateral currency-swap agreements with the central bank or currency authority of more than 34 nations and regions. By May, 2016, the total sum, effective by virtue of contract supplement or extension, amounts to 3.2885 trillion RMB.[15] In a sense, these agreements constitute a network of credit for the internationalization of RMB.

There is a high degree of overlapping between partners signing currency-swap agreements with the PBOC and prospective founding members of the Asian Infrastructure Investment Bank (AIIB), reflecting the potential of RMB to expand its influence in the Silk Road Economic Belt and the 21st-Century Maritime Silk Road (the Belt and Road). In the Belt and Road initiated by China, monetary circulation and currency cooperation play an important role, while AIIB functions as a major channel

---

[13]http://data.stats.gov.cn/workspace/index?m=hgnd.

[14]Gompert et al. (2016).

[15]Reuters (2016).

to facilitate that role. It is inherent in the innovation of regional currency cooperation to downplay the dependency of the region on external currency (e.g., US dollar) and to put regional currencies into more use. By way of this, RMB will further develop on its way to regionalization and internationalization. Among the 34 nations and regions signing currency-swap agreements with the PBOC, with the European Central Bank as a department not qualified for AIIB member, and delegates of the Hong Kong Special Administrative Region (HKSAR) participating in the Chinese Delegation to AIIB negotiations, 23 are AIIB prospective founding members. It can be taken as a kind of support of currency-swap partners for the Belt and Road Initiative, and indirectly manifests the international influence of the Chinese currency.

In terms of direct or factual international influence of RMB, more currencies are now taking RMB as "exchange rate anchor", and RMB accounts for an increasing percentage in global trading and financing, and international payment and settlement. After RMB restored the floating mechanism in June, 2010, the number of currencies with RMB as an anchor is on the rise, while that with Euro and US dollar as an anchor decreases. Actually, a RMB zone is form in East Asia. Currencies in seven out of the ten economies in Eastern Asia have a closer relation with RMB than with US dollar.[16] In October, 2013, RMB accounted for 8.66% in global trading and financing (including letters of credit and bills sent for collection). The number may look trivial in comparison with the US dollar's 81.08%, but it surpass Euro for the first time, taking its place as the second most commonly used currency in trading and financing.[17] In December, 2014, RMB became the fifth most commonly used current in international payment and settlement. After that, RMB stepped backwards in the ranking due to seasonal reasons of the Chinese New Year in February, 2015, but regained the position in March, accounting for 2.03% of the total sum.[18]

To the end of 2015, IMF decided that RMB would be added to the basket of Special Drawing Rights (SDR). Since then, China accordingly introduces many relevant measures of reform. In February, 2016, the central government of China opened its interbank bond market to foreign investors. In August of the same year, the government announced its plan to launch Shenzhen-Hong Hong Stock Connect, enlarging the scope of listed enterprises in mainland China eligible for foreign investment, and the scope of Hong Kong-listed enterprises eligible for domestic investment. In the end of the same month, upon the proposal of PBOC, the World Bank issued 500 million SDR-denominated bonds (i.e., Mulan Bond) in the interbank bond market of China, and the Bank became the first organization issuing SDR bonds in China.[19] A review points out that the Mulan Bond assumes a strong international hue and

---

[16]Subramanian and Kessler (2012).

[17]SWIFT: RMB taking place of Euro as the second most commonly used currency in trading and financing. SWIFT RMB Tracker, November, 2013. http://www.swift.com/assets/swift_com/documents/products_services/RMB_tracker_November2013_SC.pdf.

[18]Bank of China: BOC CRI Monthly, May 19, 2015. http://www.bankofchina.com/aboutboc/bi1/201505/t20150519_5047034.html.

[19]Arunma Oteh, World Bank vice president, says, the Mulan Bond named after the legendary female hero, Mulan, reflects the expectations of the World Bank for the goals of peaceful and sustainable development. See Song, Yikang and Zhou Ailin. 2016. Interview with the vice president of the World

is full of Chinese elements, marking a new milestone in the internationalization of RMB.[20] The RMB-included SDR basket was effective on October 1, 2016, laying a solid institutional foundation for RMB to wield its international influence.

An Increasing Power in Establishing International Institutions

On institutional level, China has an expanded voice in international organization, and its capacity to participate in international institutionalization improves. On the one hand, China has an increasing activeness and influence in the current system of global governance. Currently, most international economic rules are established with the developed countries as the leading force, including the IMF, the World Bank and the World Trade Organization (WTO), and other international economic and rule framework concerning economy, finance, trade, investment, labor, energy, technological standards and environment. China actively participates in international economic cooperation and competition, safeguards its own interests and those of developing countries, and has acceded to major international economic organizations such as the IMF, the World Bank and the WTO, and endeavors to actively participate in establishing and revising relevant economic rules.

Under the IMF, China takes the advantage of various opportunities to promote its rules to reflect the interests of developing countries. For instance, China promotes reforms in exchange rate surveillance so as to have a closer watch on that of the developed countries. Before the subprime crisis gave rise to a global financial crisis, IMF monitors the exchange rate of its members according to Article IV of the Articles of Agreement and the *Decision on Bilateral Surveillance over Members' Policies* (Decision 2007 for short). Since most developed countries adopt floating exchange rate, the actual surveillance focus is on the emerging economies. It is thus "non-neutral", "asymmetric", and unfair to developing countries and emerging economies. After the global financial crisis broke out in developed countries, China timely called for all parties to reflect on the IMF's failure to monitor economies and send a warning of the crisis, and contributed to the revision of the operational guideline of the Decision 2007 in June, 2009, cancelling the conduction labeling member states. In October, 2011, under the proposal of China, the Executive Board of the IMF decided to adjust its legal framework for surveillance, and to re-establish a new surveillance decision integrating bilateral and multilateral surveillance and covering wider areas of global stability. China, in the meantime, actively promoted the revision and obtained support at the G20 Cannes Summit. For another example,

---

Bank: Issuing SDR bonds will continue, G20 should encourage globalization. *Yi Cai*. September 2, 2016. http://www.yicai.com/news/5084820.html.

[20]Zhou, Ailin. 2016. A surprise before G20 summit: the World Bank issues SDR bonds named Mulan. *Yi Cai*. August 31, 2016. http://www.yicai.com/news/5080127.html.

China, together with other developing countries, promoted reforms in the quota system of the IMF. With the efforts of China and other developing countries, the IMF Board of Governors finally adopted the resolution to reform its quota system, with its current total quotas doubled, and the quota for China increased from 3.72% up to 6.39%, with its ranking climbing from No. 6 to No. 3, standing second only to the United States and Japan.

As to the World Bank, China also contributes to its institutional construction, and to its bettering policy- and rule-making for international development. For example, under the initiation of China and other countries, the World Bank/IMF Development Committee meeting adopted a reform in voting power, increasing China's voting power by 1.65–4.42%, with its ranking climbing from No. 6 to No. 3, standing second only to the United States and Japan. For another example, poverty reduction and development are the major concerns of the World Bank, for which the Bank put forward a series of rules, including quota policy for concessional funds, debt-deduction policies and sustainable standards for low-income countries, security policies for ensuring projects, project management policy, anti-corruption policy, rules for accounting, auditing and banking, and information disclosure policy. All these rules ultimately point to poverty reduction for developing countries. China is one of the most successful countries in reducing poverty. It actively cooperates with the World Bank to institutionalize and standardize its experience in poverty reduction, and provides support in intellect and rules for the World Back in its arrangement of global poverty reduction. In November, 2012, the World Bank signed an agreement with the Chinese Ministry of Finance to establish the "World Bank-China development practice knowledge center", which means that the World Bank attaches an unprecedented importance to studying and generalizing the experience of China. Kim Yong Jim, the president of the World Bank, said, "the major task of the 'knowledge center' is for Chinese and foreign experts to study and summarize the experiences of China's development, assimilate experiences of international development, and to conduct sharing and exchange with the World Bank in China and the international community."

China also improves its capacity to participate in WTO rule-establishing or revision. Although the Doha Round is currently caught in a standstill, China, since its accession to the WTO, has participated in comprehensive negotiations, contributing its due part to the Doha Round. In 2005, China held an informal ministerial meeting of the WTO, and tried its best to bridge the differences between WTO members. In July, 2008, China become one of the seven core members of the Doha Round, symbolizing that China has entered the nuclear circle of decision-making for establishing multilateral trade rules, enjoying an heightened position in the multilateral trade system and a bigger voice in rule-establishment for international trade. Besides, China has also made efforts and attempts with regard to other international trade rules of WTO, such as trade remedy measures, non-preferential agreement on rules of origin, information technology agreement, agreement on trade-related aspects of intellectual property rights, and domestic policy support for WTO agricultural agreement, playing an active part.

On the other hand, in addition to an ever more important role within the existing rules and governing system, China actively participates in establishing new mechanism for international cooperation. Both the Chiang Mai Initiative (CMI) and the mechanism for its multilateralization, in which China is a major participant, and the BRICS cooperation mechanism, which is mainly initiated and promoted by China, have made remarkable progress. The Belt and Road initiated by China alone, and the China-proposed AIIB have gained wide support from the international community.

After the Asian financial crisis, ASEAN countries and China, Japan and Korea (ASEAN+3), out of reflections on the lack of regional relief mechanism and on the low efficiency of relief organizations outside the region, started to seek mechanisms to strengthen regional cooperation and to jointly ward off risks, and finally came to the CMI and upgraded its multilateralization. China has played a positive role in this process of institutionalization. The China-proposed financial cooperation mechanism between ASEAN and China, Japan and Korea laid foundations for the CMI and later its multilateralization. In February, 1998, at the second ASEAN+3 Leaders' Summit, China first tabled a proposal for a finance vice-ministers and central bank vice-governors meeting for ASEAN+3, so as to enhance dialogue and policy coordination between these country, promoting mutual exchange and cooperation. Upon the proposal of China, the first ASEAN+3 Finance Vice-Ministers and Central Bank Vice-Governors Meeting was held in Hanoi, Viet Nam, March, 1999, focusing on issues such as the surveillance of short-term capital flow and the reform of international financial system. At the third ASEAN+3 Leaders' Summit, in November, 1999, China proposed to institutionalize the ASEAN+3 finance vice-ministers and central bank vice-governors meeting, and to hold finance ministers and central bank governors meeting as needed. After the discussions on self-relief and mutual support mechanism in East Asia at the vice-ministers and vice-governors meeting, the CMI, which aimed at establishing a network of currency-swap in the region, was adopted in May, 2000, at Chiang Mai ASEAN+3 Finance Ministers and Central Bank Governors Meeting, setting up the agenda for gradually establishing a network of bilateral currency-swap within ASEAN+3, so as to render help to relevant countries in a short-term financial problem and to ward off risks of financial crisis. In order to deepen financial cooperation in East Asia and hence self-relief capacity to fight regional crisis, China was again the first in October, 2003, to propose to "promote CMI multilateralization (CMIM)", and to transform the loose bilateral currency-swap mechanism under the CMI as to form a multilateral financial assistance mechanism. The spreading of the global financial crisis accelerated the CMIM. In February, 2009, ASEAN+3 Finance Ministers agreed to enlarge the common reserve from the originally scheduled $80 billion to $120 billion. In May of the same year, Finance Ministers of ASEAN+3 countries reached an agreement on major factors concerning the common reserve, such as quota distribution, quota structure, lending quota and decision-making mechanism. On March 24th, 2010, ASEAN+3 Finance Ministers and Central Bank Governors together with the Chief Executive of Hong Kong Monetary Authority proclaimed that the agreement on the CMIM formally went into effect. China and Japan are tied as the two biggest sponsors of the East Asia Common Foreign Exchange Reserve. In July, 2014, the revised agreement on the CMIM took effect, enlarging the fund of the CMIM from $120 billion to $240 billion, and increasing the decoupling ratio of IMF loan arrangement from 20 to 30%.

China has also played a positive role in establishing, expanding and deepening the BRICS cooperation mechanism. In December, 2010, China, assuming the rotating presidency of the BRICS cooperation mechanism, reached a consensus with Russia, India and Brazil to accept South Africa as an official member of the BRICS cooperation mechanism. At the third BRICS Summit, Sanya, China, 2011, it was announced that local currency trade settlement would be adopted, and the BRICS Interbank Cooperation Mechanism (Framework Agreement) was signed and rectified. Currency and financial cooperation became an important breakthrough to improve the level of institutionalization for the BRICS cooperation mechanism. At the fifth BRICS Summit in 2013, the leaders agreed to establish BRCIS Development Bank and prepare to establish BRICS foreign exchange reserve. At the sixth Summit, it was announced that the initial capital of the BRCIS Development Bank would be $100 billion, with the five founding members sharing an equal quota, and the Bank was headquartered in Shanghai. At the same Summit, Zhou Xiaochuan, governor of the PBOC, on the behalf of the Chinese government signed the Treaty for the Establishment of a BRICS Contingent Reserve Arrangement in Fortaleza, Brazil with delegates of other BRICS countries. This is a significant attempt for the emerging economies to deal with common global threats, and to establish a common financial network by breaking geographical restrictions. President Xi Jinping delivered a key-note speech entitled Building Partnership Together Toward a Bright Future at the seventh Summit, Ufa, Russia, 2015. He proposed a strategic blueprint for strengthening BRICS partnership from four aspects of "remembering history, safeguarding world peace", "benefits sharing, common development", "inclusiveness, inter-civilization dialogue", and "upgrading rules, promoting governance". On October 16th, 2016, the eighth BRICS Summit was held in Goa, India. He said, "this year marks the tenth anniversary of BRICS cooperation. We in China often say 'It takes a master craftsman ten years to sharpen a sword.' Indeed, through painstaking efforts, BRICS countries have traversed a rewarding journey in the past ten years. With solid steps, BRICS cooperation has grown in depth and substance and evolved into an international mechanism with major influence and a productive track record."[21] Under the strong support and driving of China, the BRICS cooperation mechanism, in the ten years, has become more multi-dimensional in contents, has deepened the depth of cooperation, and improved the level of institutionalization. On the one hand, the BRICS cooperation mechanism has its own integrity intensified, the contingent reserve arrangement has been put into operation, with global financial security network strengthened, the BRICS Development Bank has opened business, which has its first batch of loans already granted to support renewable energy projects in BRICS countries, and has issued the first batch of RMB-denominated bonds. On the other hand, the BRICS cooperation mechanism as a whole not only voices its opinion on global trend, international situation and major regional problems, show-

[21] Xi (2016).

ing a tendency to cooperate with other mechanisms as a single independent entity, but also begins to form a new concept of global economic governance of its own characteristics.

The Belt and Road Initiative and the establishment of AIIB represent new developments in China's efforts to promote the evolution of international economic rules. In terms of geographical coverage, the Belt and Road concerns more than 60 countries within the region and adopts an open attitude to stakeholders outside the region, surpassing by a large margin the ASEAN+3 cooperation and the BRICS in coverage. In terms of the fields of cooperation, the Belt and Road involves a wider range, including policy coordination, trade, currency and finance, infrastructure construction and humanities and social exchanges. In March, 2015, China issued the Vision and Proposed Actions Outlined on Jointly Building Silk Road Economic Belt and 21st-Century Maritime Silk Road, putting forward the Belt and Road Initiative in a white book-like fashion, and gaining active response from the international community. China also proposed to establish the Asian Infrastructure Investment Bank (AIIB), providing intellectual and financial support to the Belt and Road connectivity of infrastructure. In October, 2014, Finance Ministers and authorized representatives of the first 21 AIIB prospective founding countries including China, India and Singapore signed an agreement in Beijing, deciding to establish the AIIB. On June 29, 2015, the Articles of Agreement on AIIB was signed in Beijing, with Finance Ministers and authorized representative of the 57 prospective founding countries attending the signing ceremony. On December 25, 2015, the AIIB was formally established. In comparison with the currency and financial cooperation of ASEAN+3 and BRICS, the concept and rules of governance as reflected by the mechanism of AIIB give the impression of a more different concept of value from the traditional organizations. The rules or the principles of an organization are usually based on a particular concept of value. For example, the IMF and the World Bank are based on the "Washington Consensus", stressing transparency, market economy and deepening financing, and for that purpose, establish a set of "a priori" conditions for loans, disregarding the borrowing countries' facts, which often turns into bureaucratism and troublesome procedures in practice. In contrast, the AIIB takes "lean, clean and green" as its core value, emphasizing streamlined procedure and efficiency. In his speech at B20 summit opening ceremony on September 3, 2016, President Xi Jinping clarifies the motive to propose the Belt and Road Initiative, pointing out that "the new mechanisms and initiatives launched by China are not intended to reinvent the wheels or target any other country. Rather, they aim to complement and improve the current international mechanisms to achieve win-win cooperation and common development."[22] The explication shows that the revision of international rules and mechanisms by China does not aim at sabotaging the existing system or creating a parallel system, but at supplementing and perfecting.

[22]Xi (2016).

Chinese Concepts Gaining More Heart

The achievements of China in materials, currency and institution arouse the interest of other countries or regions in understanding what development concept underlies the achievement. The opinions of China of the world, development and peace, as expressed the Chinese leaders, attract more attention and obtain more agreement.

Harmonious World, which draws on the system theory and wholism of the traditional Chinese culture, is an important concept concerning international political ethics, law and international relation building. In April, 2005, Hu Jintao, the President of China proposed the concept of Harmonious World in a speech at the Asian-African Summit, Jakarta. Later, the concept was written into the Joint Statement of China and Russia on the International Order of the 21st Century, entering into the view of international community as a common understanding between countries. In September, 2005, Hu comprehensively explained the concept of Harmonious World in an address delivered at UN headquarters. In August, 2006, Hu, in a speech at the Central Meeting on Foreign Affairs Work, pointed out that it was a necessary requirement of China's peaceful development and an important condition for its realization to promote the construction of a harmonious world. On April 15, 2014, Xi Jinping, the successor to Hu Jintao, at the First Meeting of the Central National Security Commission also proposed to "seek peace, cooperation and mutual benefits and building a harmonious world"[23] A harmonious world becomes the Chinese expectation for the foreign environment.

While the concept of Harmonious World expresses China's vision for the future, the "community of common destiny" reflects the reality and urgency of comprehensive win-win cooperation and common development. In the *China's Peaceful Development* (the White Book) issued by the Information Office of the State Council of China, it is pointed out that "countries of different systems and different types and at various development stages are in a state of mutual dependence, with their interests intertwined. This has turned the world into a community of common destiny in which the members are closely interconnected"; and that we "should find new perspectives from the angle of the community of common destiny—sharing weal and woe and pursuing mutually beneficial cooperation, exploring new ways to enhance exchanges and mutual learning among different civilizations, identifying new dimensions in the common interests and values of mankind, and looking for new ways to handle multiple challenges through cooperation among countries and realize inclusive development."[24] Hu Jintao, in the report at the 18th Party Congress, went on to stress that mankind has only one earth to live on, and countries have only one world to share, and we should raise awareness about human beings sharing a community of common destiny. As Xi Jinping succeeded Hu as the General Secretary of the Party, he elaborated the concept on several occasions. While the concept focuses on the sharing of space in documents such as the 18th Party Congress Report, president Xi Jinping, in his speech at Moscow State Institute of International

---

[23]Xi (2014).

[24]Information Office of the State Council of China (2011).

Relations on March 23, 2013, extended the concept as to cover a fuller dimension including both space and time. He stressed that "it is a world where countries are linked with and dependent on one another at a level never seen before. Mankind, by living in the same global village in the same era where history and reality meet, has increasingly emerged as a community of common destiny in which everyone has in himself a little bit of others."[25] The focus on "the same era" or temporal dimension represents a call for and an expectation of mankind to fulfill the common mission which is endowed by the great times shared by mankind. Later, Xi repeatedly explicated his idea and thought of the community of common destiny, when talking about Chinese-African relation, Chinese-Arabian relations and the relation of China with neighboring countries, and on important international occasions such the UNESCO, Boao Forum for Asia, G20 Summit, APEC Conference and CICA Summit. Besides, Xi also includes the concept in the Belt and Road Initiative and the wholistic view of national security.

Both concepts of Harmonious world and community of common destiny are closely connected with the idea of "Great Harmony" in the traditional Chinese culture and thoughts. The concepts of peaceful development and non-interference, which grow out of the traditional Chinese culture and thoughts, have gained more and more understanding and agreement of the international community. The history of China undergoes a tightly connected course of events, with political, economic, military and cultural records of a 2000-year history well preserved by official historians, thinkers, literary figures, poets, novelists, playwrights and actors. This heavy history is pressed and condensed into a single point of reality, where heroes and heroines, loyalty and betrayal, miraculous tactics and conspiracies, nobility and baseness relate to the contemporaries of various dynasties and eras in manners of words, drawings, oral story-telling, and folk arts. Standing by the bank of Wujiang River, one might still hear the sigh of Xiang Yu before he cut his own throat.[26] Generations of the Chinese people grow up in a history, remote but intimate like yesterday. The history extending to the present day and the thoughts and culture accumulative over the course crystallize into the inescapable heritage of the Chinese people, exerting an influence on China's national act, which cannot be ignored.

Henry Alfred Kissinger tries to summarize in his book *On China* the motivations and principles by which China conducts its strategic acts on the basis of the Chinese traditional culture and thoughts influencing leaders of the New China. He notices the differences in the concept of history between Eastern and Western countries. First, China has an understanding of history entirely different from the West, and the difference has an important influence on China's strategic acts. The West believes that history is a process of modernity achieving a series of absolute victories over

---

[25] Xi (2014).

[26] *Shi Ji* records that Xiang Yu committed suicide in East City, not by the bank of Wujiang River. Recently some scholars propose that the Wujiang story started to prevail since Jin Renjie's play *Xiao He Chasing after Han Xin under Moonlight* in the Mid-Yuan Dynasty. However, it is what people believe that matters. The belief may not correspond to historical facts, but becomes a memory of history, reflecting the cognitive structure based on social contents and psychological development. With the method of "archeology of knowledge", the memory can be analyzed. See Hu (2004).

evil and backwardness. The tradition Chinese view of history emphasized a cyclical process of decay and rectification, in which nature and the world can be understood but not completely mastered. Consequently, China values harmony, and strategy and statecraft become means of "combative coexistence" with opponents. The goal is to maneuver them into weakness while building up one's own *shi*, or strategic position. Kissinger provides a very enlightening illustration of the contrast between China and the West with that between *weiqi* (the game of go) and chess. *Weiqi* does not focus on the elimination of an opponent's pieces. While the game is still going on, the pieces encircled will enjoy possibility of getting back to game. In terms of victory and loss, there is a concept of live chess, that is, both parties are interconnected, mutually dependent and sharing common interests on the same territory. When the game is set, the margin of advantage may be slim. At the end of a well-played game, the board is filled by interlocking areas of strength, and to the untrained eye, it is not always clear who is the winner. In contrast, the chess piece eliminated is eliminated forever. The player aims to eliminate his opponent's pieces, with the purpose to the opponent's political power as represented by the king.

Second, the traditional Chinese culture of strategy emphasized defense rather than conquest. The way to put strategy into practice was to rely on a rich array of diplomatic and economic instruments to draw potentially hostile foreigners into relationships the Chinese could manage, so as to deter invasion and prevent the formation of barbarian coalitions. When the nation was powerful, the above strategy of China did not intend to take advantage of other countries, but to seek an ideological rationalization for imperial power on its borders. During periods of decline, it served to mask weakness and helped China manipulate contending forces, so as to disintegrate them with the effect of "using barbarians against barbarians". The fact that the strategy turned out effective for China is due to a civilization far ahead of the neighboring countries. Before the modern times, China has never met a civilization comparable in volume and power, not to mention a more powerful one. So when the guns of the Great Britain broke open the door of China, the nation still resorted to "using barbarians against barbarians", inviting other European countries in for the purpose of first stimulating and then manipulating their rivalry. But the giant gap in power between China and the West could not be offset by sophisticated strategies, and the Chinese civilization confronted an unparalleled impact, which the contemporaries considered as an unknown upheaval in three thousand years.

Thirdly, the traditional Chinese mentality includes universal feelings, but no universal complex. China is proud of its ethical rules, and makes them open to "barbarians". If the "barbarians" adopted the manners of China, then they would be considered a part of China; if China lost its manners, it would be reduced to "barbarians". There was no absolute boundary between the two, and this was where the Chinese universal feelings lay. But different from the United States, which propagates its values all over the world, China adopted the method of emotional influence, or set an example without doing anything else, waiting peacefully for events to take their course. As Kevin Rudd, the former Prime Minister of Australia, said, Confucianism is not designed as a value for export to the world. In contrast, American liberal democracy, either by way of active political evangelization or simply by passive example, is precisely that.[27]

Stressing the differences of mentality between the East and the West does not mean to contradict the researches such as that of Andrew Scobell and Alastair Johnston. The former holds that China has a dualistic strategic culture: one is conflict-averse and defensive-minded, and the other favors military solutions and is offensive-oriented.[28] The latter proposes that what is truly effective is the bellicose strategic culture, while the images of Confucius and Mencius have only symbolic meanings. On this issue, the traditional Chinese culture "says one thing, does another". In essence, it has nothing different from the Western cultural tradition of assault and conquest.

In fact, as the realists believe, both the East and the West share some "basic character" of mankind, such as desire-fulfilling, profit-seeking and harm-avoiding. Such character leads to the bellicose and offensive conduct against an opponent. However, the differences in mentality between the East and the West, which Alastair Johnston believes to possess only symbolic meanings, generate substantial or essential differences in the manners and contents by which both sides shape and restrict their "basic character" with a set of customs and rules. These differences cannot be ignored in their influence on individual and collective acts.

Another aspect of interest to other countries, especially the developing countries, is China's concept of prioritization of bottom-up construction and infrastructure building, which is a lesson learned in the practice of economic development.

As always, the Chinese way of development and international cooperation is not without controversy. For example, there are criticisms of China's aiding foreign countries with no political conditions attached, saying that it offsets the effects of "high-level" assistance by organizations such as the World Bank, contributes to the dictatorship and corruption of the beneficiary country, and worsens the inequality within the beneficiary country. Before China's efforts, the developed countries of the West have provided assistance to underdeveloped countries in Africa and other areas, but to little avail. They assume that assistance to or investment in a country of low governmental transparency, high-level of economic control, and low degree of financial freedom and professionalism will run a huge risk, and worsen domestic problems such as corruption. Hence, they ask the country to conduct institutional reforms in the first place, realizing market economy and freedom economy. Their assistance and investment are bound up with such reforms: reforms as required bring assistance, no assistance or withdrawal of assistance otherwise, in which case the beneficiary country would get into trouble. This model of top-down reform and development may lower the risk of assistance, but put the country receiving the assistance under greater risk.

Infrastructure-oriented development goes a different path. Its underlying assumption is simply the bottom-up idea, "if you want to be rich, first build roads." Once there are roads, local labor force, resources, and funds will be linked to the international market by the connectivity of infrastructure, and enjoy the benefits thereof.

[27] Rudd (2015).

[28] Scobell (2002).

And when the grassroots people obtain these benefits, their conception will change gradually as well. The heightened wishes will demand opening-up and reforms in institution and idea, then promote the country to be better integrated into the network of modern world economy. This is the basic lesson of China. But only the feet can tell whether shoes fit or not. Each country ought to choose the path suiting its own need. It is the right of the country, it is its obligation. China has a lesson to learn from, and is willing to provide necessary assistance, but in the end the country has to make its own strategic judgment, and China will never impose its own ways and methods on others.

As a matter of fact, China supports most of the institutional reforms and rules of market as advocated by Western countries. China is a major beneficiary and supporter of these rules. As Xi Jinping said when discussing the pilot free trade zone, "we should gain a solid understanding of common international rules, and quicken the step to form the basic institution system and supervision model which connect to the common rules of international investment and trade."[29] But as the experiences of China in theory and practice show, it is hard for a country to make a great leap forward from the bottom echelon to the top. China would rather take the process as one of self-education and self-reform with bottom-up and gradual learning. While China may accept assistance from other countries, it would not allow its growth to be forced, let alone to be controlled. In this sense, president Xi Jinping stresses the efforts to "bravely act, boldly try and independently reform."[30] What China does to underdeveloped and developing countries is nothing other than opening routes and channels for them to connect to the international market. In terms of market-oriented development path, China and Western countries have the same goal but different methods.

The American economist A. C. Pigou adopts a dualistic view of "social product and private product" in his the *Economics of Welfare* to discuss the "educative possibilities of small businesses". He points out that in addition to production, industry units of different sizes and nature have also the function of training their workers. A rational distribution of industry units in a society will provide common workers the ladder to tap and develop their potential. If most industries of a society are controlled by several conglomerates, their private products will be maximized, but not the net products of the society, because most workers will be deprived of the opportunity to climb the "ability ladder" as provided by the training function of businesses. That is to say, a society or a well-organized economic ecology should consist of enterprises of different sizes and nation, taking the form of coexistence and diversity. The theory can also be applied to a "global society". Giving priority to infrastructure building as advocated by China is to provide an "ability ladder" to underdeveloped countries, for them to grow from underdeveloped to developed status by drawing on their own power and that of emerging economies, and not to be intimidated by the

[29]Xi (2014).

[30]Ibid.

slim prospect of turning into a developed country by a leap. Certainly, the peaceful overall international environment is a necessary condition to maintain the "ladder" or to keep the channel open.

A Hard-Won Choice of Path

As discussed above, China has achieved a lot on its road to rejuvenation in many aspects. A more essential question to other countries, however, is what China's rejuvenation brings to the world. Recent studies reflect worries over China's rejuvenation, as can be seen in such titles as *China Shakes the World: A Titan's Rise and Troubled Future—and the Challenge for America*,[31] *Eclipse: Living in the Shadow of China's Economic Dominance*,[32] *When China Rules The World: The End of the Western World and the Birth of a New Global Order*,[33] *Is China buying the world?*,[34] and *China as an Economic and Military Superpower: A Dangerous Combination?*.[35]

After a long and winding process of twists, turns and even setbacks, the fast development China is achieved under the leadership of the Communist Party of China since the reform and opening-up initiated by Deng Xiaoping. A look at the background and process by which China finally goes on the road of reform and opening-up will make more appreciated the change of world view underlying its fast development, the dependence of China miracle on the peaceful and stable internal and external environment and on the current situation of world economy, and why China cherishes so much the hard-won path of peaceful development. With these understandings, there will be no unnecessary worries, as reflected in the titles above, about a rising China or a powerful China actively seeking conflicts with the world.

We do not need to hide the fact that China was carried into the modern world in a truly awkward manner by the Western guns and ships. Though the evil habit of opium (the main ingredient for heroin) taking was introduced to China by European sailors as early as the 17th Century[36], opium ran rampant in the 19th century in China largely due to the efforts of the biggest armed organization of drug dealers, the Great Britain. Britain had a great demand for tea produced in China, but it could offer no Europeans consumer goods that were needed in large quantity by the Chinese people.[37] Hence there was a serious trade imbalance between the two countries. The commodities imported annually by the British East India Company from China were worth 7 million yuan[38], while half of that amount was exported to China. Opium

[31] Kynge (2007).

[32] Subramanian (2011).

[33] Jacques (2012).

[34] Nolan (2012).

[35] Uckert (2012).

[36] Stavrianos (2005).

[37] Fairbank (1985).

[38] The measuring unit yuan here means the then current silver dollar. The same below.

then became a major export to make up for the trade deficit (and later on generated a huge amount of surplus). The so-called "Honorable East India Company" was a conglomerate took up the political task of exercising "sovereignty of the royal family for the royal family." In 1773, the company established an organization of monopoly in India in order to sell drugs to China. Over the years from 1822 to 1830, it transported a huge amount of drugs to China by way of bribing the corrupt Chinese officials with the annual trade volume reaching 18,760 chests of opium. Up to 1836, opium exported to China amounted to 18 million yuan, and the trade became the largest single-commodity trade of the world in the 19th century. It turns the trade balance between the two countries from a surplus of 26 million yuan for China in the first ten years of the 19th century to a deficit of 38 million yuan in the years from 1828 to 1836.[39]

China took a strong hand to ban and destroy opium, and confiscated opium in the hands of the British merchants. The British trade representative to China asked the merchants to give the drugs to him, and he would then transfer them to the Chinese government, and the British government would bear the merchants' loss. The arrangement clearly shifted the responsibility of drug dealing from private sectors to the government. Under the arrangement, the British merchants handed in more opium than they had in stock, totaling 20,283 chests worth 9 million yuan.[40] Then the British government and some parliament members motivated to declare war against China. Although some conscientious members pointed at the injustice of drug dealing, the men in charge change the topic under discussion from "drug dealing" to "free trade", with the anti-war bill denied by five votes.[41] This was a war between the industrialized Britain and the agricultural China. Like a fight of a strong adult against a rebellious kid, the latter had nothing to defend itself, and in some place it was practically a one-sided slaughter. The scene was so cruel that even the slaughterers themselves would feel scared and sick.[42]

More unfortunately, while the Opium War showed that China did not possess the mean to protect itself, the Treaty of Nanjing concluded the war with a message that the Chinese government was "rich" and "generous". According to the Treaty, China ceded to the Great Britain the island of Hong Kong, opened five ports to the British merchants and paid twenty-one million yuan to the Great Britain. As mentioned above, before the 19th century, China's GDP, which was based on consumer goods such as silk and tea, was much larger than that of industrial countries including the Great Britain. Now these countries found that by way of steel-made firearms with the worth of a little amount of GDP, they could do whatever they wanted and take whatever liked. The fire of desire inflamed could not be quenched easily. Countries such as the Great Britain, the United States, France and Russia grabbed lands, properties and privileges from China by means of war and blackmail through the seemingly civilized way of "treaty". Japan, which is the close neighbor to China

---

[39]Fairbank (1985).

[40]Ibid., p. 201.

[41]Ibid., p. 209.

[42]Ibid., p. 221.

and had benefited from China for a long time in history, now came back to bite its benefactor after the country was itself invaded by Western countries and swiftly adopted the policy of "departing Asia for Europe". In 1894, the Sino-Japanese War of 1894–1895 broke out and China's failure ended up in war reparations of 230 million *liang* of silver. In 1900, the Eight-Power Allied Forces including Japan and seven Western countries broke into Beijing, burning, killing and looting, had forced China to sign the Peace Protocol of 1901, prescribing war reparations of 980 million *liang* of silver. The total sum Japan had obtained from the reparations amounted to 8 times of its annual revenue, which contributed to accelerating its modernization[43], while China lost the opportunity to participate in the modernization of the world by way of the Westernization Movement.[44]

In 1912, the government of Qing Dynasty, which was supposedly responsible for China's accumulated poverty and weakness, suddenly fell. The fortune of China, however, did not change. The newly founded Republic of China was powerless to deal with the warlords, who divided the nation by military rule under the support of one foreign nation or a combination of foreign nations. The divided situation put the international position of China in great jeopardy. Although China was luckily among the victors in the First World, the state could not take back what belonged to it from a defeated nation. The interests of Germany in the Shandong peninsula were surreptitiously transferred by Britain and France to please another victorious nation, Japan. The news caused domestic sensation. On May 4, 1919, about 3,000 students demonstrated around Ti'an Men square in Beijing, requesting the dismissal of Japanophile officials and setting fire to the residence of Minister of Transportation. Suppression of the demonstration led to bloodshed, which incited a nationwide support activities and demonstrations. The government fired three Japanophile ministers, and refused to sign the final treaty with Germany. The grassroots movement is called the "May Fourth Movement". Later on, Marxism gained public audience in China. The Communist Party of China was founded two years later.

The Nationalist Party of China (NPC or Kuomintang) headed by Sun Zhongshan (also known as Sun Yat-sen) began to cooperate with the later-founded CPC in 1924, pursuing a national control by Northern Expeditions. China would look different, if Sun's efforts had panned out. The popular revolutionary leader died on his north-heading way to negation with warlords in March, 1925. After a series of intra-Party struggles, Chiang Kai-shek seized the power of NPC. With the assistance of CPC, NPC had gained the control of Shanghai and the lower reaches of the Yangtze River, where most of China's industrial and commercial businesses were located. In 1927, Jiang conducted a purge of the Party together with Shanghai gangsters,

---

[43]Zhang (2003).

[44]During years from the 1860s to the 1890s, officials of the central and local governments in the Qing Dynasty worked hard to introduce advanced military equipment, machines and science and technology from the West, hoping to "learn from foreigners so as to ward them off" with the guideline of "treating Chinese values as essence and Western knowledge as tools". These officials are called "westernizationists", and the movement they led is called the "Westernization Movement". The Beiyang Fleet (or the Northern Navy), which was a significant fruit of the movement, was wiped out in the Sino-Japanese War of 1894–1895, symbolizing the failure of the movement.

arresting and killing CPC members. During the process, 90% of CPC members were killed, and the rest had to work undercover. Then the nationalist government moved the capital of the country from Beijing to Nanjing, and formally unified China with major warlords gathering under the flag of Nanjing, but each retaining a certain degree of independence. The stability that came with this unification in form brought an opportunity for the development of the Chinese economy. As doctor Kenneth Lieberthal observes, any government able to impose a modicum of order in China [...] would have benefited from significant economic growth. China saw many substantial economic achievements in the 1930s, when the big powers were caught in a great depression. China attained its peak levels of output in industry, agriculture, and commerce in 1936, levels that would not again be achieved until well into the communists' first decade of rule in the 1950s.[45]

The growth was again arrested by Japan. As early as 1931, Japan seized power of Northeast China, and stirred up conflicts in North China and Shanghai. In 1935, Japan took control of North China. Like the Great Britain and France who adopted an appeasement policy to German fascists, the national government adopted a policy of compromise and yielding to Japan. Chiang Kai-shek proposed a slogan of "Resisting Foreign Aggression after Stabilizing the Country", that is, to crack down on rebellious forces of the CPC and within the NPC before defending the country against the Japanese invasion. The act actually fostered the ambition of Japan. On July 7, 1937, the Japanese army caused the Marco Polo Bridge Incident (or the Lugou Bridge Incident), which marked the beginning of the full-scale Anti-Japanese War. During the war, the NPC and the CPC made a second round of cooperation, jointly fighting against Japan. On August 15, 1945, Japan surrendered unconditionally. From 1937, the beginning year of the war, to 1945, when the war was over, more than 21 million Chinese people died or were harmed in battle, about 10 million people were tortured to death, about 930 cities fell into the Japanese hands, and China suffered a direct economic loss up to $62 billion, and an indirect loss of more than $500 billion.[46] China was once again for the war with Japan excluded from the process of modernization.

With the victory of the Anti-Japanese war, while no external dangers threatened China, inter-conflict broke out. The NPC refused to govern China with the CPC and other democratic parties, and sent troops to attack the army of the CPC. After a three-year war, the CPC defeated the NPC on the mainland China, and the remnants of the NPC fled to Taiwan.

Economic development of China was repeatedly delayed by wars, and the situation continued until the founding of the New China, when stability was finally achieved. Since the founding of New China, the heavily destroyed economy began to restore its vitality, even though social reforms and the War to Resist USA and to Aid Korea (the Korean War) put a heavy pressure. In 1952, China attained the highest level of industrial and agricultural production in history. Through socialist industrialization, socialist transformation and the first five-year plan, a socialist system was basically

[45] Licbcrthal (2010).

[46] Information Office of the State Council of China (1991).

established. The successive achievements in several years, from the founding of New China to the essential completion of socialist transformation, led the CPC leadership with Mao Zedong (Chairman Mao) as head to holding an over-optimistic view of the prospect of social and economic construction, and thus to initiating the "Great Leap Forward" and the People's Commune Movement, which violated the law of social and economic development, causing serious harms to the economic construction of China. In addition, Mao Zedong, based on misjudgments of domestic and international situation, launched the Culture Revolution, which brought the most serious setback and loss since the founding of New China to the CPC, the nation and the people. China, as a result, deviated from the correct direction of development, and was detached from the international trends of development of economy, science and technology, with its gap with other countries enlarged in social and economic development.[47] It was not until Deng Xiaoping resumed his post that the Party started to put things right and redirect the country back on its route to social and economic development.

With the hardships and bitter experiences of China since the 1840s in view, we may come to the following conclusions. First, since the 1840s, the damage that foreign powers wrought on China by way of invasion and exploitation was severe, and China should constantly be vigilant to such a possibility. Second, asymmetric dependence of economy is a major factor that leads to conflicts. If the Great Britain and China had maintained a large-scale and symmetric dependence in trade since the very beginning, instability of the Chinese market would be a detriment to the interests of the British merchants, and hence it would be less likely for Britain to launch a war of invasion against China. Thirdly, internal disorder directly causes a standstill and setback of the social and economic development of China. If external invasion does not penetrate deep into the Chinese society and seriously destroy its order, China may still enjoy a certain degree of development. Fourthly, China missed an opportunity to keep abreast with the international community for a long time since the 1840s, and therefore, the nation will cherish the opportunity of development brought about by the end of internal and external disturbances.

References

Andrew Scobell, *China and Strategy Culture*, Honolulu: University Press of the Pacific, 2002.

CPC History Research Center of the CPC Central Committee. 2011. *A History of the Communist Party of China, Vol. 2*. CPC History Press.

David C. Gompert, Astrid Cevallos, Cristina L. Garafola, *War with China Thinking Through the Unthinkable*, Published by the RAND Corporation, Santa Monica, Calif., 2016. http://www.rand.org/content/dam/rand/pubs/research_reports/RR1100/RR1140/RAND_RR1140.pdf.

Derek M. Scissors, *Will China's economy be #1 by Dec. 31? (And does it matter?)*, 1st May, 2014. http://www.aei.org/article/economics/international-economy/will-chinas-economy-be-1-by-dec-31-and-does-it-matter.

[47] CPC History Research Center of the CPC Central Committee (2011).

Fairbank, J. 1985. *The Cambridge History of China: The Late Ch'ing, 1800–1911*. Trans. by Institute of History Studies, Chinese Academy of Social Sciences. China Social Sciences Press.
Guthrie, D., *China and Globalization: The Social, Economic and Political Transformation of Chinese Society*, Routledge, 2012.
Hu, Huawei. 2004. Fiction and reality: Folklore, history memory and "archeology of knowledge" of social history. *Jiangsu Social Sciences*, No. 6, pp. 162–166.
Information Office of the State Council of China. 1991. *Human Rights in China*. November, 1991. http://www.scio.gov.cn/zfbps/ndhf/1991/Document/308017/308017.htm.
Information Office of the State Council of China. 2011. *China's Peaceful Development*. September, 2011. http://politics.people.com.cn/GB/1026/15598619.html.
Jacques, M., *When China Rules The World: The End of the Western World and the Birth of a New Global Order* [*Greatly Expanded and Fully Updated*], Penguin Books Limited, 2012.
Jeffrey Frankel, "China is not yet number one", 9th May, 2014, http://www.voxeu.org/article/china-not-yet-number-one.
Jérémie Cohen-Setton, "China's GDP (PPP) to surpass the United States?". 12th May, 2014, http://www.bruegel.org/nc/blog/detail/article/1328-blogs-review-chinas-gdp-ppp-to-surpass-the-united-states/.
Kevin Rudd. "China under Xi Jinping: Alternative Futures for U.S.-China Relations", Match 2015, http://csis.org/files/publication/150313_rudd_speeches.pdf.
Kynge, J., *China Shakes the World: A Titan's Rise and Troubled Future - And the Challenge for America,* Houghton Mifflin Harcourt, 2007.
Licbcrthal, K. 2010. *Governing China*. Trans. by Hu Guocheng and Zhao Mei. China Social Sciences Press.
Liu, Peilin. 2014. China regaining world No. 1: A historical lesson. *China Economic Times*. October 16th, 2014.
Maddison, Angus. 2006. *The World Economy: A Millennial Perspective*. OECD. p. 263.
Nolan, P., *Is China Buying the World?*, Cambridge, UK; Malden, MA: Polity Press, 2012.
Reuters, "China President Xi Jinping Tells Donald Trump the 2 Countries Must Cooperate", *Fortune*. November 14, 2016. http://fortune.com/2016/11/14/china-president-xi-jinping-donald-trump-cooperation/Robert.
Stavrianos, L. 2005. *A Global History*. Trans. by Dong Shuhui et al. Peking University Press, p. 580.
Stephen G. Brooks and William C. Wohlforth, "The Once and Future Superpower: Why China Won't Overtake the United States", *Foreign Affairs*, Volume 95, Number 3, 2016.
Subramanian, A. and M. Kessler. 2012. China's Currency Rises in the US Backyard. *Financial Times*. October 21, 2012.
Subramanian, A., *Eclipse: Living in the Shadow of China's Economic Dominance*, Peterson Institute, 2011.
Uckert, M.B., *China As an Economic and Military Superpower: A Dangerous Combination?*, BiblioBazaar, 2012.
Xi, Jinping. 2014. *The Governance of China*, Foreign Languages Press.
Xi, Jinping. 2014. Promoting the Construction of (Shanghai) Free Trade Zone, Strengthening and Innovating Social Governance of Megalopolis. *People's Daily*, March 6, 2014.
Xi, Jinping. 2016. Firm up Confidence and Seek Common Development, Remarks at the Plenary Session of the Eighth BRICS Summit, October 16th, 2016. http://news.xinhuanet.com/2016–10/16/c_1119727543.htm.
Xi, Jinping. 2016. A New Starting Point for China's Development, A New Blueprint for Global Growths: speech at B20 summit opening ceremony, September 3, 2016. http://cpc.people.com.cn/n1/2016/0905/c64094-28690521.html.
Zhang, Yuyan. 2003. The influence of war on economy. *International Economic Review*, No. 2, pp. 11–13.

Chapter 2
Deng Xiaoping and China's Reform and Opening-Up

To work together with one heart and peaceful coexistence are written into the genes of history of the Chinese Nation and constitute the essence of the Eastern civilization, but the international act of China may take different forms as conditioned by different domestic and international situations. Since the founding of New China, the Chinese people are back on their feet. The Party united and led the Chinese people to have "brought about the most extensive and profound social transformation in the history of China", "laid the fundamental political and institutional foundation for all of the progress made in contemporary China and created a solid basis for the country to become strong and prosperous."[1] It should also be seen that "the construction of New China has made remarkable achievements in the history of over 60 years, and China, the biggest developing countries of the world, shakes off poverty within a short period of 30 years and becomes the second largest economy of the world",[2] which shows from a different angle that the Cultural Revolution and the old way of obturation and rigidity brought huge damages to the country with the result that the country still lived in poverty in the first 30 years since the founding of New China. In June, 1971, Deng Xiaoping, banished to Jiangxi at the time wanted to find a job for his son, Deng Pufang, asking his worker colleagues whether there were radios needing repair. A worker replies that workers could not afford a radio. Deng Xiaoping felt sad and said, we have made experiments with socialism for 20 years and now a worker family could not afford so much as a radio.[3]

In the end of the 1970s, China began to change dramatically since Deng Xiaoping resumed his position in the center of the Chinese politics. Universal material shortage came to be eased, the people were allowed to possess their own means of production and started to accumulate wealth, and pop music, film and television shows of Hong Kong and Taiwan and even of the West became popular … at present, the "Chinese

[1] Xi Jinping's Speech Marking the CPC's 95th Founding Anniversary. *People's Daily*, July 2, 2016.

[2] Ibid.

[3] Vogel (2013).

Y. Zhang and W. Feng, *Peaceful Development Path in China*, China Insights,
https://doi.org/10.1007/978-981-13-1439-1_2

dama (that is, wealthy middle-aged ladies)", whose income increases by a large margin, can purchase gold, real estate and smart toilet lid all over the world. In comparison with the life of 30 or 40 years ago, an era seemed to have passed. And all the changes began with the "Deng Xiaoping Era". To understand what Deng and his colleagues have done and what they have done right will help understand the resolution of the current and future Chinese leadership in sticking to the path of peaceful development inaugurated by them.

Historical Background Before Reform and Opening-Up

Upon the end of the World War II, the world was caught in the two parallel political and economic systems of the United State and the Soviet Union vying for world hegemony. The socialist group under the leadership of the Soviet Union established the Council for Mutual Economic Assistance (CMEA). The CMEA grew out of the "Molotov Plan", which was proposed in response to the America-led "Marshall Plan" and named after the then Soviet Foreign Minister, Vyacheslav Molotov. The former plan aimed at coping with the threats of the latter to the Soviet-controlled Eastern Europe, with the Soviet Union providing economic assistance to Eastern European socialist countries and developing trade with them. From January 1 to 8, 1949, delegates of the Soviet Union, Bulgaria, Hungary, Poland, Romania and Czechoslovakia conducted discussion in Moscow and declared to establish the CMEA. In June, 1962, the 16th Meeting of the CMEA revised the CMEA agreement so as to permit entry to non-European countries. Later on, Mongolia, Cuba and Viet Nam acceded to the CMEA. On June 28, 1991, the CMEA was dissolved at its 46th Meeting in Budapest. The CMEA, from birth to dissolution, have been one of the biggest regional economic organizations, running second only to the European Economic Community, and have played a positive role in facilitating the economic exchange between CMEA members.

On the part of the West, after the post-War economic order took shape, a hegemonic and stable international economic system was established with the United States as its head. The system persisted until the collapse of the Bretton Woods System. During the process, the United States assumed the nucleus or hegemonic position in the international economic governance of the Western World, with US dollar occupying the central position of in international currency system. As the dominant power of the Western world in the post-War era, the United States established a overwhelming part of international mechanisms and rules suiting its own interests (and its allies).[4] It was not only the case that the United States controlled the decision-making in the organizing structures, headquarters locations, and conditions of authorization for such major organizations of international governance as the United Nations, the World Bank and the IMF,[5] but also that the operations and acts of these organizations

[4] See Gao (2012), Qin (1999).

[5] See Peet (2003), Woods (2003).

largely reflected the interests of the United States. For example, an empirical research shows that World Bank loans are clearly influences by the interests of the United States,[6] and the IMF conditions for loans have something to do with the relation of relevant countries with the United States (and its allies).[7] On the other hand, international trade organizations can never reach an official agreement without the support of the United States, regardless of who is in need.[8] Certainly, it should also be noted that the economic power of the United States occupied a position of absolute superiority in the Western world at the time, and functioned as the major or even the only provider of public product to the Western world. In order to make up for the inadequacy of the IMF and the World Bank credit mechanism in deficit financing for large trade in Western Europe, the United States provided a huge amount of investment to Western European countries by way of the European Recovery Plan, supporting their post-War reconstruction. During the Korean War, the United Stated invested an enormous sum of money in Japan, which far exceeded the amount received by countries participating in the European Recovery Plan.

In this parallel system, China initially adopted a "one-sided" policy fully conforming to the system led by the Soviet Union. From 1956 to 1961, China participated in the CEMA meetings as an observer. But as the Sino-Soviet relation split, China has never joined the CEMA. Generally speaking, China stood outside of the international economic system most of the time, being neither a member of the West under the leadership of the United States, nor a member of the CEMA under the leadership of the Soviet Union.

China's transition from its detachment from the international system to its integration can be appreciated by looking at the situation of China's participation in international rules and accession to organizations. From 1949, the year of founding New China, to 1978, the year of reform and opening-up, China basically stood outside major international organizations and systems of rules. Over the 29 years, China approved or signed only 29 multilateral treaties, most of which are largely "neutral" or "instrumental" rules for international practice such as the Metric Convention, the Law of Universal Postal Union and the Geneva Convention for the Amelioration of the Condition of the Wounded and Sick in Armed forces in the Field. Until after the reform and opening-up, China started to actively participate in the existing system of international organizations. From 1978 to 1999, China has approved or signed 197 multilateral treaties, with the annual average of 8.6 treaties. Since 2000, China has seen its step quickened in the multilateral process. From 2000 to 2013, China has approved or signed over 140 multilateral treaties, 10 treaties each year on average.[9] All this started with the reform and opening-up led by Deng Xiaoping, which brought China back to the globalized world, providing an important foundation for the China economic miracle.

---

[6] Fleck and Kilby (2006).

[7] Dreher and Jensen (2007).

[8] Keohane (2001).

[9] The number is calculated with the data provided at the website of the Foreign Ministry of China. http://www.fmprc.gov.cn/mfa_chn/ziliao_611306/tytj_611312/tyfg_611314/default.shtml.

A Good Cat Should Be Good at Catching Rats

The China miracle is realized along with the wakening and growing of pragmatic spirit over the revolutionary romanticism or idealism. Mao Zedong, the core of the Party's first-generation leadership, was not only a great leader but also a romantic poet. In his poem, he boldly depicted his wish to cut the Kunlun Mountains, one of the biggest in China, into three parts, with his back leaning on the sky and a sword in hand, to give one part to Europe, one to the United States, and the last one to Japan[10] so as to make the whole world feel the same degree of warmth (from *NianNujiao Kunlun*). Deng Xiaoping would never think in this way. From Deng's personal experiences, we may see that his pragmatic spirit was a trait that showed itself long before the reform and opening-up.

On July 7, 1962, in a speech when meeting all members attending the 7th Plenary Session of the 3rd Central Committee of the communist Youth League of China, he said, "As to what kind of relations of production is the best mode, I'm afraid we shall have to leave the matter to the discretion of local authorities, allowing them to adopt whatever mode of production that can facilitate quickest recovery and growth of agricultural production. The masses should also be allowed to adopt whatever mode they see fit, legalizing illegal practices as necessary…Comrade Liu Bocheng often quotes a Sichuan proverb—'It does not matter if it is a yellow cat or a black cat, as long as it catches mice.' The reason we defeated Chiang Kai-shek is that we did not always fight in the conventional way. Our sole aim is to win by taking advantage of given conditions. If we want to restore agricultural production, we must also take advantage of actual conditions. That is to say, we should not stick to a fixed mode of relations of production but adopt whatever mode that can help mobilize the masses' initiative.…Another possibility would be to legalize the practice of fixing farm output quotas for each household.…We failed to give them enough consideration in the past, rashly placing the entire country under a unified plan. In some cases, instead of giving full consideration to the different conditions and particular circumstances of different areas, we jumped to conclusions and made everyone do the same thing. As I have mentioned on other occasions, we have had too many movements, launching a movement for each and every undertaking, and all of them were nationwide in scope. It seems that they have not worked out successfully."[11] The words in the quotation that attracted enormous attention were the so-called "cat theory": it does not matter if it is a yellow cat or a black cat, as long as it catches mice. But as a matter of fact, "legalizing illegal practices as necessary" and "to legalize the practice of fixing farm output quotas for each household" were just what villagers of Xiaogang, Fengyang County, Anhui Province did over ten years later, and the practice sounded

---

[10]In the initial version, Mao Zedong kept the third part of Kunlun in China, and changed from "keeping one part in China" to the present version "giving one part to Japan" with the consideration that a balance should be kept between Europe, the United States and Japan. See CPC Literature Research Center of the CPC Central Committee (1996).

[11]Deng (1994b).

the beginning of the reform and opening-up, which was initiated by Deng Xiaoping with the aim of "deliberating and developing productive forces"

When Deng made the above speech, China was suffering greatly from the after-effect of Stalinist mode of development (the after-effect was still felt until right before the reform and opening-up). Though the Sino-Soviet relation broke up due to open quarrels between the two, China did figure out a way of development other than the Stalinist mode. On that issue, Khrushchev, who quarreled with China, was no exception. Although he was dubbed the first reformer of the Soviet Union for his deceased-curing secret report on Stalin, what he actually "revealed, criticized and tried to defeat is Stalin, rather than Stalinism."[12] His reform did not go out of the Stalinist framework.

According to Stalinism, the government manages economy with mandatory plans. The plans enjoy legal force, and a failure to carry them out would face executive and legal punishment. In the Stalin era, the plans were handed out on a year to year basis, and divided in terms of quarters, months and days. As for the mandatory plans, it was often said that "it requires central allocation to have a piece of brick, a pair of shoes or a piece of underwear." It was no exaggeration. According to the Soviet Ministers Conference Resolution on Approving the Retail Price List of State-Operated Foods and Industrial Products, a resolution jointly issued by Stalin with the Director of the General Office of the Soviet Ministers Conference on December 14, 1947, there was a detailed prescription for prices of products such as flour, soap and match in different areas, cities and countries.

Under mandatory plan system, subordinate officials, for the sake of praise or avoidance of punishment, attempted to step up the pace to over-fulfill the plans issued by superordinate leaders, sometimes even practicing fraud for that purpose. The superordinates, misguided by the overall performance and with their goals in plans heightened, would force their subordinates to twist and fulfill the heightened plans head-on, finally leading to disastrous results. In 1947, local Soviet organizations made a competition in their report of fulfilling and over-fulfilling the plan of grain collection, with the result of forcing farmers to turn in seeds and rations. In order to fulfill plans concerning meat collection, cows (even pregnant cows) were subject to butchering for meat. Practices such as these caused a wide spread of famine.[13] The plan of 1958 included a gradual merger of tractor stations and farms. The plan to be gradually realized staged a competition among farms for merger. Till January, 1959, only 345 among the 8,000 tractor stations were left, and to the end of that year, the number was 34. The movement-like merger landed a great number of farms in bankruptcy, machines purchased operated in low efficiency for lack of mechanics and maintenance personnel, and the industrial production of agricultural machines also shrank.[14]

Similar incidents occurred in China, with even more serious results than the Soviet Union. In 1958, Mao Zedong launched a movement called the "Great Leap Forward",

---

[12]Arbatov (1998).

[13]Shen (2002).

[14]Lu (2007).

requiring village residents to join the "People's Commune", and till the end of the year all villages turned into people's communes. In order to meet the goal of national steel production, farmers stopped farming to produce steel in their backyard with their own cooking tools as raw materials, and messed together in a canteen. The practice consumed grain storages collectively owned by a village, while producing a large amount of useless steel. In the autumn and winter of 1958, agricultural production suffered a severe loss for too many farmers stopped farming. Later, grain production difficulties continued due to mistakes in policies, messy management and natural disasters. In the meantime, the leaders wanted to ensure enough grain supply to citizens. Consequently, in order to please their superordinates, local officials with the ever more common practices of being boastful and egalitarian, went so far as to hide the terrible living and producing condition of rural areas, even excessively collected farmers' rations, and caused unnatural death of over 10 million people. Besides, there was also a severe setback in industry, fiscal revenue and commercial business. By 1961, in terms of commensurable price, gross product of agriculture lowered by 2.4% in comparison with the previous year, that of light industry by 21.6%, that of heavy industry by 46.5%, fiscal revenue by 37.8%, and the total sum of retail sales of social products by 12.8%. The amount of grain, oil and cloth consumption for city and country residents decreased in three consecutive years from 1959 to 1961. The people face the hardest time since the founding of New China.[15] With the situation in view, Mao Zedong criticized himself at the Enlarged Conference of CPC central committee of 1962 (the number of persons attending the conference was 7,118, and it was then called the Seven-Thousand People Conference).

The "cat theory" speech was made upon the Chinese leaders starting to reflect upon the "Great Leap Forward". From 1961 to 1965, Deng Xiaoping together with Liu Shaoqi, Zhou Enlai and Chen Yun was in charge of drawing up a plan to restore the country's economy, and adjust the radical measures of the "Great Leap Forward". The plan they formulated nullified almost all policies of the "Great Leap Forward". In the respect of agriculture, they transferred the power of people's commune to production teams, and allowed farmers to possess a plot for their private use. In the respect of industry, the accountability system, specialized management and differentiated wage system were re-adopted. By 1965, the situation was clearly improved, with the grain produce of the year reaching 195 million tons, resuming the level of 1957 before the "Great Leap Forward", and production of most industrial products doubling that of 1957.[16] The achievements of the national economic adjustments notwithstanding, the incorrect "Left" guideline for economy did not only continue, but also developed in politic and thoughts.[17] As Deng Xiaoping himself commented, "from 1957 on, China was plagued by 'Left' ideology, which gradually became dominant."[18]

As the adjusting measures of Deng ran counter to Mao's ideas, Deng was estranged. Upon the Cultural Revolution, Deng was criticized and denounced, house-

[15]CPC History Research Center of the CPC Central Committee (2011), p. 593.

[16]Evans (1996), p. 179.

[17]CPC History Research Center of the CPC Central Committee (2011), p. 743.

[18]Deng (1993a).

arrested and banished as the second in another "Command" antagonistic to Mao. The condition persisted till 1972 when Deng, upon the information that Lin Biao, the designated successor to Mao, defected and fled the country and died in air crash in 1971, wrote a letter to Mao and the CPC Central Committee asking for work. With the support of Premier Zhou Enlai, Deng was transferred back to Beijing from Jiangxi, where he was banished in February, 1973, and re-appointed as vice Premier, assisting the cancer-afflicted Zhou Enlai to preside over governmental affairs. In 1975, Mao Zedong felt unsatisfied with Deng's work of correcting the mistakes of the Cultural Revolution, and launched a movement to "criticize Deng, and fight against Right-headed trend of redressing cases". In the year after, Deng was dismissed from his post, but his membership of the Party was retained. Now there was a period of over a year before Deng resumed his position and initiated the great cause of reform and opening-up. During the period, Mao Zedong and Zhou Enlai passed away, and the "Gang of Four" was smashed, who took advantage of the close relationship with Mao to seize power of the country, and caused huge damages to the Chinese social and economic development.

Upholding the Four Cardinal Principles

To see the pragmatic Deng Xiaoping as a pragmatist, who would say yes to any measures to facilitate reforms, is completely mistaken. On this point, Deng was quite different from the leaders of the Soviet Union in the mid and late 1980s, such as Gorbachev. At the time, some leaders of the Soviet Union (such as Ligachev, the political bureau member of the Communist Party of the Soviet Union) hoped to conduct reforms to the Soviet Union, but wanted to keep the country's international and military position and its socialist system. In contrast, the supreme leader Gorbachev and his allies in the Political Bureau did think so. They held that whatever might ensure reforms would go, and went so far as to dissolve the Soviet Union.[19]

Different from the descendants of Soviet revolutionaries as represented by Gorbachev, Deng Xiaoping and other first-generation proletariat revolutionists cherished the independent position and the socialist system of the country, which were won with a long-term arduous struggle. Besides, despite the fact that Mao Zedong made serious mistakes on issues such as the Cultural Revolution, causing severe harms to cadres and common people including Deng Xiaoping, his reputation and authority was still where the belief of most Chinese people lay. The turmoil in places like Georgia after Khrushchev's secret report was a lesson to learn from. And Deng was fully aware that China, which walked out of disasters shortly before, could not endure another splitting up and opposition.

On December 13, 1978, De Xiaoping after resuming his post for one year made a speech entitled Emancipate the Mind, See Truth from Facts and Unite as One in Looking to the Future at, saying that "the great contributions of Comrade Mao in the course

[19]Odom (2000).

of long revolutionary struggles will never fade....Mao Zedong Thought will forever remain the greatest intellectual treasure of our Party, our army and our people." He also pointed out that Mao Zedong was not infallible or free from shortcomings, and we must understand the scientific tenets of Mao Zedong Thought correctly and as an integral whole and develop them under the new historical conditions. As for the Cultural Revolution, "it may take a rather long time to fully understand and assess some of the particular issues involved. We will probably be able to make a more correct analysis of this period in history after some time has passed than we can right now."

Encouraged by the speech, a campaign to shatter the bandages of concept and liberate the mind was unfolded in the country, and some acts and activities went "too far" for Deng Xiaoping. For example, at a theoretical work meeting of 1979, someone called for denying Mao Zedong Thought and Mao Zedong himself, and even rooting out Mao Zedong Thought; it was also suggested that it was improper to write the leadership by the CPC into the Constitution. Outside the meeting room, the strong discontent emotion expressed on the "democracy wall" of Xidan worries Deng and other revolutionists a lot. Deng Xiaoping said to Hu Qiaomu, "I read the briefing of the theoretical work meeting. The more I read it, the more I feel uneasy."[20]

On March 30, 1979, Deng Xiaoping at a theoretical work meeting made a long speech entitled Uphold the Four Cardinal Principles as a response to the current thoughts within the Party and in society. He proposed that to carry out China's four modernizations, the Four Cardinal Principles must be upheld. The four principles are: We must keep to the socialist road; we must uphold the dictatorship of the proletariat; we must uphold the leadership of the Communist Party; we must uphold Marxism-Leninism and Mao Zedong Thought.

By the Four Cardinal Principles, Deng Xiaoping reiterated the goals of the socialist system, strengthened the legitimacy of the Party to lead the people in the socialist construction of the country on the principle of the dictatorship of the proletariat, and under the guidance of Marxism-Leninism and Mao Zedong Thought, and stabilized the thoughts and the cadres. The direct statement of the Four Cardinal Principles delimits the boundary of conducting reform and opening-up in a pragmatic spirit, clarifies misunderstandings in the country, and concentrates the force of construction for modernization. In fact, the CPC leadership is the core of the China path. The strong leadership provides a basic and efficient framework for the social, political and economic stability, and enhances the predictability of governmental acts.

Seen from another perspective, upholding the Four Cardinal Principles reflects the strong determination and pragmatic spirit of China's sticking to the path of independent development. In 1989, drastic changes occurred in Eastern Europe, and the socialist cause suffered a great setback. When expressing all his ideas and intentions to several key CPC leaders, Deng Xiaoping said, "if we did not uphold socialism, we would eventually become, at best, a dependency of other countries, and it would be even more difficult for us to develop. The international market has already been fully occupied, and it will be very hard for us to get in. Only socialism can save

[20] Wang (2014).

China, and only socialism can develop China."[21] It seems that Deng also considered the socialist status of China from the perspectives of national independence and even of the chances to win international market. He well understood that if China leaned on the West like the Eastern European countries, China would be one of those "banner-changers", and would probably not be a welcome one due to stark differences in culture and customs. If China exchanged its own interests for some assistance, it would be of little help to the development of such a big economy like China. Moreover, with the international market in hot competition, China would not get a market share for free, even if it comprehensively leaned on the West.

In contrast, China, with the banner of socialism upheld, will occupy a conspicuous position among various countries. Those who do not enjoy an advantage in current international market and under current international rules are likely to focus their efforts to develop a relation with China, by which China can obtain diversified supply channels in energy and raw materials. With chances of war between big powers largely excluded by the existence of nuclear weapons, developed countries may also invest more resources in China with the aim of transforming the country by ways of market. Therefore, China will become one of the countries to which developed Western countries attach attention and importance. As long as China maintains this kind of exchange and communication with these countries and sticks to the principles of market and honesty, their capital, technology and market will gradually be open to China. If China is stable, develops well, with its powerful resources of production and large scale of market, the goal of integrating into world economy, while being free from foreign influence, will be better realized. The Four Cardinal Principles lay the foundation for the socialist path with Chinese characteristics. The development of the 30 years since proves that this principled and pragmatic development path, pointed out by Deng Xiaoping, is correct.

To sum up, the socialist road is the basis of the development path with Chinese characteristics. The dictatorship of the proletariat under the leadership of the Party provides a stable and strong leading nucleus and efficient and powerful political and economic framework for exploring and practicing the social road. In this sense, leadership of the Party is the core of the Chinese path. Under the long-term leadership of the Party, all classes of the countries have a consistence expectation of China's political order, and concentrate their attention on socialist construction. The Party can carefully formulate the blueprint for national development and construction in a long-term, comprehensive and strategic manner, and practice and realize it by way of efficient political and economic framework.

Allowing Some People to Be Prosperous First

As Deng Xiaoping sees it, the concrete way for China's pragmatic development is to allow some people to be prosperous first, let the prosperous help the poor, and

[21] Deng (1993b).

finally to realize common prosperity. In the 1978 speech, Emancipate the Mind, See Truth from Facts and Unite as One in Looking to the Future, Deng Xiaoping has already proposed the "good first" policy, saying that "in economic policy, I think we should allow some regions and enterprises and some workers and peasants to earn more and enjoy more benefits sooner than others, in accordance with their hard work and greater contributions to society. If the standard of living of some people is raised first, this will inevitably be an impressive example to their 'neighbors', and people in other regions and units will want to learn from them. This will help the whole national economy to advance wave upon wave and help the people of all our nationalities to become prosperous in a comparatively short period."

On January 12, 1983, in a talk with leaders in charge of the State Development Planning Commission and agricultural authorities, he first proposed the concept of "rich first", saying, "Some people in rural areas and cities should be allowed to get rich before others. It is only fair that people who work hard should prosper. To let some people and some regions become prosperous first is a new policy that is supported by everyone. It is better than the old one." On October 23, 1985, in a meeting with a senior US business delegation organized by the Time Inc. Deng Xiaoping reiterated the "rich first" concept and talked about "common prosperity", saying that "some regions and some people may prosper before others do, and then they can help other regions and people to gradually do the same."

It is generally accepted that the theory of common prosperity is a correct rationale to realize national economic growth on the principle of efficiency and with the mechanism of incentives. It does make some sense. Later on, Deng Xiaoping on different occasions talked about the issue of allowing some regions and people to be prosperous first, and almost every time he had emphasized first prosperity is to help the poor and to realize common prosperity. Besides explicating the mechanism of incentives, it was also a justification for first prosperity under socialism. In fact, Deng Xiaoping made a clear statement that "poverty is not socialism". In an interview with Wallace, he said that during the Cultural Revolution there was a view that poor communism was preferable to rich capitalism, and he was opposed to that view, holding that there is no such thing as poor communism, and that communist society is based on material abundance. He stressed that "there can be no communism with pauperism, or socialism with pauperism. So to get rich is no sin.... The principles of socialism are: first, development of production and second, common prosperity."[22] Views such as these include getting prosperous within socialist system, and richness is not considered as a result of the sinful capitalism.

The theory of first prosperity and common prosperity contain two points which easy to be overlooked. First, the theory of first prosperity makes a fundamental contribution in that it makes clear that prosperity of the people is the basis and premise of national prosperity. The thirty redresses the imbalanced Stalin mode, under which the consumption and income growth of the people were suppressed, and state-invested projects such as the military and heavy industry were emphasized.

[22]Deng (1993c).

In a relatively closed environment, a state may realize an extraordinary development in particular fields and departments, with methods such as depending on the "price scissors" between villages and cities, and calling for or forcing the people to "tighten the belt" or "giving up butter for cannons". Against a specific historical background, such a development mode may speedily improve a country's basic productive force and level of security in a short period of time, and hence a helpful policy. But once the special measures were made permanent, the social development would undergo an abnormal road.

The Soviet Union suffered on this point. A script of Thatcher's 1991 Huston speech[23] first released on a Russian website records that the United States and the Great Britain dragged the Soviet Union into arms race by way of "leaking" the number of their nuclear weapons on purpose, forcing the country to decrease the production of consumer products and hence bringing about large-scale discontent.[24]

Such unsubstantiated evidence aside, a comparison between military investment and productive investment indeed shows that the imbalanced distribution in resources affect the country's domestic economic development. Sustainability in military expenditure for the Soviet Union, as measured by the difference of growth rates in GNP and defense expenditure from the end of 1960s to the end of 1970s, was lower than that of the United States, with the Soviet presenting a negative value for many years. It can be taken to mean that the GNP of the Soviet Union could not sustain the growth in defense expenditure, which surpassed economic growth for many years. In the 1980s, the sustainability in military expenditure for the Soviet Union improved relatively, but the performance was achieved against the background of the sliding GNP growth (in an absolute sense and in comparison with the United States). In other words, it followed from the fact that the high military expenditure in previous decades had dragged the economy down, and military expenditure growth had to be adjusted accordingly.

Deng Xiaoping's theory of first prosperity and common prosperity lays the foundation for the prosperity of the people and of the state, enables the country to sidestep the old road of the Soviet Union, and provides a solid and sustainable basis for national prosperity. Certainly, it was closely related to a different international environment which China was involved in and endeavored to safeguard. China was then in a relatively more peaceful and open international environment, providing a relatively stable external basis for the Chinese people's road to prosperity.

---

[23]Doubts were expressed as to the authenticity of the speech script, considering it to be faked by the Russian military. A special research by doctor Zhang Shuhua and others, who first introduced the speech to China, found that "Mrs. Thatcher visited Huston on November 18, 1991, and delivered a speech at a meeting organized by the US Petroleum Institute. Up till now, the contents of the speech were released and quoted by the Russian media and relevant persons. The Thatcher Foundation could not (or would not) provide the script of the speech, while the British Independent Television Network and the US Petroleum Institute remained silent on the issue. We believe that the Russian material could be trusted before the Thatcher Foundation provides credible evidence to the contrary effect." See Zhang Shuhua and Wang Wen'e. 2010. A research on the authenticity of Mrs. Thatcher's 1991 Huston Speech. *Red Flag Files*, No. 23.

[24]Zhang (2010).

The era of Soviet-US supremacy struggle was a different story. The United States treated the ideologically opposing Soviet Union as an arch rival. Despite the change of policy race to "peaceful coexistence, peaceful competitive, and peaceful transition" on the apart of the Soviet under the pressure of arms, the United States stuck to its policy of containment and its stand of hostility to the Soviet Union. Gordon H. Chang, an American scholar, in a research based on a large amount of declassified documents, reveals that since the end of the 1940s, the United Stated has conducted a "psychological warfare" with the leverage of China against the Soviet Union so as to weaken the power of the socialist camp. On the one hand, the United States, out of consideration of the Soviet leader's yearning for respect of the civilized West, expressed respect and appreciation of the Soviet Union's concessions, while repeatedly and openly condemning China's conduct; on the other, it adopted a long-term and comprehensive economic blockade against China, leaving the country no alternative but to lean on the Soviet Union and Eastern Europe, which increased their economic burden, and eventually led the dissatisfaction of the Soviet leaders. What was out of their expectations was that the United States resumed relation with China upon their split-up with China, enclosing the country from the East, the West and Central Asia, landing it in extreme fiscal difficulties and defeating this arch rival finally. This shows that the United States adopted a clear and strong strategy to pinpoint the major rival and disintegrate it with concentrated force.[25]

In comparison, the United States did not take severe containment measures against China when the country attempted to enter in the global economy after reform and opening-up. A new research by RAND make the following comment on China's globalization: China is a major contributor to the open world system advocated by the United States; "Although joining late, China has joined the globalized system much more enthusiastically than Japan. China's economy is much more open than Japan"; China has changed a lot, "among the most important of these changes are the decision to adopt the Western concept of rule of law; adoption of competition as a centrally important economic practice; and adoption of English language as virtually a second language for the educated Chinese population.…Perhaps most importantly, China has sent its elite youth abroad for education in an exercise of internationalism comparable to the Romans turning over their children to the Greeks."[26]

On June 20, 2013, we paid a visit to academician Titarenko, the director of the Far East Institute of the Russian Academy of Sciences. He complained about his experiences of attending meetings in China. He said at international meetings held in China, it was inappropriate for the Chinese scholars to express their views in English rather than in Chinese. He "felt ashamed for his Chinese comrades." As far as he can see, China is a country with a long history, and the Chinese language was an important international language as one of the UN working languages. China should value its own culture and language as Russia does. Indeed, English signboards are seldom to be seen on the streets and in subways stations of Moscow, which are more often than not indicated only in Russian. The situation constitutes a sharp contrast with Beijing,

---

[25]Gordon (2014).

[26]Overholt (2005).

where almost all public signs are written in both Chinese and English, providing convenience to foreigners. In a sense, the academician's complaint makes sense. It seems that China pays a huge amount of one-directional "language seigniorage" to English-speaking countries, but in terms of the RAND report, the amount is actually a credit deposit for China to embrace the US-led globalization.

In another word, since the 1970s when the Sino-US diplomatic relation was established, the United States never treated China as an arch rival, but hoped to weaken the Soviet Union with the power of China. The situation provided the foundation for the subsequent development of Sino-US relation. Since reform and opening-up, China has taken a series of economic measures to develop its economy with the goal toward the prosperity of the people, and also sent out clear and credible signals to embrace globalization, which helped ease the tense relations between China and the Western countries such as the United States.

The second two points which is easy to be overlooked is that Deng Xiaoping's theory of first prosperity and common prosperity is not about the commonsensical property protection. When making the policy of promoting the practice of fixing farm output quotas for each household, Deng actually set up in policy and in legal terms farmers' rights of land contract and interests. These rights have been expanded and recognized throughout the years, with the fixed number of years for land contract extended from one year, three years, 15 years to 30 years, and finally becoming "long-standing". Farmers started to possess assets (including rights of land subcontracting, as we all land use and interests) in addition to products. He who has a permanent property will have a heart of perseverance. The increasingly clear delimitation of property right inspired farmers' working enthusiasm with the result that agricultural production greatly improved without the help of remarkably improved agricultural technology. From 1978 to 1984, production per capita for grain, cotton and meat grew annually by 3.8%, 17.5% and 9% respectively, whereas from 1957 to 1977 the corresponding number was 0.2%, −0.6% and 1.7%. By the mid-1980s, radios, about which Deng Xiaoping once felt sad because a city worker family could it after 20-year socialist construction, now came into common farmers' households. Many of them bought bicycles, and were about to build a new house with bricks, cement and gravels.[27] The areas where property rights were to be recognized were also spread to other social sectors, and finally inviolability of private property was written into the country's constitution.[28] The origin in the development of private property protection was then traced back to Deng Xiaoping's recognizing and confirming the practice of fixing farm output quotas for each household in the early period of reform and opening-up.

---

[27]Evans (1996), p. 278.

[28]The Constitution of 1954 only recognized citizens' right of succession to private property, and Constitutions of 1975 and 1978 cancelled contents related to private property. The Constitution of 1982 returned to the stand of 1954, prescribing that "the nation protects citizens' right of succession to private property according to laws." An Amendment to the Constitution in 2004 eventually establishes that citizens' legal private property is inviolable, and that the nation protects citizens' right to private property and right of succession to private property according to laws. Up till this point, right of private property is established as a complete and formal right by the Constitution.

There is, however, a difference of focus. The theory of first prosperity and common prosperity stresses "priority of non-neutral property right system over property right protection."[29] As shown by the rising of the Western World, American bullions flowing into Europe resulted in a disparity in wealth and class reorganization. The rising class of merchants has gain more voice in their call for property right protection, which contributed to the development of capitalist institutions and economic growth. European property right system then (non-neutrally) emphasized the right to property for the emerging merchant class, which consisted of people of adventurous character (or entrepreneurship), the ability to produce and the desire to obtain profits. The non-neutral system was preferential to them, helping them grow strong as individuals and giving other groups impetus to bring themselves (and their resources) into their activities, which led to the rise of Europe or the Western World as a whole. The theory of first prosperity and common prosperity was somewhat similar in essence though not in practice. It aimed at protecting the group made up of people of entrepreneurship, practicing the "priority of productive non-neutral property right system over property right protection".

At that time, both protectors with Deng Xiaoping as a symbol and the protected were in a hard situation. Protectors had to make unremitting efforts to convince their conservative colleagues, while the protected might even face prison sentence for their conduct. It was the period when Deng Xiaoping just resumed his position for the third time in his "three-dismissal-and-three-resumption" life and when Nian Guangjiu, founder of Fool's Sunflower Seeds, was in the half of his life journey of three rounds of ups and downs.

In the 1960s, Nian Guangjiu inherited his father's fruit stall, but later the stall was outlawed as "the tail of capitalism" and he was put into jail for "excessive speculation". During the Cultural Revolution, Nian learnt to cook sunflower seeds and started a business, and in the end of 1979, he registered the brand "Fool's Sunflower Seeds", expanded his business range, and hired more than 100 employees. At the time, hiring more than 8 employees would be considered a conduct of exploiting workers' surplus value. The case was reported to Deng Xiaoping, and the reply was "leave him alone". On October 22, 1984, Deng delivered a speech at the Third Plenary Session of the Central Advisory Commission, mentioning that "the emergence of privately hired labor was quite shocking a while back. Everybody was very worried about it. In my opinion, that problem can be set aside for a couple of years. Will that affect the overall situation? If we act on the question now, people will say the policies have changed, and they will be upset. If you put the man who makes "Fool's Sunflower Seeds" out of business, it will make many people anxious, and that won't do anybody any good. What is there to be afraid of if we let him go on selling his seeds for a while? Will that hurt socialism?"[30] The instruction from the supreme leader made Nian go through the difficulty.

---

[29]Zhang and Gao (2004).

[30]Deng (1993d).

In 1987, Nian was investigated again for economic conducts. The case was dragged into 1991 and he was sentenced to three-year imprisonment for "hooliganism".[31] In 1992 Deng Xiaoping in "Talks during the Inspection Tour in the South" said that "in the initial stage of the rural reform, there emerged in Anhui Province the issue of the "Fool's Sunflower Seeds". Many people felt uncomfortable with this man who had made a profit of 1 million yuan. They called for action to be taken against him. I said that no action should be taken, because that would make people think we had changed our policies, and the loss would outweigh the gain."[32] After the talk was made public, the Procuratorate of Wuhu actively dropped the case, and on March 13 of the same year Nian was set free.

Nian Guangjiu or "Fool's Sunflower Seeds" was not the only one protected by Deng Xiaoping. His protection of those becoming rich first encouraged people of entrepreneurship, and a large number of entrepreneurs showed up, including Liu Chuanzhi, who started his business in roughly the same period as Nian Guangjiu after reform and opening-up. Liu founded Lenovo Group, which is the biggest producer of PC and No. 3 producer of smart phone in the world, acquiring IBM's PC and laptop business in 2004, and Motorola's smart phone business in 2014.

One Country, Two Systems

Right after the "Gang of Four" was smashed, Deng Xiaoping resumed his position in Chinese politics under the support of old cadres such as Chen Yun, and quickly eliminated the ill effects of the concept of "Two Whatevers"[33] proposed by the Mao Zedong-appointed successor. Deng was facing a China in dire need of rebuilding. In his own words, the sabotage by the "Gang of Four" of the four modernizations brought China's economy to the brink of collapse. Years of internal friction limited China's domestic accumulation, and to save the day, it was not enough for Deng Xiaoping to rely only on internal reform and the gradual first prosperity of some regions and some people. He had to resort to stable external environment and continual inflow of foreign capital and technology for fast economic development. Areas where overseas Chinese gather such Hong Kong and Taiwan served as the major potential sources where China has obtained foreign capital, technology and management experiences since reform and opening-up.

Although the policy of "One Country, Two Systems" is directly targeted at problems of China's reunification, such as Hong Kong's return and the Taiwan problem, it was first proposed, with the contemporary internal and external conditions into consideration, as an effort to safeguard international peaceful environment, including a

[31] The new Criminal Law of 1997 revokes the crime of hooliganism.

[32] Deng (1993e).

[33] That is, "whatever policy decisions Chairman Mao had made must be firmly upheld, and whatever instructions he had given must be followed unswervingly." According to the creed, there was no legitimacy for Deng Xiao, who was dismissed before the death of Mao Zedong, to resume his post.

main intent to ensure developed countries such as the United States and Japan. The germ of the idea of Deng Xiaoping first appeared in a dialogue with Japanese literary critic Jun Eto on October 8, 1978. He said that mainland China's policy towards Taiwan would take the realities of Taiwan into account, and took the investment interests of the United States and Japan in Taiwan as an example. After that, Deng Xiaoping, at many meetings with Americans and the Japanese and during his visit to the United States, reiterated his idea that as long as reunification of the country can be realized, the reality and the current system of Taiwan would be respected, and foreign investments in Taiwan and nongovernmental exchanges could go on as before.

The first article included in *Selected Works of Deng Xiaoping* (Vol. III) that discussed the idea of "One Country, Two Systems" was A New Approach to Stabilizing the World Situation, a script for his talk with a delegation from the Center for Strategic and International Studies of Georgetown University in Washington, D.C. In the very beginning, he said that "there are many disputes in the world, and we must find ways to solve them. Over the years I have been considering how those disputes could be solved by peaceful means, rather than by war." That is to say, the essence or focus of "One Country, Two Systems" is a signal of peace to the world (especially the United States).

The problem of reunification concerns the legitimacy of power for the Chinese rulers, bearing no equivocation. But how can the sincerity of peace be fully or convincingly expressed so as to win a stable external environment? It will not work with only slogans. The idea of "One Country, Two Systems" provides a concrete workable measure "to solve disputes by peaceful means", taking into account the interests of the whole nation, of both parties involved and of third parties which are involved due to investment and trade relations. The idea, by way of repeated expositions and promotions by top leaders, was made a state policy at the Third Session of the Sixth National People's Congress (the highest organ of state power). It then constituted an endorsement of the sincerity of China's intent to reunify the country by peaceful means.

The policy of "One Country, Two Systems" also plays an important role in attracting overseas Chinese to put their energy and resources into China's economic construction. If a divided China returned to the situation of confrontation, overseas Chinese of different backgrounds would hardly avoid the troublesome question who to support and who to be opposed to. In a peaceful situation, there will be no question as to the common wish of overseas Chinese for mainland China to be prosperous. The policy of "One Country, Two Systems", as a peace plan on the part of mainland China, encourages overseas Chinese to participate in China's development. At a meeting with Dhanin Chearavanont, Chairman of the Board of the Chia Tai Group in Thailand, on April 7, 1990, Deng Xiaoping made an explanation of the policy of "One Country, Two Systems", saying that we have already shown our broad-mindedness by proposing the policy of "One Country, Two Systems". He also mentioned that "we have tens of millions of overseas compatriots, and they want to see China grow strong and prosperous. We are unique in that respect." In order to eliminate the worries of overseas Chinese to invest in China, Deng purposefully explained that "Last year there was some unrest in China. As was necessary, we brought the situation under control. I asked others to tell President Bush that if the political situation in China became unstable, the trouble would spread to the rest of the world, with consequences that would be hard to imagine. Stability is essential to economic development, and only under the leadership of the Communist Party can there be a stable socialist China."[34]

Ensured by the promise of "One Country, Two Systems", the capital of overseas Chinese flowed into mainland China via places such as Hong Kong, making a significant contribution to China's economic construction. From 1986 to 1994, foreign direct investment (FDI) flowing into China by way of Hong Kong accounted for 61.2% in the overall amount that China received from abroad. The percentage lowered since, but still maintained a high level of over 30%. When the American subprime crisis induced a global financial crisis, FDI that comes from Hong Kong remarkably improved, with an average percentage of 58.1% from 2009 to 2013. This shows from another aspect the strong attachment of overseas Chinese to their cultural roots and their passion and importance to participate in China's economic construction.

The policy of "One Country, Two Systems" vouchers the inclusiveness of China-style socialist system. The inclusiveness shows to the Western developed countries that China's system is expansive or aggressive, but open and cooperative. As the realization that "poverty is not socialism" adds inclusiveness and flexibility into China's socialist system, the policy of "One Country, Two Systems" manifests its vitality.

At a meeting with the members of the Committee for Drafting the Basic Law of the Hong Kong Special Administrative Region on April 16, 1987, Deng Xiaoping said, "Our socialist system is a system with Chinese characteristics. One important characteristic is our way of handling the question of Hong Kong, Macao and Taiwan, or the policy of 'One country, Two Systems'. This is something new. It was created not by the United States, Japan, the Soviet Union or any European country, but by China; that is why we call it a Chinese characteristic."[35] As Deng Xiaoping sees it, a system other than that of China could not be so inclusive. The United States would not allow communism to be practiced in some of its regions, neither would the Great Britain and Japan. In a similar fashion, the Soviet Union would not bear capitalism to be practiced in its regions. The peaceful competition between two systems as mentioned by the Soviet Union was between one country with another. Only China in reform and opening-up can be so inclusive as to allow the competition to go on within a country. Deng Xiaoping has confidence in the system, saying "We believe the existence of capitalism in limited areas will actually be conducive to the development of socialism...will favor the growth of the socialist economy there."[36]

[34]Deng (1993f).

[35]Deng (1993g).

[36]Deng (1993h).

Peace and Development Are the Two Issues in the World Today

The strategic transformation of China, with focus on internal economic construction and external peace by openly resorting to the formula of "One Country, Two Systems" for reunification, results from the change in Deng Xiaoping and the CPC's judgment about the world. In the era of Mao Zedong, war and revolution were considered the main themes of the world. Although China did not seek war, the country presupposed that a war was bound to break out and it would take the position of defense in the war. Then the war had better break out sooner, in a more extensive manner and be fought with nuclear weapons. China hoped to delay or even eliminate the possibility of war with such determined preparations. "War has its own laws, which are not subject to human will. If we are not prepared, things will worsen; if we are prepared, either the enemies will be deterred from coming, or they will be eliminated, if they do come.".[37] This was why it was always stressed then that "there was an imminent danger of war".[38]

Since the 1980s, the CPC's judgment about the international situation began to change. The National Congress of the CPC, the highest organ of Party power, is convened every five years by the Central Committee of the CPC. The report at the Party Congress summarizes the principal work of the country and the Party, and lays out the plan for work in coming years under essential judgments of internal and external situations. A comparison of the part on international situation in the reports since the Eighth Party Congress (convened from September 15 to September 27, 1956) reveals that the CPC's judgments about the world gradually changed from "rampantly anti-China", "a world in turmoil" and "factors leading to war clearly on the rise" before reform and opening-up to a mild formulation. In the report of the 12th Party Congress of 1982, it was stated that "the danger of a world war is more pressing than ever", but also pointed out that "the people of the world can sabotage their strategic deployment". By the 13th Party Congress, the report presented a changed description that "the East and the West have seen a certain degree of easing in their relations", and since the 14th Party Congress, the judgment on international situation has been constant to the effect that a new world war can be avoided or never breaks out. The report of the 15th Party Congress proposes that "for a fairly long period of time to come, it will be possible to avert a new world war and secure a favorable, peaceful international environment and maintain good relations with the surrounding countries", while the report of the 16th Party Congress points out in an assured manner that "A new world war is unlikely in the foreseeable future." The reports of both the 17th Party Congress and the 18th Party Congress make assessments of the underlying forces contributing to peace in the future, stating that "the international balance of power is changing in favor of the maintenance of world peace." It can be seen that

[37] CPC Literature Research Center of the CPC Central Committee (1997).

[38] Deng (1993i).

China's positioning and stand in foreign affairs as reflected in the reports of Party Congresses change from confrontation to safeguarding peace.

Moreover, a comparison between Party Congress reports shows that the part on international situation accounts for a noticeably shorter length after reform and opening-up, signifying that the ruling party of China has restored its long tradition of focusing on internal affairs, emphasizing internal construction rather than external conflict, and creating conditions for internal development by the means of external cooperation (Table 2.1).

The change in the judgments of the CPC concerning international situation came as a result of a new understanding of the main themes of the times by the collective leadership with Deng Xiaoping at its core. On December 28, 1977, right after resuming his post, Deng Xiaoping made a new judgment on international situations, holding that "it is possible to win a delay in the outbreak of war". On the one hand, China enjoyed the conditions to work from inside: "applying Comrade Mao Zedong's strategy of differentiating the three worlds and following his line in foreign affairs, we can contribute our share to the international struggle against hegemonism"; on the other hand, objective conditions were also in favor of maintaining the current peaceful situation: "the Soviet Union has not yet finished its global strategic deployment. And the global strategy of the United States, after its defeat in Southeast Asia, has shifted to the defensive. The United States isn't ready to fight a world war yet either."[39] Only with a judgment to such an effect could Deng Xiaoping make the decision to step up the country's economic construction along aside strengthening the peaceful environment. When looking back on the decision in 1987, Deng Xiaoping candidly said, "With regard to the international situation, it seems to me that relatively long-lasting peace is possible and that war can be avoided…. It was on the basis of this appraisal of the international situation that in 1978 we decided to devote all our energies to economic development. Without a peaceful environment, economic development would be out of the question. At the same time that we determined the policies for domestic development, we also made some adjustments in our foreign policy. We pursue an independent foreign policy of peace, a policy that helps to preserve world peace."[40]

In May and October, 1984, Deng Xiaoping, at meetings with Brazilian president Figueiredo and Burmese president U San Yu, mentioned that there were two outstanding issues in the world, one is the issue of peace, and other is the issue of North-South. At a meeting with Japanese businessmen, he formally proposed that the two really great issues confronting the world today, issues of global significance, are: first, peace, and second, economic development.[41] Deng Xiaoping summarizes the two issues in terms of East, South, West and North. The issue of peace involves East-West relations, while the issue of economic development involves North-South relations. As for the first issue, he made a clear statement that "China seeks to preserve world peace and stability, not to destroy them. The stronger China grows, the

[39]Deng (1994a).

[40]Deng (1993j).

[41]Deng (1993k).

Table 2.1 Formulations on international environment in Party Congress reports since the founding of New China

Year	No.	Total words	Words	Percentage (%)	Judgment on international situation	China's positioning and stand
1956	8th	44,502	4828	10.85	The international situation tends to ease, and it is possible to realize a long-lasting peace	A member of the camp of the Soviet
1969	9th	22,430	5256	23.43	The imperialist United States and the revisionist Soviet Union are rampantly anti-China	The practitioner of proetariat international obligations, carrying the struggle through to the end
1973	10th	9886	2760	27.92	The current international situation can be characterized by a world in turmoil	Adhering to proletariat internationalism, uniting the Third World in their opposition to the hegemony of the United States and the Soviet Union
1977	11th	31,081	3499	11.26	As revolutionary factors increase, factors leading to war are also clearly on the rise	China is a developing socialist country, belonging to the Third World
1982	12th	31,713	4439	14.00	The danger of a world war is more pressing than ever, but the people of the world can upset their strategic deployment	Socialist China belongs to the Third World
1987	13th	32,125	364	1.13	The East and the West have seen a certain degree of easing in their relations	–
1992	14th	26,351	2116	8.03	For a fairly long period of time to come, it will be possible to secure a peaceful international environment and avert a new world war	China is a developing country, willing to develop friendly and cooperative relations with all countries on the basis of the Five Principles of Peaceful Coexistence

(continued)

Table 2.1 (continued)

Year	No.	Total words	Words	Percentage (%)	Judgment on international situation	China's positioning and stand
1997	15th	28,410	1546	5.44	For a fairly long period of time to come, it will be possible to avert a new world war and secure a favorable, peaceful international environment and maintain good relations with the surrounding countries	We oppose hegemonies and safeguard world peace. China will never seek hegemony even when it becomes developed in future
2002	16th	28,196	1254	4.45	A new world war is unlikely in the foreseeable future. It is realistic to bring about a fairly long period of peace in the world and a favorable climate in areas around China	China will never seek hegemony and never go in for expansion. We stand for fighting against terrorism of all forms
2007	17th	28,084	1575	5.61	The international balance of power is changing in favor of the maintenance of world peace, and the overall international situation is stable	Unswervingly following the path of peaceful development; China opposes terrorism of all forms; China will never seek hegemony or engage in expansion
2012	18th	29,115	1490	5.12	…tipping the balance of international forces in favor of the maintenance of world peace. All this has created more favorable conditions for ensuring general stability in the international environment	China will continue to hold high the banner of peace, development, cooperation and mutual benefit. We are firm in our resolve to uphold China's sovereignty, security and development interests and will never yield to any outside pressure. China opposes any foreign attempt to subvert the legitimate government of any other countries

Sources Report scripts released on xinhuanet.com

better the chances are for preserving world peace." As for the second issue, he proposes that the developed countries, such as Japan and the countries in Europe and North America, have to seek outlet for their capital and commodities, and the outlets can only be found in Southern countries such as China. Only when developing countries become more prosperous can developed countries expand their market. These words show that China does not only consider peace and development to be the main themes of the times, but also actively send the judgment to developed countries, with the hope to deepen economic and trade relations with developed countries so as to safeguard world peace and development.

Generally speaking, the process in which Deng Xiaoping promoted China's participation in globalization and integration into international market is also the process of China's giving up the philosophy of struggle and becoming the mainstay of peace and stability. It is not a makeshift. In the early 1990s, he proposed the policy of "hiding our capabilities and biding our time". Together with the idea of "never acting as the leader (in confrontation with the West)", it has become a long-standing strategy practiced by China. The underlying logic is that the more deeply China is involved in international market, the more China will rely on the economic system of the world. Under such a condition, an unstable world economic system will be more detrimental to China's interests, as there are more common interests shared between China and the world. Consequently, on the premise that "the international balance of power is changing in favor of the maintenance of world peace and there are more favorable conditions for ensuring general stability in the international environment", China will attach more and more importance to peaceful development, stress that the country will "unswervingly follow the path of peaceful development", and will "continue to hold high the banner of peace, development, cooperation and mutual benefit."

Crossing the River by Feeling for the Stones

But what is the method to find the path to peace and development, and what is the standard of a desirable development? The answer of Deng Xiaoping to the first question was to try bold experiments and blaze new trails. Later on, it was summarized as "crossing the river by feeling for the stones", and his answer to the second is the "Three Benefits".

While defining and protecting property right lays the foundation for development, it does not point the concrete development path. The Chinese leaders of the time had no better way than going forward by trial and error. Chen Yun first proposed that we should take "crossing the river by feeling for the stones" as a working method. Chen and Deng joined the Party in the same year, and became a member of the Political Bureau 21 years earlier than Deng. For many years, Chen was the superordinate of Deng. In the early years of New China, top leaders were ranked in the order of Mao Zedong, Liu Shaoqi, Zhou Enlai, Zhu De, Chen Yun, Lin Biao and Deng Xiaoping, with Chen ahead of Deng by two places. Chen was famous for his ability in economic work within the Party.

As documents available to us show, Chen Yun first put forward the method of "crossing the river by feeling for the stones" at a meeting of the Government Administration Council on April 7, 1950, saying that both rising prices and lowering prices are harmful to production, we may as well cross the river by feeling for the stones, sticking to a safe path. On July 20, 1951, Chen Yun proposes in the article, Do a Better Work of the Federation of Industry and Commerce, "the method should be steady. I call it 'crossing the river by feeling for the stones.' Rash actions would cause damages. Between being rash and dangerous and being slow and safe, I'd prefer the latter. We should pay attention to it, especially in national economic work."[42]

On December 16, 1980, Chen Yun delivered an important speech entitled Economic Situation, Experiences and Lessons at the Working Conference of the CPC Central Committee. In the speech, he summarized the principles and methods that should be applied in the reform and opening-up, saying "we have to reform, but the steps must be steady. Because problems concerning our reform are complication, we cannot be impatient. It is true that the reform needs theoretical research, economic statistics and expectations, but what is more important is to adopt a pilot project, summing up its experience at whatever time appropriate, that is 'crossing the river by feeling for the stones.' In the beginning the steps taken have to be small, slow and steady." At the closing session of the meeting on December 25, Deng Xiaoping expressed full agreement with Chen Yun's speech, saying that Chen Yun "correctly summed up our experience in handling a series of problems in economic work over the past 31 years and the lessons we have drawn from it. His statement will serve as our guide in this field for a long time."

In Chen's formulation, "crossing the river by feeling for the stones" focuses on its literal meaning, i.e., to take things slow, being realistic and steady. But when we talk about "crossing the river by feeling for the stones" now, it means more than Chen's original idea, also implying Deng Xiaoping's idea of "trying bold experiments and blazing new trails". On April 30, 1987, Deng at a meeting with the Spanish vice Prime Minister said, "China is such a big country and what we are doing is something that has never been done here before. Since China has its own characteristics, we can only run our affairs in accordance with the specific conditions in China. Of course, we can learn from the experience of others, but we must never copy everything. Since reform is a brand-new undertaking, mistakes are inevitable. We must not be afraid of making mistakes, and temporary setbacks must not make us abandon the reform and just mark time. We have to be daring, or we shall never be able to modernize. But we also have to be cautious about introducing particular reforms and review our experience regularly. Minor errors are inevitable, but we should try to avoid major ones."[43] On November 16 of the same year, Deng in the talks with Japanese guests stressed "ours is an entirely new endeavor, one that was never mentioned by Marx, never undertaken by our predecessors and never attempted by any other

[42]Chen (1995).

[43]Deng (19931).

socialist country. So there are no precedents for us to learn from. We can only learn from practice, feeling our way as we go."[44] During his inspection tour in the South, Deng Xiaoping further proposed that "we should be bolder than before in conducting reform and opening to the outside and have the courage to experiment. We must not act like women with bound feet."[45] Chen Yun and Deng Xiaoping shared the idea of feeling the war forward, but the latter lay more emphasis on making bold experiments and breaking into the forbidden zone of old patterns.

In economic development, what was in need of breaking then was the bondages of the highly totalitarian command-like planned economy, a mode borrowed from the Soviet Union. Under planned economy, a leader's will usually enjoys rapid execution without being tested or constrained by a scientific mechanism of experiment feedback. For example, Khrushchev extended his corn-planting experiences in Ukraine throughout the Soviet Union as a major part of agricultural reform. He collected intelligence on agriculture via "agricultural attaché" of the embassy in the United States. During his visit to the United States, the idea of large-scale corn-planting was supported by the owner of Garst's farm, Iowa, and he learned that corn stalk could serve as silage besides grain. However, before the large-scale extension occurred, he tested the American "Sterling" hybrid corn seed[46] only in the vegetable garden beside his villa and neighboring farms. Under forceful mobilization, the corn-planting area expanded enormously in the Soviet Union, from less than 3.50 million hectare in 1953 to in 37 million hectare1962, accounting for 1/6 of the overall planting area of the Soviet Union. Resources of other department were also put into corn-related fields.[47] This rash expansion led to a per unit yield of corn as grain only 1/4 of that of the United States, and as silage only 12%. The corn plantation movement ended up in a double failure of economy and politics.

Deng Xiaoping's version of "crossing the river by feeling for the stones" attaches more importance to "bold experiments and scientific verification". No one knows in advance what foreign institutions and methods can be used. Special economic zones and open cities are instituted to provide places for such bold experiments. What turns out successful can be extended to other areas, and the risk of what turns out unsuccessful can be taken under control. The task that Deng Xiaoping gave to Shenzhen was clear, that is, making bold experiments and breaking a new path. "Every year leaders should review what they have done, continuing those measures that have proved correct, acting promptly to change those that have proved wrong and tackling new problems as soon as they are identified. It will probably take another

[44] Deng (1993m).

[45] Deng (1993e).

[46] Harry Stine, Board Chairman of Stine Seed Company, US, who came to China to promote his short-straw high-population corn in March, 2015, also comes from Iowa. It is unclear whether he has any relation with the "Sterling" corn seed or Garst's farm. See http://world.people.com.cn/n/2015/0326/c1002-26754499.html for the visit.

[47] Machine manufacturing departments invested a lot in making corn seeding machines, and established corn research institute. In order to better the work of introducing American hybrid corn, agricultural authorities created an academic journal entitled *Corn*. Besides, corn foods were researched and development by food authorities, and special core food shops were opened in cities.

thirty years for us to develop a more mature and well-defined system in every field. The principles and policies to be applied under each system will also be more firmly established."

Three Benefits

But what practice or institution can be firmly established? Deng Xiaoping, during his inspection tour in the South, gave an answer: the chief criterion for making that judgment should be whether it promotes the growth of the productive forces in a socialist society, increases the overall strength of the socialist state and raises living standards. The criterion is known as the Three Benefits.

Productive forces constitute the foundation for sustainable social development, continual increase of the overall strength of state and constant living standards improvement. Without the development and progress of productive forces, all other matter would be a river without sources, or a tress without roots. Deng Xiaoping emphasized, "development is the absolute principle"[48] The absoluteness of the principle lies in the fact that development enjoys a priority over other issue. The Third Session of the 11th Party Congress confirmed that except for large-scale foreign invasion, developing economy and realizing modernization are the core work for the Party. Even if invasion occurred, "China has a wealth of experience in resisting foreign aggression. We would first defeat the invaders and then start reconstruction."[49]

What is of particular significance is Deng Xiaoping's command of the law of development for great powers. He pointed out that for a big developing nation like China, it is impossible to attain faster economic growth steadily and smoothly at all times; stable and proportionate development are relative terms, not absolute; we cannot deny development itself for fluctuations and setbacks in the process of development. "… If we become overcautious, not daring to emancipate our minds and act freely, we shall lose opportunities as a result. Like a boat sailing against the current, we must forge ahead or be swept downstream."[50]

The increase of the overall strength of state requires the development and progress of productive forces, and stresses the comprehensiveness of development. It is an absolutely unacceptable situation of falling behind and suffering, and it is not desirable to be a rich but weak nation, either. In fact, the overall strength of state includes not only material elements or hard power such as economic prosperity, security, social harmony and environmental cleanness, but also soft power, that is, to build China into a country manifesting its superior socialist system and humanitarianism, full of charm, attractiveness and appealingness.

Raising the living standards of the people is a further requirement on the inclusiveness of improving productive forces and the overall strength of state. The improve-

[48]Deng (1993m).
[49]Deng (1993e).
[50]Deng (1993n).

ment in productive forces and the country's strength has to bring tangible benefits to the people. The purpose of the CPC is to serve the people. Going against the people, or without their support, the Party would lose its foundations, like Antaeus losing its power when leaving Gaea.[51]

The Three Benefits, together with the method of "crossing the river by feeling for the stones", break the bondage of the Chinese people to make their efforts to improve their life, enable the Party to lead the country in completely breaking the forbidden zone of ideology, and in whole-heartedly seeking or giving priority to development in internal economy, society and people's livelihood by all possible means such as extensive international cooperation, and in making due contribution to consolidating world peace.

Science and Technology Constitute a Primary Productive Force

While the Three Benefits provide fundament goals and criterion of development, it makes a vital problem as to how to efficiently develop the productive forces of a socialist society. It should not be denied that New China has undergone a period of "romantic" anti-intellectualism, as manifested by the slogan "however bold you are, however large the yield would be." As mentioned above, the boastful and fraudulent working style brought the nation into disaster. The cause was institutional rather than man-made. A person's subjective initiative shall never contradict realistic and objective conditions. Productive forces cannot be expected to improve "by leaps and bounds" with little-by-little accumulation of common factors of production such as labor force and capitals, expect when the progress in science and technology changes the situation.

Deng Xiaoping was fully aware of it. In his talk with the Czech President on September 5, 1988, and in his speech at the briefing meeting on the preliminary reform plan of prices and salaries on September 12 of the same year, Deng Xiaoping discussed the issue of science and technology. Excerpts of the two discussions are combined to form the essay Science and Technology Constitute a Primary Productive Force, included in the *Selected Works of Deng Xiaoping, Vol. III*. The article shows a significant change of idea and policy of the Party's leader. It can be summarized into three points. First, it heightens the importance of science and technology, from Marx's idea of "science and technology as productive force" to "science and technology as a primary productive force".

Second, it acknowledges the role of opening to outside world in the improvement of productive forces. "To expand productive forces, ..., we must open our country to the outside world." It stresses the necessity and importance of achiev-

[51]In Greek mythology, Antaeus was the son of Poseidon, the God of Sea, and Gaea, the Mother Earth goddess. He is powerful and invincible as long as he is contact with the earth, since he can obtain limitless power from his mother by the contact.

ing progress in technology by introducing from external sources, and thus shows an open-minded view of technology progress. Besides introducing advanced technology so as to improve productive forces, Deng Xiaoping laid a special emphasis on creating conditions for Chinese students studying aboard to come back and work in China, bringing advanced science and technology together with them. In the respect of opening to the outside world, externally-sourced technology progress has a special meaning. When China introduces technologies from European developed countries and the United States, it always implies the concurrent acceptance of their technical norms. Once they are accepted, it will be very difficult to change, and China will face extremely high withdrawal cost. This in turn reflects the credibility and sincerity of China's drive to join the current system of rules.

Third, it attaches a great importance to internally-source technology progress, proposing to increase the material benefits for top intellectuals, to arouse their enthusiasm and show them more respect. "Haven't we developed the atomic bomb, the hydrogen bomb, satellites and space technology on our own? The engineering of the electron-positron collider that we have completed also ranks among the world's most advanced technologies."Deng Xiaoping has realized that in addition to material incentives to scientists and top intellectuals, respect or intellectual encouragement were also important. Besides, Deng Xiaoping was also aware of the importance of education in internally-sourced technology progress, saying that we would rather make sacrifice in other aspects or even in development speed in order to solve the problem of education. It was for this idea that Deng Xiaoping volunteered to take charge of education, science and technology when resuming his post.[52] On August 8, 1977, at a forum on work in science and education presided by him, Deng Xiaoping proposed to restore the College Entrance Examination and to stop the Cultural Revolution practice of recommendation by the masses.[53] The decision changed the fate of a generation of young students, and provided the basis of human resources for internally-sourced technology progress and science development.

The emphasis on science and technology was of particular significance to the country recovering from the Cultural Revolution, in which intellectuals had been treated with no respect. Even without the situation, it is also necessary to attach importance to science and technology. Science and technology can work on labor force and capital equipment, can improve productive forces by means of enhancing many factors of production, such as the ability and quality of labor force and the efficiency of tools of production. The improvement in quality can have a more remarkable effect on productive forces than increasing the number of workers and equipment.

During his inspection tour in the South, Deng Xiaoping stressed again the idea of "science and technology as a primary productive force", pointing out that "rapid development of the economy can only be based on science, technology and education"; that "one breakthrough in the field of high technology promotes the growth of several industries"; that "we must promote science, for that is where our hope lies";

---

[52]CPC Literature Research Center of the CPC Central Committee (2004).

[53]Ibid., p. 179.

and that "China should take its place in the world in the field of high technology too." The talks of Deng Xiaoping in his inspection tour in the South summarized his thoughts of reform and opening-up, and put top priority on science and technology in the cause of reform and opening-up.

It seemed that many thoughts of Deng Xiaoping were expressed unintentionally in his meeting speeches, especially in his talks with foreign visitors. The seemingly easy and carefree talks actually contained deep considerations. He sometimes asked his audience to convey his message to those absent. These talks mixed declaration, promise and mobilization together. It was like bidding in his favorite pastime of bridge, by which he transmitted the key message of the game. Richard Evans, former British ambassador to China, summed up the messages of Deng Xiaoping's talks: first, the ten-year turmoil of the Cultural Revolution was over, and would never occur; second, the development of China required a peaceful international environment, and China was willing to contribute to world peace; third, China wanted to learn from other countries, but China should maintain its independence in politics and economy.[54] These thoughts were actually shared by those reformers seeing China encounter "an unknown upheaval in thousands of years", that is, China should accept the Western ideas, but not be subject to its control, and China should try to gain a position equal to the West.

In general, Deng Xiaoping radiated the glory of pragmatic spirit. The principles he upheld ensure China's characteristics, independence and inclusiveness, and his pragmatic spirit enabled China to adopt an attitude of being open-minded and courageous in experiments, and to improve economy, productive forces and living standards of the people in a practical way. His policy convinced the world of the importance of peaceful environment to China, and of the ability of China to provide the world with development opportunities. This in turn brings China development opportunities. China views the era of Deng Xiaoping as an important period of development opportunities.

References

Arbatov, G. A. 1998. *The Soviet Politics: Inside Information*. Trans. by Xu Kui et al. Xinhua Press.

Chen, Yun. 1995. Do a better work of the Federation of Industry and Commerce (July 20, 1951). *Selected Works of Chen Yun Vol. II*. People's Press.

CPC History Research Center of the CPC Central Committee. 2011. *A History of the Communist Party of China, Vol. 2*. CPC History Press.

CPC Literature Research Center of the CPC Central Committee. 1996. *Poems of Mao Zedong*. CPC Literature Press, p. 62.

CPC Literature Research Center of the CPC Central Committee. 1997. *A Chronicle of Zhou Enlai Vol. II*. CPC Literature Press, p. 731.

CPC Literature Research Center of the CPC Central Committee. 2004. *A Chronicle of Deng Xiaoping: 1975–1997, Vol. I*. CPC Literature Press, p. 164 and p. 178.

[54] Evans (1996), p. 271.

Deng, Xiaoping. 1993a. We shall expand political democracy and carry out economic reform (April 15, 1985). *Selected Works of Deng Xiaoping Vol. III*. People's Press, p. 115.
Deng, Xiaoping. 1993b. Urgent Tasks of China's Third Generation of Collective Leadership. *Selected Works of Deng Xiaoping Vol. III*. People's Press, p. 311.
Deng, Xiaoping. 1993c. Replies to the American TV correspondent Mike Wallace (September 2, 1986). *Selected Works of Deng Xiaoping Vol. III*. People's Press.
Deng, Xiaoping. 1993d. Speech at the Third Plenary Session of the Central Advisory Commission of the Communist Party of China (October 22, 1984). *Selected Works of Deng Xiaoping Vol. III*. People's Press.
Deng, Xiaoping. 1993e. Excerpts from talks given in Wuchang, Shenzhen, Zhuhai and Shanghai (January 18 to February 21, 1992). *Selected Works of Deng Xiaoping Vol. III*. People's Press, p. 371.
Deng, Xiaoping. 1993f. We are working to revitalize the Chinese nation (April 7, 1990). *Selected Works of Deng Xiaoping Vol. III*. People's Press.
Deng, Xiaoping. 1993g. Speech at a meeting with the members of the Committee for Drafting the Basic Law of the Hong Kong Special Administrative Region (April 16, 1987). *Selected Works of Deng Xiaoping Vol. III*. People's Press.
Deng, Xiaoping. 1993h. China will always keep its promises (December 19, 1984). *Selected Works of Deng Xiaoping Vol. III*. People's Press.
Deng, Xiaoping. 1993i. Speech at an Enlarged Meeting of the Military Commission of the Central Committee of the Communist Party of China (June 4, 1985). *Selected Works of Deng Xiaoping Vol. III*. People's Press.
Deng, Xiaoping. 1993j. Reform and opening to the outside world can truly invigorate China (May 12, 1987). *Selected Works of Deng Xiaoping Vol. III*. People's Press.
Deng, Xiaoping. 1993k. Peace and development are the two outstanding issues in the world today (March 4, 1985). *Selected Works of Deng Xiaoping Vol. III*. People's Press.
Deng, Xiaoping. 1993l. We shall draw on historical experience and guard against wrong tendencies (April 30, 1987). *Selected Works of Deng Xiaoping Vol. III*. People's Press.
Deng, Xiaoping. 1993m. Two features of the Thirteenth National Congress of the Communist Party of China (November 16, 1987). *Selected Works of Deng Xiaoping Vol. III*. People's Press.
Deng, Xiaoping. 1993n. With stable policies of reform and opening to the outside world, China can have great hopes for the future (September 4, 1989). *Selected Works of Deng Xiaoping Vol. III*. People's Press.
Deng, Xiaoping. 1994a. Restore agricultural production (July 7, 1962). *Selected Works of Deng Xiaoping Vol. I*. People's Press.
Deng, Xiaoping. 1994b. Speech at a Plenary Meeting of the Military Commission of the Central Committee of the CPC (December 28, 1977). *Selected Works of Deng Xiaoping Vol. II*. People's Press.
Dreher, A. and N. M. Jensen. 2007. Independent Actor or Agent? An Empirical Analysis of the Impact of U.S. Interests on International Monetary Fund Conditions. *The Journal of Law and Economics* 50(1): 105–124.
Evans, R. 1996. *Deng Xiaoping*. Trans. by Wu Shihong. Shanghai People's Press.
Fleck, R. K., and C. Kilby. 2006. World Bank Independence: A Model and Statistical Analysis of US Influence. *Review of Development Economics* 10(2): 224–240.
Gordon, H. Chang. 2014. *Friends and Enemies: The United States, China, and the Soviet Union 1948–1972*. Trans. by Gu Ning et al. Central Compilation & Translation Press.
Gao, Cheng. 2012. On institutional hegemony in the new empire system and governance pathway. *Teaching and Research*, No. 5.
Keohane, R. O. 2001. *After Hegemony: Cooperation and Discord in the World Political Economy*. Shanghai People's Press, p. 180.
Lu, Nanquan. 2007. *A History of Economic Reform in the Soviet Union*. People's Press.
Odom, W. E. 2000. *The Collapse of the Soviet Military*. Trans. by Wang Zhenxi. Xinhua Press, pp. 99–101.

Overholt, W. H. 2005. *China and Globalization: Testimony presented to the US-China Economic and Security Review Commission on May 19, 2005*. Santa Monica, CA: RAND Corporation.

Peet, R. 2003. Unholy Trinity: The IMF, World Bank and WTO. Zed Books. Wade, Robert Hunter. 2002. "US hegemony and the World Bank: the fight over people and ideas." *Review of International Political Economy* 9(2): 215–243.

Qin Yaqing. 1999. *Hegemony System and International Conflict: Acts of Support of the US in International Armed Conflicts*. Shanghai People's Press, p. 13.

Shen, Zhihua. 2002. *Selected Historical Archives of the Soviet Union, Vol. 23*. Social Sciences Academic Press.

Vogel, E. F. 2013. *De Xiaoping and the Transformation of China*. Trans. by Feng Keli. SDX Joint Publishing Company.

Wang, Tao. 2014. The theoretical work meeting of 1979. *Party History and Literature*, (13): 36–42.

Woods, N. 2003. "The United States and the international financial institutions: Power and influence within the World Bank and the IMF." Foot, McFarlane and Mastanduno (Eds.), *US Hegemony and International Organizations*, Oxford: 92–114.

Zhang, Shuhua. 2010. Mrs. Thatcher on the downfall of the Soviet Union. *Red Flag Files*, No. 11.

Zhang, Yuyan and Gao Cheng. 2004. *American Bullion and the Rise of the Western World*. Citic Press Group.

Chapter 3
The Chinese Dream: Rejuvenation of the Nation and the Outside World

The economic growth of China has benefited from the globalization that emerged in a peaceful environment, which in turn increases China's dependence on a peaceful environment and globalization. To economists, globalization is nothing but a process with an ever-increasing market. Production elements and commodities scattered in different parts of the world are constantly involved in an increasingly integrated global market and the expansion of the market will lead to the enhancement of labor division and specialization, one direct result of the latter is the increase of productivity of labor and long-term economic growth. The above has been the ideal paradigm portrayed by the classical economic growth theory. Given deepening insights into the market mechanism, there has been greater recognition that the expansion of the market size is not non-conditional. A legitimate government with the capacity of identifying and protecting property rights is an important premise for the expansion and strengthening of the market. A vital defect of globalization lies in the absence of such an expanded and strengthened marketized government across the world which can formulate rules and regulations for globalization. Even so, human kind has never given up its efforts to tame globalization. The current USA-dominated global economic system with the Bretton Woods System as its pillar serves as an imperfect alternative of some functions of a desirable global government featuring an expanded and strengthened market.

It should be noted, however, the impact of the American subprime crisis and the following global financial crisis it triggered indicates that the existing world economic governance system is approaching a "critical point" in terms of its inclusion of global economic growth. The vision that globalization would be defeated by its own success is looming. China, as one of the beneficiaries of world peace and globalization, has also made contribution to world peace and development in proportion to its own identity and capacity. Some of its contribution has been domestically-oriented. For instance, as it has iterated, the sheer fact that China is able to feed one fifth of the world population shall be deemed as its largest contribution to human beings.[1] Moreover,

[1] Wen (2008).

Y. Zhang and W. Feng, *Peaceful Development Path in China*, China Insights,
https://doi.org/10.1007/978-981-13-1439-1_3

starting from the overall situation of regional and world peace, China has been making concessions for the sake of everyone and dealing with crises in rational and moderate manners when faced with unjust treatment imposed on by outside powers. On the other hand, China is making more foreign-oriented contribution in this respect in a more systematic way. China is sure to join in the efforts of taming globalization and contribute its leading power. It doesn't mean that China simply seeks to join in the "leadership" of current system so as to obtain more privileges in the international system. On the contrary, China aims to push the current international governance system in terms of its functions forward rather than taking it away from the just, inclusive "global government" featuring an expanded and strengthened market by working together with other countries.

To sort out whether the interaction between the Chinese dream of rejuvenation of the nation and the outside world can facilitate the establishment of a global system featuring an expanded and strengthened market peacefully, it is imperative to understand China's identity in the world today and the fundamental goals of foreign strategy that China aspires to achieve. The identity issue is concerned with what kind of country China is on the international community today. The answer lies in six aspects, that is, China is a socialist, developing, fast growing, not yet unified, large and indispensable country right on its way of reform and opening-up.

Socialism

Firstly, China is a socialist country. The socialism that China follows is socialism with Chinese characteristics. Unlike "welfare state socialism", "Congress Party socialism", "Program Party socialism", "Renaissance Party socialism", "Buddhism socialism", "Islamic socialism", "Arab socialism", "Ujama (village commune) socialism", "African socialism", "Sandino socialism" and so on, the socialism with Chinese characteristics came into being on the basis of inheriting and developing the scientific socialism put forward by Karl Marx and Friedrich Engels. It means that China will, under the leadership of the Communist Party of China (CPC) and basing itself on China's realities, take economic development as the central task and adhere to the Four Cardinal Principles and the policy of reform and opening-up. It means China will release and develop the productive forces, develop the socialist market economy, socialist democracy, an advanced socialist culture and a harmonious socialist society, and promote socialist ecological progress. It also means China will promote well-rounded development of the person, achieve prosperity for all over time, and make China a modern socialist country that is prosperous, strong, democratic, culturally advanced and harmonious.

The essence of socialism with Chinese characteristics is reflected in writings of Deng Xiaoping, the proponent of socialism with Chinese characteristics. On April 29, 1983, in a talk with a delegation from the Central Committee of the Communist Party of India (Marxist), he mentioned, "In a socialist country, a genuinely Marxist ruling party must devote itself to developing the productive forces and, on that basis, gradually raise the people's living standards. This means building a society with high material standards. ... At the same time, we are building a socialist society with high cultural and ethical standards, which essentially means that our people should have communist ideals, moral integrity, a good education and a strong sense of discipline. Internationalism and patriotism also belong to this realm."[2] That means the socialism with Chinese characteristics, on the one hand, emphasizes that the economic growth and its fruits are for the people; on the other hand, emphasizes the need to adhere to the lofty ideal of and belief in communism and always maintain the momentum and mindset towards further development instead of being content with accomplishments it has harvested in practice.

On June 30, 1984, in a talk with the Japanese delegation to the second session of the Council of Sino-Japanese Non-Governmental Persons, Deng Xiaoping made more thorough interpretation of what is socialism with Chinese characteristics and how to build socialism with Chinese characteristics. He first reviewed the modern history of China then presented the necessity for China to follow the socialist road that fits in with the realities of China instead of taking the capitalist road. He stressed that socialism is the primary stage of communism, "the fundamental task for the socialist stage is to develop the productive forces. The superiority of the socialist system is demonstrated, in the final analysis, by faster and greater development of those forces than under the capitalist system. As they develop, the people's material and cultural life will constantly improve. ... Socialism means eliminating poverty. Pauperism is not socialism, still less communism." To him, although capitalism can only enrich a minority of the people, only socialism can solve the problem of "enriching the remaining more than 90 per cent". "But if we adhere to socialism and apply the principle of distribution to each according to his work, there will not be excessive disparities in wealth. Consequently, no polarization will occur as our productive forces become developed over the next 20–30 years." He also emphasized the importance of opening-up, arguing no socialism shall be built with the doors closed and domestic barriers between different regions, industries and departments should be removed as well. "We welcome foreign investment and advanced techniques. Management is also a technique." He mentioned in the end of his speech, "We shall accumulate new experience and try new solutions as new problems arise. In general, we believe that the course we have chosen, which we call building socialism with Chinese characteristics, is the right one."[3] It can be noted from above, the socialism with Chinese characteristics advocated by Deng Xiaoping means: in terms of its goals, it requires development of productive forces (faster than that in capitalist countries) and restricting polarization (in current term, achieve inclusive development); in terms of means, it requires reform and opening-up (import capital, management and technology and realize domestic and international economic integration). It also requires not limiting specific ways of building socialism to fixed principles. Instead, China must take a creative perspective and an attitude of "learning by doing" and always deal with new problems with new approaches (which highly corresponds

[2] Deng (1993a).

[3] Deng (1993b).

with earlier analysis of the nature and essence of growth identified by Joseph Alois Schumpeter).

Deng Xiaoping supported the distinction between market economy and capitalism so that those mechanisms in capitalist countries that may promote economic growth or development of productive forces may be separated from capitalism itself, an opposite ideology of socialism, and China (or informed Chinese people) may better study and use those mechanisms with no fear of being labeled capitalist. On October 23, 1985, in an interview with a delegation, including senior American entrepreneurs, organized by Time Inc., Deng pointed out, "There is no fundamental contradiction between socialism and a market economy."[4] To him, as long as the public sector remains the mainstay of the Chinese economy and collective prosperity is pursued, it will not violate the principles unique to socialism. Correspondingly, those good methods (market economy) previously labeled capitalist can be imported and used with no worries at all.

Apart from developing productive forces and holding on to collective prosperity, socialism with Chinese characteristics is also about holding on to peace. On October 26, 1989, in a talk with Prime Minister Chatichai Choonhavan of Thailand, Deng argued, "The socialism we are building is a socialism that is adapted to our own conditions, a socialism that helps to constantly develop the productive forces and that favours peace. Only by constantly developing the productive forces can a country gradually become strong and prosperous, with a rising standard of living. Only in a peaceful environment can we develop smoothly. China will safeguard its own interests, sovereignty and territorial integrity. It also maintains that a socialist country should not infringe upon other countries' interests, sovereignty or territory."[5] Judging by "Only in a peaceful environment can we develop smoothly", "peace" is seemingly a precondition (although necessary) of "development", yet "a socialist country should not infringe upon other countries' interests, sovereignty or territory" indicates that peace actually remains an absolute "moral-law-type" requirement of the nature of socialism with Chinese characteristics.

The peace attribute of socialism with Chinese characteristics was never a sudden inspiration of Deng Xiaoping. As early as April 4, 1986, in a talk with Radovan Vlajkovic, President of the Presidium of the Socialist Federal Republic of Yugoslavia, Deng specially associated socialism and peace. He argued, "Keeping to socialism is of vital importance for China. If China, with its one billion people, took the capitalist road, it would be a disaster for the world. It would be a retrogression of history, a retrogression of many years. If China, with its one billion people, abandoned the policy of peace and opposition to hegemonism or if, as the economy developed, it sought hegemony, that would also be a disaster for the world, a retrogression of history. But if China, with its one billion people, keeps to socialism and adheres to the policy of peace, it will be following the right course and will be able to make greater contributions to humanity."[6] In a word, the very underlying requirement that a

[4]Deng (1993c).

[5]Deng (1993d).

[6]Deng (1993e).

socialist country should not infringe upon other countries' interests means that China will not risk expansion or exploiting other countries unless it gives up on socialism. Meanwhile, socialism also requires China to protect its own interests from being infringed upon by other countries. The peace advocated and required by socialism with Chinese characteristics is by no means passive "peace" without any principles or dignity. As Deng has said, "Our political line is to focus ... on continued development of the productive forces. Nothing short of a world war could tear us away from this line. And even if a world war broke out, we would engage in reconstruction after the war."[7]

Entering the era of Xi Jinping, socialism with Chinese characteristics has been passed down as an essential part of the national ideology. A coherent political orthodoxy[8] has established itself as follows: the first generation of leaders of the Communist Party of China offered "precious experience, theoretical preparation and material foundation" for it, the second made "successful exploration" of it and the third "pushed it into the 21st century" and the Central Committee of the Communist Party of China (CCCPC) with Hu Jintao as the general secretary "succeeded in persisting on and developing it at a new historical starting point". Based on a review of long-term practice of the socialist period, the new CCCPC with Xi Jinping as the general secretary theoretically refined and sublimed socialism with Chinese characteristics, arguing it is a trinity of path, theory system and institutions.

As for path, taking economic development as the central task, releasing and developing the productive forces, realizing collective prosperity and adhering to the Four Cardinal Principles and the policy of reform and opening-up remain vital to the socialism with Chinese characteristics. Apart from economic development, more significance is attached to the all-round development in politics, culture, society, ecology and so on as well as the human all-round development. As for the theory system, the new CCCPC showcased the relationship between the latest development of localization of Marxism in China (Deng Xiaoping Theory, the important thought of "three representatives", the scientific outlook on development) and Marx-Leninism and Mao Zedong Thoughts, arguing that "in contemporary China, adhering to the socialist theory system with Chinese characteristics is really adhering to Marxism." As for institutions, it highlights the organic synthesis of the fundamental political system (the People's Congress system), the basic political system (multi-party cooperation and political consultation under the leadership of the Communist Party of China, regional ethnic autonomy and self-governance at the primary level of society, etc.), the basic economic system (with public ownership playing a dominant role and diverse forms of ownership developing side by side) and other specific systems.[9] In a

---

[7]Deng (1993b).

[8]Orthodoxy was originally a term the Confucians used to shed light on the system of propagating the doctrine. The Mencius was the first to construct the systems of propagating the doctrine of Yao, Tang, Emperor Wen of Zhou Dynasty, the Confucius as well as his own. Zhu Xi was the first one to put forward this term. He argued that Zhou Dunyi and the two Chengs (Cheng Jing and Cheng Yi) inherited from the Mencius while he himself the Confucian legacy from Zhou and the two Chengs. The term orthodoxy reflects the inheritance-based authenticity and legitimacy of ideologies.

[9]Xi (2014c), pp. 6–20.

word, from Deng Xiaoping to Xi Jinping, the socialism with Chinese characteristics has become more complete in form, more consistent and consolidated in core content and more legitimate and unshakable as ideology.

Relevant ideas about developing productive forces, reducing the gap between rich and poor, promote all-round development of individuals, peaceful development and so on in the socialism with Chinese characteristics will not incur disapproval from other countries. Its essential feature, that is, upholding to the leadership of the country by CPC, however, is not an option to the bulk of other countries in the world today. Most of the countries in the world today are not socialist countries, which means socialist countries are in the minority with different values, ideology, political structures, social goals from those of the mainstream countries. For China, it's not surprising that disparities exist between different countries and it's not impossible for countries with different institutions to bring about good cooperation. Deng Xiaoping once told Prime Minister Chatichai Choonhavan of Thailand, "The relations between our two countries are a model of friendship between countries with different social systems."[10] But some people from certain countries insist on the assumption that "all the countries ruled by communist parties are dictatorships, China, therefore, is a dictatorship as it is ruled by CPC", arguing that "democratic countries" featuring multiparty elections and "dictatorships" are just like herbivores and carnivores, certainly impossible to live under the same sky. Such recognition, once applied in a country's policy-making, may lead to severe damages to international relations.

Reform and Opening-Up

Secondly, China is a country in reform and opening-up. Reform and opening-up are the two sides of the same coin. On October 10, 1984, in a talk with Chancellor Helmut Kohl of the Federal Republic of Germany, Deng Xiaoping said, "The basic content and experience of both rural and urban reform is to invigorate the domestic economy and open China wider to the outside world."[11] On March 28, 1985, in a talk with Susumu Nikaido, Vice-President of the Liberal Democratic Party of Japan, Deng Xiaoping argued again, "We have two types of opening-up, i.e., opening-up domestically and internationally. The policy of opening-up domestically and internationally will not change. The reform we are undertaking is the continuation and extension of that policy."[12] The basic content of the reform at that time was the transformation from being closed to opening-up. Judging from the above, the inseparability (or organic synthesis) between reform and opening-up is the first attribute of reform and opening-up.

Irreversibility is the second attribute of reform and opening-up. Reform and opening-up has smashed the old production and distribution patterns, creating new

[10]Deng (1993d).

[11]Deng (1993f).

[12]Deng (1993g).

stakeholders both domestically and internationally, who, benefited from reform and opening-up, are much more powerful than those whose interests are damaged. In accordance with Ashley Madison's data, from 1950, the next year after the founding of New China, to 1978, the year reform and opening-up was launched, the total sum of China's GDP amounted to about $15.1 trillion, while the total sum of China's GDP from 1979 to 1989 reached about $16.3 trillion, more than the accumulation of almost three decades from the founding of New China to the year before reform and opening-up. Obviously such rapid economic growth would have been impossible if reform and opening-up had not been launched. It means the beneficiaries of reform and opening-up could negotiate the vested interests that oppose reform and opening-up even if the former had to redeem their gains. Deng Xiaoping had a clear understanding and an acute sense of such irreversibility. In 1985, when talking to Susumu Nikaido, Deng Xiaoping made it clear, "Some commentators abroad say that China's current policy is irreversible. I think they are right."[13]

Comprehensiveness is the third attribute of reform and opening-up. It lies not only in the requirement for reform in the economic structure but also in the political structure; not only in reform in national fundamental policies at the macro level but also in reform in company management at the micro level; not only in opening-up to developed countries in the Western world but also in opening-up to other transforming or developing countries. From September to November, 1986, Deng Xiaoping repeatedly talked about the problem of reform in the political system. He pointed out that the reform of the economic structure was going smoothly on the whole but the problem that the political structure did not meet the needs of the economic reform was becoming more and more serious. To him, the general objectives of the reform of political structure should at least include consolidating the socialist system, developing the socialist productive forces and expanding socialist democracy in order to bring the initiative of the people into full play. As for the content of political reform, it mainly include separating the Party from the government, transferring some of the powers of the central authorities to lower levels, streamlining the administrative structure and having younger leading cadres.[14] It can be noted that Deng's political reform was actually enhancement and consolidation of existing political structure, with the purpose of increasing efficiency so as to enable the existing political structure to meet the needs of the economic reform and promote the development of productive forces. It is a kind of technical adjustment or revision, having nothing to do with the so-called "change of banner". Although Deng Xiaoping was the general designer of reform and opening-up, it didn't mean he only concerned about the macro level but neglected specific details. He especially emphasized the importance of the quality of industrial products, arguing the central task of industrial products especially exporting goods was to improve quality. He said, "quality should be placed above everything else. Township enterprises should pay attention to quality, too. If we are going to improve quality, we must carry out reform. We should make some laws regarding quality, establish criteria for quality inspection and set up a

[13]Deng (1993g).

[14]Deng (1993h).

powerful body to ensure that the criteria are strictly adhered to."[15] Ever since the 18th National Congress of the Communist Part of China, the CCCPC has further inherited and developed the comprehensiveness of reform and opening-up. When presiding over a group study held by the CPC Central Committee Political Bureau, Xi Jinping pointed out, "Reform and opening-up is a systematic project, which should be conducted in persistent all-round reform in a coordinated way and needs supporting measures."[16] *The Decision on Major Issues Concerning Comprehensively Deepening Reforms* adopted on the Third Plenary Session of the 18th CPC Central Committee lifted the comprehensiveness of reform and opening-up to a brand new level. Looking back on the comprehensiveness of the reform and opening-up since Deng Xiaoping, its opening-up has been rather practical and comprehensive. Deng Xiaoping argued: China should not only mean opening to the West, instead, China should open to the West, the Soviet Union and the East European countries and developing countries of the Third World. Even though state-to-state relations are not normal, exchanges can go on, for instance, in commercial transactions, technology and even in joint ventures and technical innovations.[17] It means that, as long as there were chances for win-win cooperation at the micro level, relevant parties could go and achieve "interests in trade" by breaking through the hindrance of macro policies. Although the Soviet Union has disintegrated and the East Europe undergone drastic changes, this kind of practical and comprehensive outlook of reform and opening-up is not out of date.

Experimentality is the fourth attribute of China's reform and opening-up. Deng's experimentality didn't mean that China's reform and opening-up was just a temporary expedient, which would be readily abandoned in case of set-backs. As a matter of fact, with "irreversibility", Deng Xiaoping has indicated that the general direction of reform and opening-up would never change. Experimentality means the recognition that "there is no perfect program for reform"[18] and "our entire policy of opening to the outside is an experiment too, and a big one from the world point of view."[19] On the one hand, it requires reformers to advance and experiment daringly, carry out and push forward reform and opening-up actively and creatively by putting aside the mental burden of taking responsibility for failure. On the other hand, we must proceed with caution during the process of reform and opening-up and stay modest, advancing in a relatively prudent manner. We may as well overestimate possible risks and try to find a solution based on difficult situations. "It is impossible not to make mistakes, but we should try to avoid serious ones and modify the program if problems arise. At the same time, we should base our work on the possible emergence of serious problems and prepare for them. In this way, even if the worst should happen, the sky will not fall."[20] Xi Jinping also pointed out, "Wading across the river by feeling

[15]Deng (1993i).

[16]Xi (2014e).

[17]Deng (1993j).

[18]Deng (1993k).

[19]Deng (1993l).

[20]Deng (1993k).

for the stones is a reform method with Chinese characteristics and in line with the prevailing conditions in China. Wading across the river by feeling for the stones, we can identify the laws that apply, and acquire knowledge in practice. Wading across the river by feeling for the stones and top-level design are two component factors for our reform effort. Reform and opening-up in a region at a certain stage should be subject to top-level design; top-level design should be strengthened on the basis of progressive reform and opening-up in the region at a certain stage. To continue reform and opening-up, we need to strengthen our macroscopic thinking and top-level design, and make sure that reform is systematic, integrated and coordinated. At the same time, we must still encourage bold experiments and breakthroughs in our efforts to further advance reform and opening-up."[21] Judging from the development of the special economic zones, especially Shenzhen, China's experimental methods of reform and opening-up have been successful. This kind of success is of significance even in terms of methodology. Inspired by the experience of Shenzhen, American economist Paul M. Romer put forward the idea of Charter Cities, which suggests some cities in underdeveloped countries could "get off the ground through identifying and adapting to modeling rules introduced from other places of the world, for instance, some policies adopted by Shenzhen, which enabled China to benefit from participating in global economy after long-term recessions." By adopting international rules, which are different from local laws, and management teams, these reform pilot zones "supply people with more job opportunities and new approaches that are able to improve their living conditions and those of their children" and speed up the reform process in those rapidly urbanizing countries.[22]

Long-term or strategic is the fifth attribute of China's reform and opening-up. Reform and opening-up is a basic state policy of China. As early as 1985, Deng Xiaoping made it clear that "The purpose of the reform is to lay a solid foundation for sustained development over the next decade and throughout the first half of the next century. Without the reform, there could be no sustained development. So, we should think not in terms of just three to five years, but in terms of the last 20 years of this century and the first 50 of the next. We must persist in the reform.[23] On June 7, 1988, in a talk with Zbigniew Messner, member of the Political Bureau of the Central Committee of the United Workers' Party of Poland and Chairman of the Polish Council of Ministers, Deng Xiaoping once again mentioned that China's reform was a long-term endeavour, saying that "China is deepening its reform, trying to create more favourable conditions for future development. We attach importance not only to our development in this century, but even more to our development in the next. The choice before us is either to continue to make economic progress or to retreat. But to retreat will get us nowhere. Only by deepening reform in every field of endeavour can we ensure that the people will live a relatively comfortable life by the end of this century and that more progress will be made in the next."[24]

---

[21] Xi (2014a), p. 68.

[22] For more information about Charter Cities, see http://urbanizationproject.org/blog/charter-cities.

[23] Deng (1993i).

[24] Deng (1993m).

Xi Jinping made further interpretation of Deng Xiaoping's assumption that reform and opening-up is a long-term cause, arguing that "reform and opening-up is always ongoing and will never end" and "reform and opening-up is a long-term and arduous cause, and people need to work on it generation after generation."[25]

Revolutionary is the sixth attribute of China's reform and opening-up. Revolutionary means: on the one hand, the reform and opening-up cause, compared with previous causes, is considerably different with brand new requirements and content which may lead to drastic changes; on the other hand, the reform and opening-up cause will be extremely arduous so the whole party and all the people must make tremendous efforts. On August 21, 1985, in a talk with President Julius Kambarage Nyerere of the United Republic of Tanzania, Deng Xiaoping began with his interpretation of the "revolutionary" aspect of reform and opening-up. He said, "the reform is designed to clear away the obstacles to the development of the productive forces and to lift China out of poverty and backwardness. In this sense, the reform may also be called a revolutionary change."[26] Xi Jinping also has a keen observation about the "revolutionary" aspect of reform and opening-up. He argued, "reform and opening-up is an in-depth revolution, and we must follow the correct direction and stay on the correct path.… Reform and opening-up is a cause that has never before been pursued. We must adopt the right methods and advance this cause through continuous exploration and practice."[27]

Having affinity to the people is the seventh attribute of China's reform and opening-up. It means the correct and smooth advance of reform and opening-up shall rely on the people and its fruits shall be enjoyed by the people. When talking about reform in 1988, Deng Xiaoping said, "when handling matters we should consult the people, act resolutely but prudently, analyze our experience from time to time and correct inappropriate plans and methods so as to prevent minor mistakes from becoming major ones."[28] The people provided prior intellectual support and mass foundation for reform and opening-up, carry out supervision along the way and make summary and assessment afterwards. Xi Jinping's understanding of the affinity to the people of reform and opening-up is of a piece of that of Deng Xiaoping's. In his speech at the second plenary meeting of the Third Plenary Session of the 18th CPC Central Committee, he argued, "we must rely on the people to promote reform. The people are the creators of history and the source of our strength. The fundamental reason why our reform and opening-up has won the people's wholehearted support and vigorous participation all along lies in the fact that from the very beginning we let the cause strike deep roots among the people… the valuable experiences of our reform and opening-up, one of which highlighted the importance of putting people first, respecting their principal position in the country, giving free rein to their creativity, and promoting reform with the close support of the people. In the absence of people's support and participation, no reform can possibly succeed. No matter

[25]Xi (2014a), p. 67.

[26]Deng (1993n).

[27]Xi (2014a).

[28]Deng (1993m).

what difficulties and challenges we may encounter, we will prevail as long as we have the people's support and participation. We must implement the Party's mass line and rally closely with the people, sharing weal and woe with them, and working vigorously by their side."[29]

Generally speaking, reform and opening-up is an important experience for the successful economic development up to date and its content and forms have aroused the interest of the international community especially that of a growing number of developing countries. In fact, as early as 1985, the visiting Vice-President Ali Hassan Mwinyi of the United Republic of Tanzania told Deng Xiaoping that Tanzania would like to learn from China's experience.[30] On October 7, 2013, Xi Jinping delivered a speech titled Deepen Reform and Opening-up and Work Together for a Better Asia Pacific at the APEC CEO Summit, sharing with the attendees the experiences of China's growth. He argued that the drivers of growth could only be found through reform, readjustment and innovation. China is in the process of deepening reform and expanding opening-up. As an organic whole, reform and opening-up, may it be introducing or going out, needs to sustain a favorable, stable and friendly external environment for a long time so that China may continue to harvest achievements in its reform and opening-up and benefit its people and friendly countries through trying and innovation.

Developing Countries

Third, China is a developing country. There are two connotations behind the emphasis on the identity as a developing country. For one thing, judging from the objective stage and level of China's development, China can only be regarded as a developing country. For another, judging from the stand that China sticks to in the international society, China insists on the identity as a developing country, commits to speaking for the interests of developing countries and opposes the practice that some developed countries infringe upon the rights and interests of developing countries by adopting partial international rules.

Judging China whether by "per capita" benchmarks, may it be the economic or consuming level or the amount of social public goods enjoyed by the public, it's obvious that China is still a developing country. In terms of GNI per capita, it was $7380 in China in 2014, much lower than that of high-income countries ($38,392), higher than that of middle-income countries ($4690) but still lower than that of upper-middle-income countries ($7893). In terms of specific countries, it was somewhere between that of Belarus ($7340) and Bulgaria ($7420). In terms of household final consumption expenditure per capita, it was $1307 in China in 2013, much lower than that of high-income countries ($18,492) and that of upper-middle-income countries ($2238) and even lower than that of middle-income countries ($1446). In terms

[29] Xi (2014b), p. 18.

[30] Deng (1993o).

specific countries, China's household final consumption expenditure per capita was somewhere between that of West Bank and Gaza (Palestine) ($1294) and Angola ($1379). In terms of health expenditure per capita, it was $367 in China in 2013, much lower than that of high-income countries ($4463), lower than that of upper-middle-income countries ($465) and a little bit higher than that of middle-income countries ($256). In terms of specific countries, China ranked somewhere between Peru ($354) and Paraguay ($395). In terms of improved urban sanitation facilities, China's urban population with access to improved sanitation facilities[31] was 74.1% in 2012, lower than that of high-income countries (97.0%), upper-middle-income countries (81.5%) and middle-income countries (74.6%). In terms of specific countries, China ranked higher than Djibouti (73.1%) but lower than Russia (74.4%). In terms of telephone lines (per 100 people), it was 19.3 in China in 2013, though higher than that of upper-middle-income countries (18.6) but still much lower than that of high-income countries (41.1). In terms of specific countries, China ranked somewhere between Qatar (19.0) and Armenia (19.4). In terms of internet users (per 100 people), it was 45.8 in China in 2013, higher than that of upper-middle-income countries (44.2) but still much lower than that of high-income countries (77.1). In terms of specific countries, China ranked between Jordan (44.2) and Dominican (45.9). In terms of mobile cellular subscriptions (per 100 people), it was 88.7 in China in 2013, lower than that of high-income countries (121.8), upper-middle-income countries (98.7) and middle-income countries (90.3), a little bit higher than that of lower-middle-income countries. In terms of specific countries, China ranked between Dominican (88.4) and Bosnia and Herzegovina (91.1) (Table 3.1).

Generally speaking, China's indicators of household final consumption expenditure, urban population with access to improved sanitation facilities, mobile cellular subscriptions and so on were lower than those of middle-income countries; China's indicators of GNI per capita, health expenditure per capita and so on are lower than those of upper-middle-income countries; though China's electric power consumption (a better indicator is electric power consumption of residents, for electric power consumption cannot fully reflect living standard of residents and is more related to the fact that China is a manufacturing power), telephone line per 100 people and internet user per 100 people has reached the level of upper-middle-income countries, there is still a huge gap between China and high-income countries. As for those countries with similar indicators to those of China, Belarus, Bulgaria, Palestine, Angola, Peru, Paraguay, Djibouti, Russia, Qatar, Armenia, Jordan, Dominican and Bosnia and Herzegovina, none of them is a developed country. Therefore, judging from these per capital and social development indicators, China is obviously a developing country.

[31] Improved sanitation facilities (percentage of urban population with access) refers to the percentage of the population using basic facilities of human excreta. Improved sanitation facilities can effectively ensure hygienic separation of human excreta from human, animal, mosquito and fly contact. They include flush/pour flush (to piped sewer system, septic tank, pit latrine), ventilated improved pit (VIP) latrine, pit latrine with slab, and composting toilet. To guarantee the effectiveness of these facilities, they must be built in correct methods and maintained properly.

Table 3.1 Various indicators show China is still a developing country

	GNI per capita (current US $) (2014)	Household final consumption expenditure per capita (constant 2005 US$) (2013)	Health expenditure per capita (current US$) (2013)	Electric power consumption (kWh per capita)	Improved sanitation facilities (% of urban population with access) (2012)	Telephone lines (per 100 people) (2013)	Internet users (per 100 people) (2013)	Mobile cellular subscriptions (per 100 people) (2013)
High-income countries	38,392	18,492	4463	8573	97.0	41.1	77.1	121.8
Upper-middle-income countries	7893	2238	465	2916	81.5	18.6	44.2	98.7
China	7380	1307	367	3298	74.1	19.3	45.8	88.7
Middle-income countries	4690	1446	256	1714	74.6	10.9	31.2	90.3
Lower-middle-income countries	2037	787	82	689	65.5	4.5	20.2	83.2
Low-income countries	635	311	38		39.1	0.9	5.2	50.8

Sources World Bank data

Apart from per capita indicators, many other indicators that depict the unbalanced economic development structures also suggest that China is still a developing country. Generally speaking, the development levels between different regions and those between urban areas and rural areas are relatively balanced while the disparities between different regions and those between urban areas and rural areas are rather obvious.[32] Judging from the income, spending and public service indicators, considerable disparities exist between urban areas and rural areas in China. In 2014, the annual disposable income per capita of rural households in China amounted to

[32]Liu (2011).

10488.88 yuan while that of urban households reached 28843.85 yuan, 2.75 times the former, meanwhile the annual living expenditure per capita of rural households reached 8382.57 yuan while that of urban households reached 19968.08 yuan, 2.38 times the former. In 2013, the annual health expenditure per capita of rural households reached 1274.44 yuan while that of urban households 3234.12 yuan, 2.54 times the former. The differences between different regions were also rather huge. In 2014, the provincial GDP per capita of Tianjin Municipality, the highest of all, was 105,202 yuan, 3.99 times that of Guizhou province (26,393 yuan), the lowest of all. In 2013, the annual living expenditure per capital of Shanghai was 39,223 yuan, the highest of all, 6.25 times that of Tibet Autonomous Region (6275 yuan), the lowest of all.[33]

Besides, we can determine whether a country is a developing or developed country according to whether its innovation mainly derives from external technology or internal technology. As a rule, developed countries, with an edge of technology, are exporters of technology while developing countries need to import, learn from and imitate others so as to achieve their technological advancement. Former Chairman of the Federal Reserve of the United States, Alan Greenspan, noted that China's rapid growth in recent years relied mainly on imported technology while, so far, only very little derived domestically. He also cited the study of Thompson Reuters, arguing that none of the top 100 most innovative companies in the year of 2011 was a Chinese one but there were 40 American companies among them.[34]

In fact, it has become a thinking ritual to criticize China for relying on technology in the USA or other developed countries due to its lack of domestic technological innovation. Only a few have realized or recognized the periodicity of such a situation. Regarding the presumption that China "steals" Western technology, Charles R. Morris, a winner of the Gerald Loeb Award in the business book category, a most prestigious award in American business and financial journalism, noted in his writing that what China is doing to USA had been done by both USA and UK two centuries ago. If anything, the Americans were even more brazen about their ambitions. At that time, American entrepreneurs advertised openly for skilled British operatives who were willing to risk arrest and imprisonment for sneaking machine designs out of the country and then starting up their business in the new continent. Tench Coxe, Alexander Hamilton's deputy at Treasury, created a system of bounties to entice sellers of trade secrets, and sent an agent to steal machine drawings. Samuel Slater answered an ad and sneaked British textile technology against national sanctions into America. Former president Andrew Jackson called Slater "The Father of the American Industrial Revolution". In a word, the 19th century Americans would steal all the technology they could from Britain. In contrast, what China has done so far is virtually nothing.[35]

An article in *Foreign Affairs* (Issue 7/8 2013) also argued that the China's "piracy" and imitation is not always an enemy of innovation, for nearly all creations rest on prior work and the ability to freely copy and refine existing designs fuels fields as

[33]For more statistics, see http://data.stats.gov.cn/.

[34]Greenspan (2013).

[35]Morris (2012).

varied as fashion, finance, and software. Copying can also foster stronger competition, grow markets, and build brands. Millions of Chinese have gained new skills, which will enhance their income and aid the growth of an emerging Chinese middle class, which represents a massive potential pool of new customers for Western firms and will ultimately boost the American economy with its increasing purchase of American goods. "Therefore, the idea that USA should take a tougher stance so as to prevent China from copying of intellectual property is also wrong."[36]

The above discussion indicates that, judging by its major source of innovation, China is still a developing country and its reliance on external innovation benefits not only itself. The differences between various developmental stages in China, which is now on its way of development, are bound to offer opportunities for the economic growth of the world. As a matter of fact, Deng Xiaoping made his observation in this regard long time ago. On October 6, 1984, during an interview with Chinese and foreign delegates to a symposium on China's economic cooperation with foreign countries, Deng Xiaoping said, "while holding to self-reliance, we should open our country to the outside world to obtain such aid as foreign investment capital and technology. This kind of assistance is not unilateral. While China will obtain investment capital and technology from other nations, particularly the developed ones, it will in turn make a greater contribution to the world economy. Its expanded foreign trade in recent years has borne this out. So we say that the assistance and the contribution are mutual."[37]

In terms of subjective choice, it has been a basic and long-term standpoint that China is a developing country. On February 22, 1974, Mao Zedong set forth his strategic thinking of the division of the three worlds when he met with Kenneth David Kaunda, President of Zambia. He observed, "In my view, the United States and the Soviet Union belong to the First World. The in-between Japan, Europe and Canada belong to the Second World. The Third World is very populous. Except Japan, Asia belongs to the Third World. So does the whole of Africa and Latin America".[38] About two months later, on April 10, 1974, Deng Xiaoping, on behalf of the Chinese government, thoroughly explained the Three Worlds Theory in a speech to the United Nations at the 6th special session of the United Nations General Assembly. Deng Xiaoping once summed up China's foreign policy in two sentences. First, "to safeguard world peace we oppose hegemony". Second, "China will always belong to the Third World." He said, "It belongs to the Third World today, and it will do so even when it becomes prosperous and powerful, because it shares a common destiny with all Third World countries. China will never seek hegemony or bully others, but will always side with the Third World."[39] The viewpoint of Deng has been stuck to till the present day. On April, 22, 2015, president Xi Jinping, at the Conference of Asian-African Leaders, pointed out, "China will always be a dependable friend and

---

[36]Raustiala and Sprigman (2013).

[37]Deng (1993p).

[38]Mao (1994), pp. 600–601.

[39]Deng (1993q).

sincere partner of developing countries, regardless of international situations. This is the basis of China's foreign policy, and it will not change now and in the future".[40]

Nowadays, some argue that China's insistence that it is a developing country aims to avoid its international obligations and responsibilities and enjoy greater rights. For instance, a developed country is supposed to undertake more responsibilities than a developing one in terms of such problems as climate change. The truth is that what China first recognized was responsibility and morality instead of rights ever since China put forward the theory of the division of the "three worlds" and its self-recognition as a developing country.[41]

Mao Zedong's division of "three worlds" was closely related to his support to equality among large and small countries. He argued that, "A large country is superior to a small one. That is a capitalistic theory. A country, no matter how small, even only with a population of several hundred thousand or tens of thousands, and another country with a population of hundreds of millions should be totally equal. That is a basic principle instead of an empty talk. Now that we are talking about equality, a large country shall not impair a small one by exploiting the latter financially, oppressing the latter politically or imposing its own will, policies or thoughts on the latter."[42]

When it comes to the Third World or developing countries, most official documents of the Communist Party of China tend to convey its aspirations to implement its responsibility of providing foreign aid, strengthening unity and cooperation among developing countries and expanding their right to speak etc. For instance, the Report to the Twelfth National Congress of the Communist Party of China said, "Socialist China belongs to the Third World… China is still a developing country. However, we have been providing assistance to the best of our ability to other countries in The Third World with whom we share weal and woe…. Whether we are to carry out mutual beneficial cooperation with them or provide foreign assistance, we give our full respect to the sovereignty of the recipient countries and adhere to the principles of not imposing any political conditions, not interfering in the internal affairs of the recipient countries. In the future, we will increasingly expand the friendly cooperation between other countries and people in The Third World and us." The Report to the Fourteenth National Congress of the Communist Party of China said, "China is a developing country. A key element of our foreign policy is to strengthen our solidarity and co-operation with other Third World countries. China and the other developing countries will, as always, support each other in safeguarding their independence and sovereignty and will increase their economic and cultural exchanges. "The Report to the Fifteenth National Congress of the Communist Party of China said, "We should further strengthen our solidarity and cooperation with the Third World countries…. China will, as always, join the vast number of developing countries in mutual support and close cooperation in all areas to safeguard our lawful rights and interests." The Report to the Sixteenth National Congress of the Communist Party of China said, "We will continue to enhance our solidarity and cooperation with other Third World

[40] Xi (2015).

[41] Yu (2013).

[42] Mao (1994), p. 190.

countries, increase mutual understanding and trust and strengthen mutual help and support. We will enlarge areas of cooperation and make it more fruitful." The Report to the Seventeenth National Congress of the Communist Party of China said, "While securing our own development, we will accommodate the legitimate concerns of other countries, especially other developing countries.... We support international efforts to help developing countries enhance their capacity for independent development and improve the lives of their people, so as to narrow the North-South gap.... we will continue to increase solidarity and cooperation with them, cement traditional friendship, expand practical cooperation, provide assistance to them within our ability, and uphold the legitimate demands and common interests of developing countries." The Report to the Eighteenth National Congress of the Communist Party of China said, "We will increase unity and cooperation with other developing countries, work with them to uphold the legitimate rights and interests of developing countries and support efforts to increase their representation and voice in international affairs. China will remain a reliable friend and sincere partner of other developing countries."

All in all, although the reform and opening-up of China has made considerable achievements and its economic aggregate has been increasing over the years, China actually faces such problems as its level of development per capita is still low, the structural imbalance is rather serious, its internal innovation dynamics is relatively weak, problems that are prevailing in many developing countries. Subjectively, China adheres to the stand that China is a developing country, willing to make more contribution to the cooperation and unity among developing countries and safeguard the overall interests of all developing countries.

Rapid Growth

Fourth, China is a country featuring rapid economic growth. According to data of the World Bank on record, China's real GDP growth rates in most years since 1961 especially 1978 have been higher than those of other countries with different levels of growth. From 1978 to 2014, the actual full-year expansion of China's GDP averaged 9.8%, only lower than that of three small countries, namely, Equatorial Guinea, Qatar and Bosnia and Herzegovina while it is more steady. The standard deviation of China's real GDP growth rates from 1978 to 2014 was only 2.69% while that of Equatorial Guinea, Qatar and Bosnia and Herzegovina was 29.34%, 7.08% and 20.19% respectively, which means the reason why the average real GDP growth rates of these countries was relatively higher was because of their particularly high growth rates in certain years. As a matter of fact, among the five countries with a standard deviation lower than 5%,[43] the average standard deviation of real GDP growth rate of China was the highest of all (Chart 3.1).

[43]The average standard deviation of real GDP growth rate of all economies from 1978 to 2014 was approximately 5%.

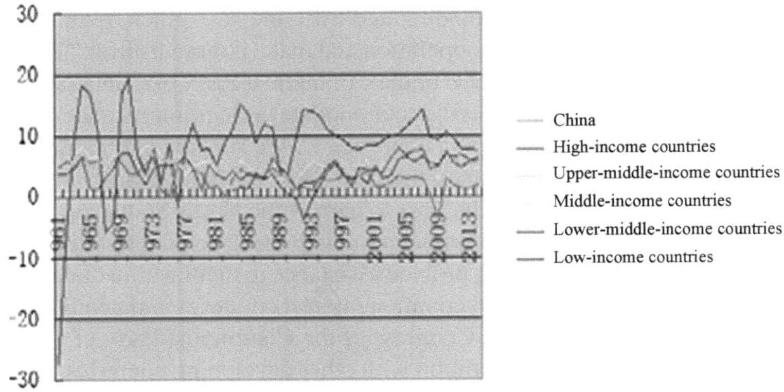

Chart 3.1 GDP Growth Rates of China and Other Countries with Various incomes: 1961–2014. *Source* Data of The World Bank

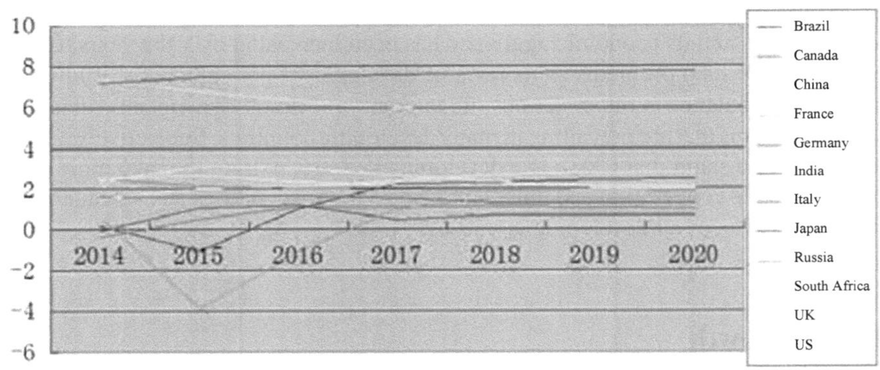

Chart 3.2 Forecasts of Real GDP Growth Rates of the Four Golden Brick Countries and G7 Countries (2014–2020). *Source* Data of IMF

In contrast, we showcase here the real GDP growth rates and their standard deviations of ASEAN countries and G20 countries. As shown in the following table, in terms of growth speed and stability, East Asian countries including China are reasonably seen as the engine for global economic growth and no doubt China draws most attention (Table 3.2).

According to forecast of the IMF, from 2015 to 2020, China will still be able to maintain a relatively high economic growth rate (with an average of about 6.3%), only second to that of India among the Four Golden Brick countries and G7 countries and apparently higher than the rest of them (that of the USA will be lower than that of China, the average real GDP growth rate of former during this period will be 2.5%) (Chart 3.2).

Looking further into the future, some institutions have forecast the GDP and ranking of the top five economies of the world by 2050. Our calculation by the

Table 3.2 Average real GDP growth rates and standard deviations of ASEAN countries and G20 countries (1978–2014)

Country	Average (%)	Standard deviation (%)
China	9.82	2.69
Cambodia	7.69	2.81
Singapore	6.87	4.04
Vietnam	6.42	1.64
Laos	6.42	2.87
Republic of Korea	6.41	3.94
Malaysia	6.06	3.67
Burma	5.99	5.43
India	5.95	2.84
Indonesia	5.64	3.75
Thailand	5.40	4.36
Turkey	3.96	4.30
The Philippines	3.63	3.35
Australia	3.16	1.57
Mexico	3.05	3.69
Saudi Arabia	3.01	4.94
Brazil	2.93	3.18
USA	2.75	1.98
Argentina	2.60	6.16
Canada	2.54	1.99
South Africa	2.47	2.29
UK	2.24	2.05
Japan	2.22	2.52
France	1.90	1.47
Germany	1.80	1.99
Italy	1.41	2.07
Brunei	1.37	5.68
Russia	0.80	6.89

Source Calculated in accordance with data of the World Bank

constant dollar in 2005 shows: the forecast of the CEPII adopted by the European Commission indicates the GDP of China will be 34.7 trillion, the USA, 26.7 trillion, India, 8.8 trillion, Japan, 8.1 trillion and the UK, 5 trillion; the forecast of Hong Kong and Shanghai Banking Corporation indicates the GDP of China will be 28.5 trillion, USA, 25 trillion, India 9.2 trillion, Japan, 7.2 trillion and Germany, 4.2 trillion; the forecast of Carnegie Endowment for International Peace indicates the GDP of China will be 46.3 trillion, the USA, 38.6 trillion, India, 15.4 trillion, Japan, 6.2 trillion and Brazil, 6 trillion; the forecast of Price Waterhouse Coopers indicates the GDP of China will be 51.9 trillion, India, 35.9 trillion, the USA, 35.2 trillion, Indonesia,

10.4 trillion and Brazil, 7.8 trillion.[44] Despite the noticeable differences between the forecasts of these institutions, China will rank highest on all the lists, which would be impossible without a relatively high speed of economic growth. For China, the speed of economic growth is more a political matter concerning the superiority of socialism than an economic matter. As cited above from Deng Xiaoping, "The superiority of the socialist system is demonstrated, in the final analysis, by faster and greater development of those forces than under the capitalist system." The Chinese government has put forward a "New Normal" theory, ready to accept the fall from "ultra-high speed" of economic growth to "a relatively high" speed of economic growth. Nevertheless, from the political perspective, the speed of economic growth is a relative concept but not an absolute one. It suggests that as long as China, thanks to its superiority, sustains an economic growth speed higher than that of developed capitalist countries in Europe and America, it will be largely "reasonable".

In a word, whether in the past, the near future or distant future, China's economic growth has remained and will remain a relatively high level, which means there's no urgent need for China to "solve" those "knotty problems" immediately and it is not in the interest of China to plummet its peaceful and stable developmental environment by stirring things up. "China will not stir up trouble, but we are also not afraid of trouble" is a true portrayal of China's status quo.

Not Yet Reunified

Fifth, China is not yet reunified. At present, China is still a divided country. In addition to being divided, China also faces the threat of internal separatists and the intertwined separatism, ethnic problems and religious problems.

The Taiwan issue remains unsettled. On September 1, 1982, in the opening speech at the Twelfth National Congress of the Communist Party of China, Deng Xiaoping said, "To accelerate socialist modernization, to strive for China's reunification and particularly for the return of Taiwan to the motherland, and to oppose hegemonism and work to safeguard world peace—these are the three major tasks of our people in this decade."[45] Now looking back, the central task among the three, namely, economic development has made considerable achievements while, given the fact that a third World War did not break out in the 1980s and much practical progress has been made in terms of reunification, the other two tasks may be considered basically fulfilled.

---

[44]These reports include the *Global Europe 2050* of the European Commission, http://ec.europa.eu/research/social-sciences/pdf/global-europe-2050-summary-report_en.pdf, the World in *2050: From the Top 30 to the Top 100* of Hong Kong and Shanghai Banking Corporation, http://www.hsbc.com/~/media/HSBC-com/about-hsbc/advertising/pdfs/the-world-in-2050.pdf, *The World Order in 2050* of Carnegie Endowment for International Peace, http://carnegieendowment.org/files/World_Order_in_2050.pdf and *The World in 2050: Will the shift in global economic power continue?* of Price Waterhouse Coopers, http://www.pwc.com/gx/en/issues/the-economy/the-world-in-2050.html.

[45]Deng (1993r).

Apparently the three major tasks were not fully accomplished in the 1980s. Now these tasks have been passed on in the Era of Xi Jinping. When presiding over the first group session of the Political Bureau of the CPC Central Committee, Xi Jinping said, "We must continue to work for the three historic missions of modernization, reunification of the motherland, and world peace and the common development of all nations. These are missions of historic importance that have been bestowed on our generation of Communists, and to which we must dedicate all our wisdom and strength."[46] Judging solely by this statement, it seems that a timetable for solving the Taiwan issue has been (at least implicitly) drafted, that is to say, the reunification shall be accomplished by this "generation of Communists" represented by Xi Jinping. However, taking into account related statements of Deng Xiaoping back in the 1980s, it can be noted that "the realization of the reunification of the motherland" is just an important mission for "this generation of Communists", who will put strenuous efforts toward it yet still regard it as a process, i.e., "it doesn't have to be me to make it."

The reality that China is not yet reunified means that, as far as territory is concerned, China will never put up an aggressive posture of "expansion" for the "legitimacy" of its whole territory is not yet wholly established due to the unaccomplished task of national reunification. China, however, will resolutely defend its territory especially when it is under the threat of other countries. In his speech at the symposium to commemorate the 120th anniversary of Mao Zedong's birth, Xi Jinping said, "We…never seek hegemonism nor engage in expansion. We will resolutely defend our sovereignty, security and development interests. No country should assume that we will trade away our core interests, nor will we accept anything that harms our sovereignty, security or development interests."[47]

Apart from Taiwan issue, separatist forces such as "Hong Kong separatists", "Xinjiang separatists" and "Tibet separatists" are also threatening or damaging the integrity of the nation. With these domestic problems unsolved, conflicts with other countries may aggravate such domestic problems.

An Indispensable Large Country

Sixth, China is a large country. It is an undisputed large country whether in terms of population or economic aggregate or political influence. It is indispensable mainly because that China has profoundly engaged itself in the current international system. Its identity as a large country means that, although China's approval may not elicit international consensus or promote collective actions, China's opposition or absence almost always suggest critical imperfection in the legitimacy or enactment of international actions or mechanisms.

---

[46]Xi (2014c).

[47]Xi (2014d).

Ever since the founding of the UN, China has been one of the five permanent member states of the UN Security Council. Since the People's Republic of China regained its UN membership in 1971, it has been playing an important part in it as one of the five permanent member states of the UN Security Council. Since China implemented its reform and opening-up, it has joined in a large number of economic cooperation organizations (for instance, China has signed the *Agreement of the International Monetary Fund, the Convention Establishing the Multilateral Investment Guarantee Agency, Agreement Establishing the African Development Fund,* to name a few.), signed many agreements on protection of human rights (For example, *The International Convention on the Suppression and Punishment of the Crime Apartheid, the Vocational Rehabilitation and Employment (Disabled Persons) Convention, 1983, the* Equal Remuneration Convention, etc.) and also joined many industry-related organizations (through agreements such *as the ITU Convention,* the *Agreement for the Establishment of the Indian Ocean Tuna Commission*, the Agreement for the Establishment of the International Network for Bamboo and Rattan). Besides, China has put an end to the marathon from "resumption of its contracting party status in the GATT" to "entry into the WTO", becoming a member of the WTO and part of all important economic organizations. Based on the platform of G20, China has been active in promoting the governance structure reform of IMF and the World Bank and has wherein achieved considerable positive results.

The cooperation organizations and agreements that China has joined in or advocated are increasing in both number and diversity. In particular, in Asia and surrounding areas of China, so far China has not only signed agreements like the *Statute of the Secretariat of the Conference on Interaction and Confidence Building Measures in Asia, the Treaty of Amity and Cooperation in Southeast Asia and the Greater Mekong Sub-region Cross Border Transport Agreement but also the Shanghai Cooperation Organization Charter, the Convention on the Privileges and Immunities of the Shanghai Cooperation Organization, the Agreement of Shanghai Cooperation Organization Members on Regional Anti-terrorism Structure, the Agreement of Shanghai Cooperation Organization Member Governments on Educational Cooperation, the Agreement of Shanghai Cooperation Organization Member Governments on Health Care Cooperation and many other conventions and agreements* under the framework of the Shanghai Cooperation Organization but also promoted the establishment of multilateral financial institutions such as BRICS New Development Bank and Asian Infrastructure Investment Bank. In addition, statistics of the CIA World Factbook 2015 show that China has joined 75 international organizations (including organizations in which China is an observer state). In other words, China has become a member in most leading global and regional transnational organizations.

Let's take G20, the most important international economic governance platform for many, as an example. The total GDP of these countries in 2014 took up about 85.2% of that of the world. In contrast, the voting rule of the IMF provides that 85% of the total votes means super-majority for any important topic for discussion. However, if China were spurned, the total GDP of G20 would fall to 71.93%, thus their weight would reduce sharply. In terms of demography, the total population of G20 countries took up about 64.08% of that of the world, which, though lower than that of GDP, also made a simple majority for it was way above the bottom line of 50%. If China were cast aside, the population proportion of G20 countries in the total population of the world would be lower than 50%, to be precise, 45.1%, which would also lead to dramatic loss of their weight in the world.

Additionally, as far as international climate talks are concerned, China also plays an indispensable role. In 2012, a scientific report titled "The challenge to keep global warming below 2 °C" by Tyndall Centre for Climate Change Research, United Kingdom was published online in *Nature Climate Change*, a special issue of the most cited scientific journal *Nature*. The report concludes that in 2011 China became the world's biggest carbon emitter, closely followed by the USA, European Union and India. We could hardly, therefore, expect the measures taken around the world to make any positive progress without the participation and support of China. Fortunately, China submitted a document titled *Enhanced Actions on Climate Change: China's Intended Nationally Determined Contributions* to the Secretariat of the United Nations Framework Convention on Climate Change on June 30, 2015. It shows the nationally determined actions of China by 2030 as follows: to lower carbon dioxide emissions per unit of GDP by 60–65% from the 2005 level; to increase the share of non-fossil fuels in primary energy consumption to around 20%; to increase the forest stock volume by around 4.5 billion cubic meters on the 2005 level and to achieve the peaking of carbon dioxide emissions around 2030 and making best efforts to peak early. As a developing country, some experts argue, China's objectives of peaking of carbon dioxide emissions, carbon intensity and consumption of non-fossil fuels are all impressive even if we compare them to those of developed countries. The document also declares that China is committed to the full, effective and sustained implementation of the Convention and to working with other Parties to achieve a comprehensive, balanced and ambitious agreement at the UN Climate Change Conference (Paris) to be held at the end of that year.[48]

Limited by its existing resources, the national identity of a country has a profound influence on its foreign behavior. No matter which stage it finds itself in, being a large country has been a key factor in China's self-identity. A country which is basically a recipient of the influence of actions of other countries, international theory, institutions and products is a small country, otherwise, a large one. A large country does not passively accept the influence from the outside world or the globalization trend, instead it noticeably influences or shapes, more or less, (one or more facets of) the outside world or the globalization trend. Being a large country means its domestic behavior has an impact on "international relative prices" (or a standard that determines the competition results of international actors). Taking that into consideration, other large countries react to such behavior of this country, the so-called Boomerang Effects.[49] After realizing the reaction, this country will take into account possible reactions of other countries while deciding how to respond accordingly. The process

---

[48]China's New Move against Climate Change, http://www.gov.cn/zhengce/2015-07/05/content_2890538.htm.

[49]In 1957 Gunnar Myrdal put forward the idea of Backwash Effects, which argues that the increase of a certain country's export and economic activities will lead to inflow of other countries' capital and labor and consequently damage the country from which productive factors flow out. Zhang

goes on and on like this. At this point, it is desirable to adopt an interactive or gaming perspective and stand in others' place while drafting foreign policies. In other words, no large country, especially a responsible one, shall be unrestrained.

China's Expectations for the Outside World: A Metaphor *in Journey to the West*

So far we have examined the national identity of China or the practical basis for its rejuvenation. As a large, developing, rapidly growing yet not yet reunified socialist country that devotes itself to reform and opening-up, China's expectations for the outside world are in close ties with the above-mentioned characteristics. These expectations, or basic goals of China's foreign strategy, can be understood in terms of the following five dimensions: One, product dimension, to be specific, rich people and a strong country, vast and overall increase in economic scale, per capita income, scientific and technological levels and military strength compared with other countries; Two, institution dimension, or final establishment and insistence of institutions suitable for the steady development of China through constantly exploration and learning in reform and opening-up. In a globalized world, the realization of fair and rational international institutions or order is also the external conditions for the realization of the Chinese Dream. Three, the fiscal and monetary dimension, it refers to diversifying the international monetary system by making the Chinese yuan a key currency of the world while maintaining a healthy and sustainable balance sheet. Four, the value dimension, it means the values and cultural traditions and customs held and observed by China are not only respected by the world but also seen as an essential part of the widely accepted values world-wide. Five, the national reunification dimension, the key to which lies in the idea that a rejuvenated country must be a reunified one, no matter how the approaches and forms of realizing reunification may vary. It is impossible for any divided country to speak of national rejuvenation.

To achieve the foreign-oriented goals in respect of products, institutions, currency, values, reunification, etc., the biggest hindrance that China faces today is the USA, which also intends to systematize China by international rules and regulations led by and favorable to the USA. In responding to the USA, China must strengthen

---

(2014) defines the effect that the initiation and enactment of a certain country's foreign policies "can change the utility functions of its competitors or cooperators" and in return influence its own development opportunities or conditions as Boomerang Effects. This definition is different from that of Gunnar Myrdal's for its emphasis on the influence on the country itself instead of that on the outside. In contrast, this definition is closer to the idea of Spillbacks put forward by IMF sometime later in April 2014, which means to warn the USA of such economic feedback loops as "if Federal Reserve withdraws from QE too soon, the emerging markets will slide into chaos and in return the American economy will also be affected". Here Boomerang Effects stand for the (both positive and negative) feedback effects (not only limited to economic spillbacks) of foreign policies in a broader sense. The term "Boomerang Effects" is used here in contrast to Gunnar Myrdal's "Backwash Effects". See Myrdal (1957), Zhang (2014).

existing risk management so as to avoid any lose-lose situation and strive for more win-win outcomes so as to inject more substantive content in the establishment of a new relationship between large countries. Despite the rather wide gap between the two countries in terms of strength, it is actually possible to envisage in a couple of decades the two countries will be able to provide the world with public goods through their difficult yet effective communication.

As a matter of fact, in contrast to the era featuring evolution of hegemony cycle centuries ago, the nature of current international power has undergone radical changes. The international power, or the ability of a country to influence other countries or international actors, can be broadly divided into hard power that the hegemony state takes the initiative to exercise and the soft power that a non-hegemony state chooses to exercise (the non-hegemony state readily recognizes the influence imposed on by the hegemony state). From the perspective of the hegemony state, the realization of its influence can be achieved through two approaches: inducement and coercion. In other words, the hegemony state can influence other countries by providing public commodities. Those public commodities in the form of benefits can be called public goods while those emerge as threats public bads. Several centuries ago, much or most of the power of the hegemony state was realized through providing public bads, such as plundering resources, raw materials of its colonies and robbing their markets of wealth by dumping their good there. In exercising power through public bads, the marginal cost involved was almost zero, which means once deterrent force was in place the hegemony state was able to achieve its purposes of coercion and exploitation without actual use of force.

In the world today, there's much less space for achieving influence through coercion. In particular, the appearance of nuclear weapons brings about even tighter restrictions to the competition between large countries. More often than not the hegemony state seeks support and recognition by providing public goods. The "power" competition in this field is mainly about rushing to provide public goods to the international society. For example, after China proposed the establishment of Asian Infrastructure Invest Bank, Japan also earmarked 110 billion dollars (its legal capital was 10 billion dollars more than that of AIIB) for building infrastructure in Asia. However, the marginal cost for exercising influence through public goods is much higher than that of through public bads. As public goods are consumptive, the constant supply of public goods in order to maintain "power" entails use of large amounts of domestic resources, which may greatly infringe upon the welfare of its own people. Therefore, the supply of public goods is inherently bounded by domestic politics.

It's impossible to pursue and exercise the "power" obtained through providing the international society with public goods infinitely. It is said that Japan will raise the capital for building infrastructure in Asia in five years through public funding and loans of Asian Development Bank. Given the high level of government debt, it's still hard to tell to what extent this goal may be achieved. Nevertheless, it's always a good thing for the international society that any country is willing to provide public goods.

As a whole, power politics still exists within a certain range yet the logic of power politics is increasingly restricted. The change of the nature of power has considerably alleviated the rivalry during power transfer because the source of power has largely turned to the implementation of international obligations. The Sino-US relationship will also turn into a cooperative and competitive relationship in implementing international obligations or providing international public goods.

In Chinese culture, nothing portrays the Sino-US relationship more vividly than the relationship between Lord Lao Zi of the Great Monad and Tathagata Buddha. Briefly, *Journey to the West* tells a story in which the powerful, ambitious yet rebellious Monkey King, Sun Wukong, is completely subdued by Tathagata Buddha, Lord Lao Zi of the Great Monad and the Jade Emperor. Born in the burst of a magic stone which received the truth of Heaven, the beauty of Earth, the essence of the Sun and the splendour of the Moon, Sun Wukong first occupied a hill and acted as a king, then he learned extraordinary skills from the Patriarch as his pupil. Later he obtained the miraculous cudgel from the Old Dragon King of the Eastern Sea. After being visited twice by the Great White Planet, a messenger of Jade Emperor, he accepted the amnesty. He made the Heavenly Palace a wreck after being discriminated at work in heaven. His later arrest turned out to be a blessing in disguise for his torture in the furnace of Lord Lao Zi of the Great Monad unexpectedly gave him fire eyes with golden pupils. Although he became even more powerful with those eyes, he ended up being held down a mountain by the Buddha. Five hundred years later, he was assigned to escort Xuan Zang, a great monk of Tang Dynasty, to fetch the scriptures from India in the West. Finally Xuan Zang and his three disciples were rewarded, Sun Wukong being "the Victorious Fighting Buddha". At the end of the novel there is a rather meaningful detail. When Sun Wukong begged Xuan Zang to remove the golden bank on his head soon after he had become a Buddha, Xuan Zang replied there was no reason for it to stay any longer since he had become a Buddha. When Sun Wukong raised his hands to feel he found that it had indeed gone.

In studies of international problems, a country is often "personified" or seen as an individual who pursues maximized interests for the sake of analysis. In some cases, things may go the other way, that is, a person may be "nationalized". As a logical consequence, the relationship between key characters in *Journey to the West* may be transformed into relationship between countries. The relationship between Sun Wukong and Tathagata Buddha and that between Tathagata Buddha and Lord Lao Zi of the Great Monad reminds us of *Empire—the Political Order of Globalization* by Michael Hardt and Antonio Negri.[50]

Traditionally when an empire sought to expand it would first occupy a certain place by force then send officials to rule there and ultimately let its merchants plunder there. To both authors, the empire today is rather different from those in history. In nature, it has become a set of legal systems, a normative or legal tool that protects contracts and resolves conflicts. It does not rely on fixed geographic borders and takes the form of centralization or hegemony over the world market and global power. As an empire, the USA is the very political subject that dominates the global governance structure and the top authority that rules the world. In its open and ever expanding territory, this ruling machine constantly tightens its integration of the globe. The establishment of

[50]Hardt and Negri (2005).

such an empire basically undergoes three phases, namely, "inclusion-differentiation-manipulation".

In the inclusion phase, the empire fully displays its generosity, freedom and diversification. It "opens its mouth with an infinite appetite", trying to absorb or drag all other countries into the order network it weaves carefully while turning a blind eye to all differences. Since the differences are deliberately contained or ignored, the empire becomes "smooth space" in which all subjects "can freewheel in it without any risk of encountering big hindrance or conflicts". After those subjects outside the system voluntarily enter or forced into the empire system, the empire sets out to enter the second phase of its rule, or the "differentiation phase", which features the recognition of and emphasis on the differences among the accepted subjects. Generally speaking, the empire does not create differences but admit existing or potential differences then categorize and judge those varied newcomers in the system. In the final "manipulation phase", the empire makes full use the these differences to level out the newcomers in law, hierarchize them in politics, integrate them in economics and arrange their specific positions in the system effectively manipulated and controlled by the empire so as to maximize the interests of the empire.

It is not difficult to note that the relationship between Sun Wukong and Tathagata Buddha is similar to that between those subjects outside the empire system and the empire, in which Sun Wukong is the former and Tathagata Buddha the latter. The story of *Journey to the West* may also be split into three phases. The first phase witnessed the transformation from Monkey King, the outsider, to the Protector of the Horses and Great Sage Equalling Heaven. The second phase witnessed Monkey King's making great havoc in the palaces of heaven and later escorting Xuan Zang to the West to fetch the scriptures as Sun Wukong. The third phase witnessed the success of the journey after the four had gone through "81 ordeals" and Sun Wukong's being rewarded as the "Victorious Fighting Buddha". To a great extent, these three phases are a good match for those the Empire maintains and develops its system. In the first phase, "Tathagata Buddha or the Empire" includes "Monkey King or subjects outside the system" with an open spirit. In the second phase, "Tathagata Buddha or the Empire" identify, position and institutionalize the "Sun Wukong or newcomers in the system". In the third phase, "Sun Wukong or the Victorious Fighting Buddha" is completely institutionalized and totally integrated into "Tathagata Buddha or the Empire", automatically nullifying the golden Band on his head as soon as he became a Buddha.

The rules of the Empire, which functions as a set of legal systems, are highly partial, that is, the same set of rules mean different results for different subjects of the Empire. It's more so for those rules that are discriminatory themselves. Given that the protection and expansion of interests mainly derives from rules and their partiality, the founder of the rule system or the Empire naturally becomes the largest beneficiary of the system. After becoming a Buddha, Sun Wukong finds himself entering a stage of life in which he can do whatever he wants to do without breaking any rules. Now it looks the "Victorious Fighting Buddha" has obtained his reward such as an admirable entitle and recognition and respect of other members in the system and gradually become a beneficiary of the current system. The truth, however, is that all he has is what the Empire system is willing to give him and he will always stay in a subordinate position. Besides, his function in the system must be subordinated to the overall interest of the Empire.

It may not be quite appropriate to draw an analogy between "Sun Wukong versus Tathagata Buddha" and "USA versus the Law Empire", yet the former necessarily reminds us of the current Sino-US relationship. However, divergent thoughts sometimes may lead to some interesting questions such as should it be a development goal for China to be completely institutionalized in a US-dominated Empire system just like how Sun Wukong was institutionalized by Tathagata Buddha? If yes, how can China realize the vision advocated by those great minds about a century ago, "(China should) accept the influence of the West without being controlled by the West"? Also, how stable is the American Empire system? Is there any powerful challenger to that system? Is there any space or possibility that other system might exist outside the US-dominated world?

If we look into the distant future, the relationship between Tathagata Buddha and Lord Lao Zi of the Great Monad may be even more interesting. They belong to two overlapping worlds, the Buddhist world and the Taoist world respectively. They have rather different beliefs yet extensive and solid common interests and work closely together. Their powerful magic or skills are different yet they stand as equals instead of emperor and his subject, which should be the desirable orientation for the Sino-US relationship in three to five decades.

References

Charles R. Morris. We were pirates, too: China is stealing our trade secrets – just as we stole Britain's. December 16, 2012. http://www.post-gazette.com/stories/opinion/perspectives/we-were-pirates-too-china-is-stealing-our-trade-secrets-just-as-we-stole-britains-666529/#ixzz2aCgncdrg.

Deng, Xiaoping. 1993a. We are building a socialist society with both high material standards and cultural and ethical standards (April 29, 1983). *Selected Works of Deng Xiaoping*, *Vol. III*. Beijing: People's Press.

Deng, Xiaoping. 1993b. Building a society with a special Chinese character (June 30, 1984). *Selected Works of Deng Xiaoping*, *Vol. III*. Beijing: People's Press.

Deng, Xiaoping. 1993c. There Is No Fundamental Contradiction Between Socialism and a Market Economy (October 23, 1985). *Selected Works of Deng Xiaoping*, *Vol. III*. Beijing: People's Press.

Deng, Xiaoping. 1993d. No one can shake socialist China (October 26, 1989). *Selected Works of Deng Xiaoping*, *Vol. III*. Beijing: People's Press.

Deng, Xiaoping. 1993e. Keeping to socialism and the policy of peace (April 4, 1986). *Selected Works of Deng Xiaoping*, *Vol. III*. Beijing: People's Press.

Deng, Xiaoping. 1993f. We regard reform as a revolution (October 10, 1984). *Selected Works of Deng Xiaoping*, *Vol. III*. Beijing: People's Press.

Deng, Xiaoping. 1993g. Reform Is China's Second Revolution (March 28, 1985). *Selected Works of Deng Xiaoping*, *Vol. III*. Beijing: People's Press.

Deng, Xiaoping. 1993h. On reform of the political structure (September-November, 1986). *Selected Works of Deng Xiaoping*, *Vol. III*. Beijing: People's Press.

Deng, Xiaoping. 1993i. Seize the opportune moment to advance the reform (July 11, 1985). *Selected Works of Deng Xiaoping*, *Vol. III*. Beijing: People's Press.

Deng, Xiaoping. 1993j. The Army Should Subordinate Itself to the General Interest, Which Is to Develop the Country. *Selected Works of Deng Xiaoping, Vol. III*. Beijing: People's Press.
Deng, Xiaoping. 1993k. We Should Draw On the Experience of Other Countries. *Selected Works of Deng Xiaoping, Vol. III*. Beijing: People's Press.
Deng, Xiaoping. 1993l. Special Economic Zones Should Shift Their Economy From A Domestic Orientation To An External Orientation. *Selected Works of Deng Xiaoping, Vol. III*. Beijing: People's Press.
Deng Xiaoping. 1993m. We Should Maintain Moderately Rapid Growth of Production (June 7, 1988). *Selected Works of Deng Xiaoping, Vol. III*. Beijing: People's Press.
Deng, Xiaoping. 1993n. Two Kinds of Comments About China's Reform (August 21, 1985). *Selected Works of Deng Xiaoping, Vol. III*. Beijing: People's Press.
Deng, Xiaoping. 1993o. We Shall Expand Political Democracy and Carry Out Economic Reform (April 15, 1985). *Selected Works of Deng Xiaoping, Vol. III*. Beijing: People's Press.
Deng, Xiaoping. 1993p. Our Magnificent Goal and Basic Policies (October 6, 1984). *Selected Works of Deng Xiaoping, Vol. III*. Beijing: People's Press.
Deng, Xiaoping. 1993q. We Must Safeguard World Peace and Ensure Domestic Development (May 29, 1984). *Selected Works of Deng Xiaoping, Vol. III*. Beijing: People's Press.
Deng, Xiaoping. 1993r. Opening Speech At the Twelfth National Congress of the Communist Party of China (September 1, 1982). *Selected Works of Deng Xiaoping, Vol. III*. Beijing: People's Press.
Greenspan, A. 2013. *The Age of Turbulence: Adventures in a New World*, Yu, J. Trans. CITIC Press, p. 135.
Hardt, M. and A. Negri. 2005. *Empire—the Political Order of Globalization*, Trans. by Yang Jianguo, et al. Jiangsu People's Press.
Kal Raustiala and Christopher Sprigman. Fake It Till You Make It: The Good News About China's Knockoff Economy. Foreign Affairs. Volume 92, Number 4. Aug/Jul. 2013.
Liu, Shijin. 2011. Why China's identity as a "developing country" is problematic? *Qiushi*, No. 11, pp. 33–36.
Mao, Zedong. 1994. *Selected Works of Mao Zedong on Diplomacy*, Beijing: Central Party Literature Press, Beijing: World Knowledge Press.
Myrdal, G. 1957. *Myrdal Gunnar, Economic Theory and Underdeveloped Regions*. Gerald Duckworth.
Wen, Jiabao. 2008. The Chinese are fully able to feed themselves. *Farmer's Friend,* No. 9.
Xi, Jinping. 2014a. Reform and Opening-up Is Always Ongoing and Will Never End. *Xi Jinping: The Governance of China*, Foreign Languages Press.
Xi, Jinping. 2014b. Align Our Thinking with the Guidelines of the Third Plenary Session. *Xi Jinping: The Governance of China*, Foreign Languages Press, p. 97.
Xi, Jinping. 2014c. Study, Disseminate and Implement the Guiding Principles of the 18th CPC National Congress. *Xi Jinping: The Governance of China*, Foreign Languages Press.
Xi, Jinping. 2014d. Carry on the Enduring Spirit of Mao Zedong Thought. *Xi Jinping: The Governance of China*, Foreign Languages Press, p. 32.
Xi, Jinping. 2014e. No stop in reform, no stop in opening-up. *Xi Jinping: The Governance of China*, Foreign Languages Press, p. 68.
Xi, Jinping. 2015. Advance the spirit of Bandung and promote cooperation and mutual benefits: Speech at the Conference of Asian-African Leaders. April 22, 2015. http://news.xinhuanet.com/politics/2015-04/22/c_1115057390.htm.
Yu, Yixuan. 2013. On China's identity as a developing country. *Fudan International Studies Review*, pp. 87–107.
Zhang, Yuyan. 2014. Periods of important strategic opportunities: exogenous and endogenous. *World Economics and Politics*, No. 1.

Chapter 4
Peaceful Development: Restrictions and Challenges

China's adherence to peaceful development bears on the influence of its cultural traditions, the needs of practical interests, the binding of the market mechanism and the restrictions of international rules. Nevertheless, it's not an easy road. China must overcome all those challenges, may it be domestic or foreign, subjective or objective, short-term or long term. Some require China to carry out adaption, reform or even revolution by itself, some go beyond the self-adaption of behaviors and institutions, requiring international coordination and banishing other countries' doubts so as to obtain the understanding, approval and support of the international society and still some are not simply challenges to China but also challenges to many countries or even the whole world as a "community of shared future", requiring China and other countries to work together and cooperate sincerely in their response. This chapter mainly examines the embodiment and source of these challenges. Possible ways and assumptions about how to respond to them will be explored in the next chapter.

The Natural Resource Choke Point

Sound economic development is the precondition and lung power that enables China to cope with various challenges. Resources are a driving force that helps the Chinese economy to soar on the global arena and the shortage of resources will seriously impede the growth of the Chinese economy. Nowadays China has become one of the largest energy consumers in the world as well as one of the largest energy importers. For instance, in 2003 the volume of crude oil imported into China was 91.1 million tons, only 5% of the total oil imports of the world, while in 2013, China became the second largest oil importer (only next to the US) with a volume of oil imports of 280 million tons, about 15% of the total volume of oil imports in the world, and foreign oil dependence as high as 59%. Besides, China is also the world's largest iron ore consumer and importer. Statistics in *Steel Statistical Yearbook 2015* show that Japan had been the world's largest iron ore importer until outrun by China in 2003. The

Y. Zhang and W. Feng, *Peaceful Development Path in China*, China Insights,
https://doi.org/10.1007/978-981-13-1439-1_4

iron ore imports of China in 2012 took up 67.9% of the world's total volume. In 2014, 933 million tons of iron ores were imported into China, 13.8% higher than that of the previous year, while China's iron ore dependence rose further to 78.5%. The natural resource choke point is more and more likely to be a challenge that will hinder the development of China's domestic economy.

To meet with the resource demand, the following three must be guaranteed: capacity to pay (affordable), stable sources (accessible) and delivery security (deliverable). "Affordable" is mainly concerned about demand, that is, whether China is able to maintain a relatively stable price system against the seller's monopoly on the international resource market and whether China has enough capacity to pay. "Accessible" is more concerned with supply, or the distribution and reserves of natural resources and the corresponding resource diplomacy between China and other resource producers. "Deliverable" is mainly concerned with transportation security. On the international market, China must have enough capacity to pay. However, what is affordable may not be accessible and what is accessible may not be able to deliver.

At present, the world is in a recovery phase after a series of crises. In the long run, the world will witness the collective rise of developing and emerging countries and the re-rise of developed countries through re-industrialization or "Industry 4.0". All this will increase the demand for resources. Competition for resources will be even more fierce in the future and prices of resources tend to increase steadily again in the long haul. However, the issue whether China "will be able to afford" caused by rising prices will not be the hardest nutshell to crack. The tremendous size of China's manufacturing system determines that it will be a main buyer of important resources. Although at present China's pricing right does not match its demand in terms of important resources like iron ores due to its unfamiliarity to industry rules and its trade practices, which, however, is likely to change in 5–10 years. The spontaneous growth and decline of relative strength on the market is favorable to China. Putting aside the intervention of non-market factors, China's resource pricing capability will increase substantially in the future.

The "accessible" issue is worthy of more consideration than the "affordable" issue, the latter is more about the challenge of market forces while the former concerns how to cope with the intervention of non-market factors. Normally, a buyer with powerful paying ability owns relatively larger market rights and a guaranteed and sustainable supply of resources. However, in case the world is besieged by recurring challenges and antagonistic contradictions occur among major economies, who is able to guarantee a reliable supply of resources will be vital. "Accessible" not only requires paying ability but also requires certain control over the production systems in major producing areas of resources. Even in normal situations, the investment required to exercise this kind of control may be even higher than the cost needed to purchase resources directly on the international market. From the strategic perspective, however, it's still necessary to make a certain amount of investment oriented at building connections. The design of a global scheme is also favorable for diversification of risks. For instance, apart from investing in minerals, investment should also be made in land resources and part of grain production should be transferred to Africa so as to enhance the security of domestic grain production.

For China, the "deliverable" issue is a more strenuous task. On emergent occasions of terrorist threats, war and other extreme events, the most vulnerable link for China is still, I'm afraid, pipes and routes. Today the fact is China has to deliberately avoid efforts to maintain the security of its pipes and routes. What's worse, some activities of multinational companies unrelated to security of these pipes and routes are distorted as evidence of China's ambition for increasing control over other areas. For example, China's commitment to building Chittagong Port and Hambantota Port, which is purely business, has been interpreted as a "String of Pearls Strategy" aimed at besieging India. In fact, as the "World's Factory", China's concern about the security of its pipes and routes should be well understood by all countries. Of course, all these suspicions mainly originate from unverified information. In the future, it will be necessary for China to make clear of its need to maintain the security of its pipes and routes and the rationality of guaranteeing those pipes and routes. China should invest more in safeguarding international routes especially the security of those pipes and routes, which are closely related to China's demand for resources, in the form of international cooperation and accumulate its global power projection capability of delivering emergent response so as to fundamentally solve the "deliverable" issue.

Tocqueville Effect

At present, China also faces the potential challenge of "Tocqueville Effect", that is, with the rapid growth of economy, the social transformation that lags behind may lead to increasing risks of turbulence. Rapid economic growth is generally considered to be a good thing, which assumes that with the accumulation of wealth and the improvement of living conditions, the people's sense of satisfaction will increase accordingly and the society will become more and more stable. A relevant belief holds that poverty is the root of social upheaval or violence. However, the reality doesn't fully support such judgment. The three centuries since the Industrial Revolution has witnessed countless reforms, revolutions and wars although the overall level of per capita income has been rising all along. More ironically, history showed a somewhat regular phenomenon: social turbulence actually happens more frequently when the economy grows ultra rapidly, especially during the transition from a country with low per capita income to a country with middle per capita income. In *Political Order in Changing Societies*, Samuel P. Huntington points out that during British period of India political violence was prevalent in those economically developed states while before the start of the French Revolution in 1789 it was the people in those people in the most developed areas that were most unsatisfied.[1]

The above phenomenon was explored by Mancur Olson in his paper "Rapid Growth as a Destabilizing Force" in 1963.[2] His argumentation is rather easy to follow: rapid growth means profound changes in the modes of production, the trade-off

[1] Huntington (1989).

[2] Olson (1963).

between the importance of different industries and regions as well as the reshuffling of the rarity of different types of labor force. All this is bound to cause broad and huge adaptation of income distribution. Generally speaking, there are large numbers of beneficiaries and sufferers in a society with rapid growth, in which some people are better off than the families where they were born and raised while the rest are the opposite. Whether they are beneficiaries or sufferers, their social classes or their "typology" are undermined and falling apart. What's worse, their household relations will also change accordingly with the change of their income and work places. As a result, the mentality of both groups is shattered by the economic growth and they become two destabilizing forces.

Olson also pointed out in this paper that the rapid growth usually creates two new groups, or the so-called "new rich people" and "new poor people". With their number increasing, the "new rich people" are sure to change social and political order by using the economic power at their hands so as to better safeguard their invested interests. To Olson, these people are "resentful beneficiaries". In contrast, the "new poor people", whose living conditions become worse instead of better, have a far greater grudge than that of the grassroots against poverty because of the fall of their absolute and relative welfare. Given the great interdependence of economic, social and political order, the resetting of economic power will certainly be reflected in social respect and the distribution of political power, making the process toward new social and political balance highly unstable.

The speed of economic growth of a country, especially the different regions in a large country, is usually uneven. The uneven regional development is also a reason for social turbulence. In *Memorial to the Throne on Political Affairs* (Chen Zheng Shi Shu), Jia Yi, a famous minister of Former Han Dynasty, looks into historical cases in this respect. The enfeoffed lords in Former Han Dynasty were different from each other in terms of wealth and strength. It was the people that suffered the most when the country was in chaos. Concerned about the emperor, the country and the people, Jia Yi put forward his "Discourse on Governance", which can be called a "Jia Yi's Law", that proposed, "To maintain the loyalty of all enfeoffed lords, nothing works better than treating each of them as King of Changsha… To maintain order and stability under the sky, nothing works better than conferring more kingdoms and weakening their strength. A weak kingdom is more easily commanded to fulfill its duties while a smaller kingdom has no intention to rebel." Due to the degradation of their social status, the sufferers, no doubt, will become a tremendous destabilizing force.[3] In particular, the middle income level of a society will be decreased with the increase in per capita income when the total benefits of a small number of beneficiaries are excessively huge and possessed by just the few of them. That is to say, it is absolutely possible that economic growth may incredibly lead to the increase of sufferers. Although the increase of sufferers due to the rise of per capita income seems to be a paradox, yet the coexistence of rapid growth and the increase of pauperizing population is not only theoretically possible but also actually exists in

[3] Sun and Zhang (1997).

reality. Kuznets's research in his renowned paper "Economic Growth and Income Inequality" clearly supports this assumption.[4]

Economic growth is bound to lead to increase of income. However, it has been a controversial issue that whether extensive income increase or allowing the vast majority of people to share the benefits of growth is helpful to social stability. To Alexis de Tocqueville, the author of *The Old Regime and the Revolution*, one of the causes of the French Revolution was not the long-term poverty suffered by the people but the great enhancement of their living conditions caused by economic growth, the unprecedented, continuous and steady growth and prosperity prior to the French Revolution and the following unsettling feeling prevailing among them.[5] This argument may seem confusing at first look but may turn out to be "truth in disguise" and the key message lies in that the dissatisfaction of the people was mainly rooted in the anticipation of their future welfare. To Tocqueville, when one is restrained by handcuffs and shackles, he has hardly any expectation for freedom, yet once the handcuffs are smashed, the mere existence of shackles will become much harder to bear, which is usually referred to as "Tocqueville Effect".[6]

In terms of vested interests, rapid growth and the interactive institutional changes are often one of the reasons for social instability. In "Economic backwardness in political perspective", D. Acemoglu and J. Robinson conclude that the popular "incremental reform or institutional change" does not necessarily accompany the stable development of social economy for there's no reliable or appropriate mechanisms to make it up for the political elites who lose power during or after the economic or institutional changes. Economic growth also render the people a better understanding of the possibility of a better life, a new ideology and a new governmental regime, arousing their expectations for "what the government should do" and "how to do". As a result, conflicts will occur between the elites with vested interests and the emerging interest groups for the former will become a hindrance to changes and social turbulence will follow.[7]

What has been discussed above only concerns the amount of absolute income. Once it comes to the field of relative income, another important source of instability comes to surface: part of the beneficiaries may also cause social instability. The reason lies in that even if economic growth enables the number of beneficiaries outrun that of sufferers by the absolute standard some or even the majority of the beneficiaries may be depressed or unsatisfied because their benefits are lower than those of others. In other words, what people really pursue is the increase of their relative welfare instead of absolute welfare. It readily reminds us of the famous saying of Confucius, "I have heard that rules of states and chiefs of families are not troubled lest their people should be few, but are troubled lest they should not keep their several places; that they are not troubled with fears of poverty, but are troubled with a fear of a want of contented repose among the people in their several places; For when the people

[4]Kuznets (1955).

[5]Tocqueville (1992).

[6]Bell (1984).

[7]Acemoglum and Robinson (2006).

keep their several places, there will be no poverty; when harmony prevails, there will be no scarcity of people; and when there is such a contented repose, there will be no rebellious upsettings." (Book XVI:16, The Analects of Confucius). The partiality of economic growth or economic growth means different things for different people or groups in a society indicates that, broadly speaking, people usually attach more importance to relative income.

Rapid economic growth may incur unwanted outcomes. The relationship between rapid economic growth and social turbulence is rather complicated, although in history examples in which rapid economic growth led to social upheavals could be seen almost everywhere. As far as China is concerned, what marks on its history is mainly those revolutions triggered by economic stagnation or setbacks such as the Revolution of 1911. However, no one can afford to ignore historical lessons. Given the rapid economic growth today, it is particularly important to be aware that the income distribution in both the absolute and relative sense may have adverse effect on social stability. We must stay alert against unequal income distribution following the rapid growth, a violation of Deng Xiaoping's principle of allowing some people and some regions to prosper first before they bring along others and ultimately achieving common prosperity and accumulating and expanding dissatisfaction caused by the lack of a redemptive arrangement of institutions so as to prevent any possible social crisis from happening.

Middle-Income Trap

Domestic stability and growth is the basis and guarantee for the peaceful development of China. After more than thirty year's rapid development, China has shifted from a low-income country into a middle-income one and the risk of middle- income trap is looming ever larger. The so-called "Middle-income Trap" refers to the phenomenon that a country suffers from declining overall competitiveness, insufficient growth momentum and finally economic stagnation because its low-end industries face even fiercer competition from other developing countries after losing its labor force advantage while its high-end industries are still unable to compete against developed countries when its per capita income has reached the middle level.

The academic world basically agree on the definition or symptoms of the "Middle-income Trap", yet main Chinese economists hold varied judgment on causes of "Middle-income Trap" especially the threats it imposes on China. Li Yining, Honorary Dean of Guanghua School of Management, Beijing University, argues, the Middle-income Trap includes three "high mountains", namely, "institutional trap of development", "social crisis trap" and "technology trap", which should be overcome by deepening reform, properly implementing macro policies and promoting technological innovation.[8] Lin Yifu, Honorary Dean of National School of Development, Beijing University, argues that we can stride over the middle-income trap by relying

[8]Li (2016).

on technology innovation and industry upgrade, in which respect we still have our late- developing advantage. Besides, with a great potential in domestic demand and adequate financial resources, China is well placed to stride over the trap.[9] Hai Wen, Dean of HSBC School of Business, Beijing University, attributes the fall into the middle-income trap to "hysteresis of industrial structure adjustment" and suggests surmounting the trap by pushing forward industry upgrade by upgrading demand, urging further opening-up in service sector and stimulating manufacturing industry upgrade by innovation.[10] Cai Fang, Deputy Dean of Chinese Academy of Social Sciences, points out the middle- income trap provides reference to China for faulty response to economic slowdown, adoption of populist policies at times of worsening income distribution and inability to break the vested interest groups that set the income distribution pattern are some important reasons for some countries' fall into the middle-income trap. He believes that China should stride over the trap by pushing forward the supply-side structural reform, speeding income distribution reform and preventing excessive welfare.[11] Hu Angang, Dean of the National Research Institute of Tsinghua University, holds that the "Middle- income Trap" is a false proposition for China for the series of policies including promoting development by innovation recently put forward by the Central Government of China are able to lead 1.4 billion Chinese people to the high-income phase featuring common prosperity.[12] Li Daokui, Director of Center for China in the World Economy, Tsinghua University, believes that a stable government that constantly supports market economy, increasingly improving human capital and consistent opening-up to developed countries are "three favorable conditions" for China to surmount the middle- income trap.[13] Zheng Xinli, Executive Vice Chairman of China Center for International Economic Exchanges, argues China can stride over the middle-income trap by advancing integration of urban areas and rural areas, enhancing investment mechanism and attaching greater importance to scientific and technological innovation.[14]

It can be noted in the above-mentioned economists' judgment and propositions about the middle-income trap that most scholars emphasize the function of innovation (including function of technological innovation and institutional innovation) and industry upgrade and the resolution of unfair distribution during economic growth and its consequent social problems is also a key condition for surmounting the middle-income trap. Although many scholars have examined the importance of opening-up economic mechanism to surmounting the middle-income trap, as a whole, however, most of them place more emphasis on domestic factors or difficulties in causing the

---

[9]Lin (2016).

[10]Hai (2016).

[11]Cai (2016).

[12]Hu (2016).

[13]Li (2016).

[14]Zheng (2016).

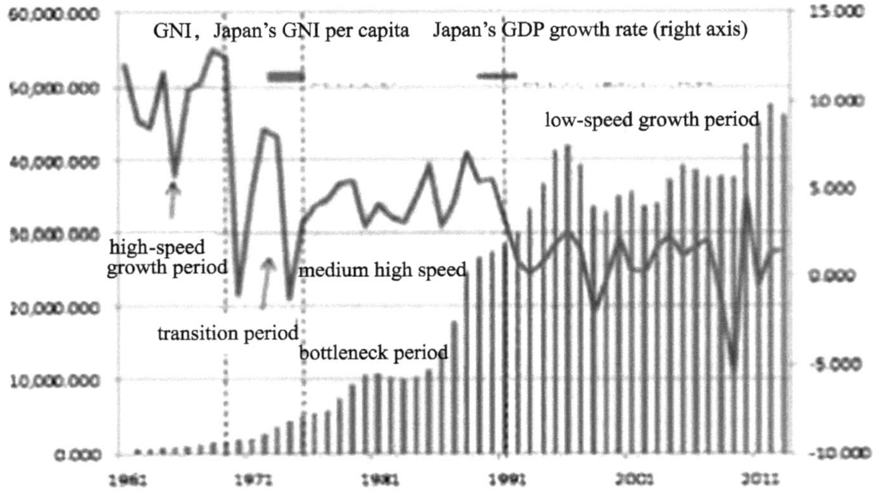

Chart 4.1 Japan's GNI per capita and the growth rate of GDP. *Source* Data from the World Bank

middle-income trap while relatively not so many people have explored the involved foreign or international factors or difficulties.[15]

In terms of the experiences of large economies in the international society, so far only Japan and South Korea have negotiated the middle-income trap into developed countries. As far as Japan is concerned, its economy had been growing rapidly before 1969, with an annual average GDP growth rate of around 10.45% and an average GNI per capita of $1039. After 1969, the Japanese economy underwent a transition period, during which its annual average GDP growth rate plunged to 3.6% and its average GNI per capita was $3260. From 1976 to 1985, the Japanese economy came to a relatively lasting and stable period featuring medium high speed growth, with an annual average GDP growth rate of 4.56% and an average GNI per capita of $13,439 (from $5310 to $27,560). In particular, from 1980 to 1985, when its average GNI per capita just reached $10,000 and Japan was transforming from a medium high-income economy to a high- income one, there was a bottleneck (stagnation) period of about 5 or 6 years, after which its GNI per capita rose sharply but its growth rate turned to be low but stable. Japan's annual average GDP growth rate after 1991 was 0.95% and its average GNI per capita was $37,593 (from $28,290 to more than $45,000), which means the Japanese economy was entering a period featuring low speed growth (Chart 4.1).

The soar of the economy of South Korea stated relatively late but followed a similar runway to that of Japan. The economy of South Korea had been growing at a rather high speed before 1988, with an annual average GDP growth rate of 9.68%

[15] Jia, Kang and Su Jingchun both talked about that, as "world No. 2", China might be opposed by No. 1 and be troubled by others below. "Poor brothers" deviate from us. However, it is beyond the topic here. See Jia and Su (2016).

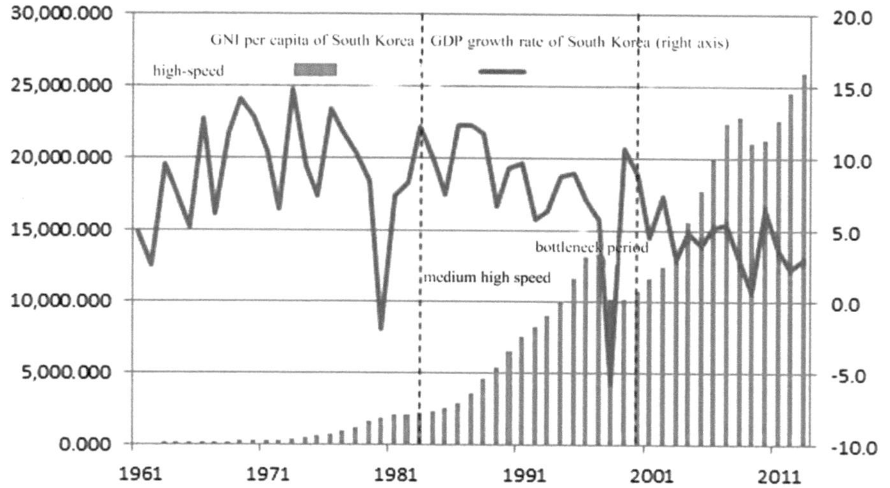

Chart 4.2 GNI per capita and GDP growth rate of South Korea. *Source* Data from the World Bank

and an average GNI per capita of $1206. From 1989 to 2000, the economy of South Korea grew at a medium high speed, with an annual average GDP growth rate of 6.86% and an average GNI per capita of $9651 (during which period its average GNI per capita rose from about $5440 to over $10,000). In particular, the period from 1996 to 2000 was a bottleneck (recurrence) period of about 5 years, during which a fall in its average GNI per capita appeared when South Korea was becoming a high-income country (with an average GNI per capita of over $10,000) before a dramatic rise of average GNI per capita that followed after that period, with its growth speed slowing down from a medium high to a low but stable speed. After 2001, the growth of the economy of South Korea become slow but steady, with an annual average GDP growth rate of 4.1% and an average GNI per capita of $19,368 (from $11,630 to $25,920) (Chart 4.2).

Judging from the experiences of Japan and South Korea, for those countries that have successfully surmounted the middle-income trap there was clearly a medium high speed growth period of 12–15 years, with an annual average GDP growth rate of 5–7% and a bottleneck (stagnation or recurrence) period, which might appear at the beginning or end of the medium high speed growth period when the GNI per capita was about to go beyond $10,000. Once going through the bottleneck period, those countries would rapidly become developed countries and gain another round of rapid economic growth.

When it comes to China, the years from 1978 to 2011 saw ultra high speed economic growth in China, with an annual average GDP growth rate of 9.96%, a relatively high one, leaving some space for a medium high speed growth period in the future (which is similar to that of Japan and South Korea-with a growth rate of about 10% in the high speed growth period. In contrast, the GDP growth rates in

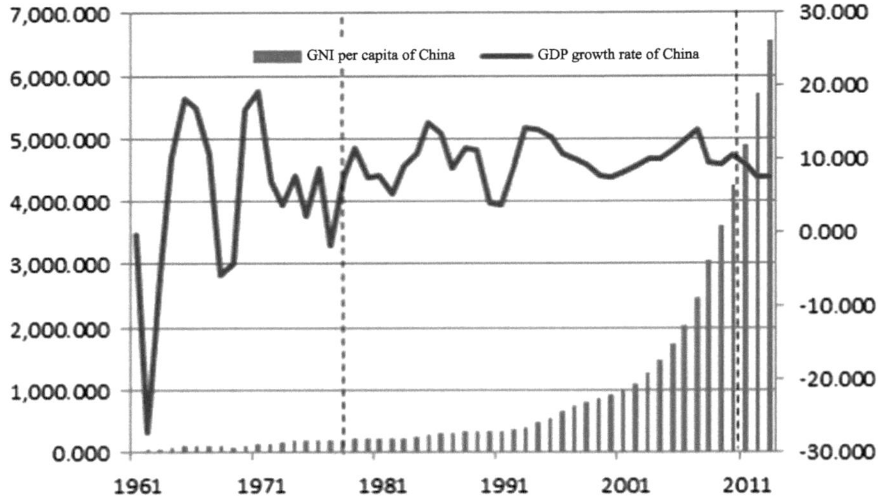

Chart 4.3 GNI per capita and GDP growth rate of China. *Source* Data from the World Bank

the high speed growth periods of Brazil and Argentina, which have fallen into the middle- income trap, were only around 4–7%, leaving no space for the medium high speed growth period) (Chart 4.3).

In 2012 China's GNI per capita amounted to $5000, beyond which the economic growth rate may enter the medium high speed phase. Judging from the experience of Japan and South Korea, the growth rate from 5% to 7% should pass for medium high speed. After entering the medium high speed growth rate phase, the Chinese economy still maintained certain growing momentum. Its GNI per capita in 2013 reached $6500 unlike that of Brazil, which fell to $5000. However, China still faced the even greater challenge, that is, lifting its GNI per capita to more than $10,000. When approaching that goal, it is likely that the Chinese economy may be plunged into stagnation or decline of 10–20 years, or, like Japan and South Korea, a bottleneck (stagnation/ recurrence) period of about 5 years. That means China must hold on to its faith in its road and policies. As long as China can steady itself in keeping its GNI per capita at around $10,000 and go through the bottleneck period of about 5 years, it will be quite possible that China can become a developed country or a high-income country without much difficulty.

The study of Zhao Dingxin shows that leading economic growth is an important source of performance legitimacy. The performance legitimacy can maintain some effectiveness and serious turbulence won't happen as long as the Chinese economy can maintain its current growing momentum,[16] which also helps the safeguarding of peace in both China and the world. Judging by the experiences of major economies in striding over the middle-income trap, plus the huge size of the Chinese econ-

[16]Zhao (2012).

omy, China will be able to maintain a relatively desirable absolute value-added and obtain steady development of economy and society if China can make the transition of medium high speed growth after its ultra high speed growth. In this process, those production elements subsided in old sectors and industries must be restructured before they enter new industries. Frictional unemployment will be interwoven with start-up ventures. The vested interests will be undermined while new and tremendous interest will not have been completely generated and will not be powerful enough to redeem the previous interest groups in an all-round way. The government will also be questioned and stressed out because of the temporary decline of revenues and the slowdown of growth. It is also likely that foreign competitors might take advantage of these temporary setbacks so as to damage the external environment of the country on its way of adjustment. That was also the very reason why most of those countries would undergo a bottleneck period of 5 years after surmounting the middle-income trap. China must take all these possible difficulties seriously: on the one hand, China must unswervingly hold on to deepening reform, strengthen innovation and transformation upgrade, on the other hand, China should make appropriate explanation and adopt proper policies, trying its best to alleviate the pain in striding over the middle-income trap while enhancing the transformation survivability of the people and all other walks as well.

Dilemma of International Division of Labor

The economic globalization dominated by the developed countries bred a new pattern of international division of labor. Economic globalization is mainly about the changes of international trade, direct investment and technology diffusion in depth, width and quantity. Developing countries usually benefit from the technology diffusion and market opening-up of developed countries while the application and diffusion of new technology also accompanies the increase of large-scale trade and investment. Many developing countries are also able to accumulate its human capital in this process. History shows us that the increase of a country's economic opening-up is in proportion to the increase of its GNI per capita. We should admit that the experience of developed countries and part of the developing countries endorses the "win-win" thinking.

However, on the one hand globalization provides the world with "win-win" opportunities, on the other hand, it imposes a threat of falling into the "trap of international division of labor" on developing countries. In the chain of international division of labor, the developed countries, relying on its advantages or favorable position, have occupied the market with high value-added, high technology products and services while most developing countries, due to its position at the end of the chain of international division of labor, have become suppliers of labor-intensive, low value-added and low technology products and services. With the extremely rapid progress of information and communication technology, obvious "digital division" appears between different countries or economies in respect of winning opportunities to access information and communication technology and doing business by using the Internet. In other words, most benefits of globalization go to developed countries and only a rather small proportion go to developing countries. In addition, developing countries fight hard against each other for this small proportion of benefits. In order to win, they rush to provide various favorable terms, such as providing tax incentives, promising to open their domestic markets to the maximum, promising to abide by those severe economic rules made by developed countries and even making political compromises.

As a result, developing countries and emerging economies find themselves caught in a dilemma. Without access to the global economic system, they would miss out on the growth opportunity of gaining access to international capital or technology. After entering the system of international division of labor, they might fall into the trap of international division of labor, being tied to the low-end manufacturing industry and subject to perpetual exploitation of those high-end countries.

As the largest developing country in the world, China also faces the severe challenge of being dragged into the trap of international division of labor. The prevalent stories on the Internet such as those about Barbie dolls and iPhones "Made in China" suggest that the value captured by the Chinese manufacturing industry only takes up less than 10%% of the product price while 90% or more comes from product design, purchase of raw materials, logistics, ordering, wholesale, retail at the terminal, to name a few. Well, these most profitable links are mainly in the hands of the developed countries in the West who occupy the top end of the industrial chain. The study of Jason Dedrick provides relevant proof about the above-mentioned phenomenon. Reality, he argued, is more severe than what we can imagine, the profits distributed to the Chinese labor is less than 2% of the total (Table 4.1).[17]

Of course, moping does no good to increase the capture of "Made in China" in the international value chain. Only by enhancing our own capability and strengthening innovation can the Chinese industries climb up the value chain to a link with higher value-added.

First of all, China must increase its innovation ability directly concerning technology and economic structure upgrade. Structural adjustment is no more than adjustment in two aspects: one is eradicating the old, the other is fostering the new. The old industries made much contribution in history, such as generating profits, and promoting employment, safeguarding the stability of the Chinese economy in a worsening external environment. However, they have shown backward or excess production capacity due to their low technique content and low level redundancy. If we continue to allow the precipitation and accumulation of social resources in them instead of eliminating or restructuring them, there will be more and more loss of social welfare. Industry structure adjustment and upgrade means turning those production elements previously precipitated in backward or excess industries such as those featuring high energy consumption and high emission into elements in those emerging and strategic

[17]Jason Dedrick, "Who Profits from Innovation in Global Value Chains? iPhones and Windmills," http://www.usitc.gov/research_and_analysis/documents/Dedrick_USITC_3-21-12_0.pdf.

Table 4.1 Global distribution of the value capture of Apple products

iPod	iPhone	iPad
Other inputs and direct labor: 36%	Apple: 58.5%	Apple: 30%
Apple: 25%	Other US companies: 2.4%	Distribution and retail: 15%
Distribution and retail: 25%	European companies: 1.1%	Other US companies: 2%
Japanese companies: 9%	Chinese Taiwan companies: 0.5%	Chinese Taiwan companies: 2%
Other US companies: 2%	Japanese companies: 0.5%	Japanese companies: 1%
Korean companies: 1%	Korean companies: 4.7%	Korean companies: 7%
Chinese Taiwan companies: 1%	Other margins: 5.3%	Other margins: 5%
	Cost of raw materials: 21.9%	Cost of raw materials: 31%
	Cost of Chinese labor: 1.8%	Cost of Chinese labor: 2%
	Cost of other labor: 3.5%	Cost of other labor: 5%

Source Jason Dedrick, "Who Profits from Innovation in Global Value Chains? iPhones and Windmills," http://www.usitc.gov/research_and_analysis/documents/Dedrick_USITC_3-21-12_0.pdf

industries. Fostering the new means to discover new areas with growth potentials and channel resources into these areas.

What is even more important is the institutional (policy and mechanism) innovation that fosters and supports technology innovation. Technology innovation is the effect while institution the cause; institution innovation and technology innovation are the ins and the outs respectively; technology innovation is the course while institution innovation the source. In terms of institutional innovation, the policy innovation is even more direct and flexible. Judging by the practice of China, the macro-economic policies in the past were mainly quantity control and there was no detailed guidance for the behavior of micro economic entities. Ever since the establishment of the new administration, China has taken such fiscal and taxation measures as "targeted tax cuts" and "targeted tax reductions" and targeted steps in forms of "minimal stimulus", "targeted policies", "invigorating the stock" and "interval management", avoiding drastic economic ups and downs caused by extensive stimulus, guiding the distribution optimization of social resources and effectively supporting the development of the service sector, "three rural issues", small and micro business, the private sector, emerging industries, new urbanization and other areas that enjoy policy priority. Yet the most essential and most difficult thing is institution innovation. Institution here refers to all the basic ideas and rules that are supposed to abide by in policy-making. It may be easy to change a policy but really difficult to change the mechanism. After reflecting upon the international financial crisis, the developed countries assumed that rising economies including China have been benefiting from previous international economic rules, blatantly accusing them of conducting "national capitalism" or "mercantilism" and threatening to replace "free trade" with "fair trade" and establish a competitive neutrality framework which aims to undermine the competition advantage of state-run enterprises. In nature, it was an attempt to establish a new set of mechanisms that aims to increase the costs of emerging countries in international competition so as to safeguard their own competition advantages. Nevertheless, it is not impossible to uncover some positive factors out of the unfavorable conditions. There is often great improvement in efficiency under the stress of costs. In building the Shanghai Free Trade Zone, China has decided to proactively seek to build highlands of reforms instead of rolling out preferential policies in certain places. That means China has taken the initiative to carry out pressure testing to find out whether the Chinese economy is able to take off against the institutional impact of "Pre-establishment National Treatment", "Negative List", "Competitive Neutrality", and so on.

Innovation momentum is mainly about motivation, or invigorating active innovation so as to provide innovation with sufficient material, policy and institution resources. Besides, efforts must be made to pay attention to and solve the direction issue of innovation. If the direction taken is wrong, stopping is actually moving forward.

In essence, the process of innovation is an experiment with both our thinking and behavior open to criticism, so restraining factors including power should hold enough tolerance or even respect to the innovation entities and their behaviors. However, effective innovation never means purposeless fancy. In other words, say, at least innovation without certain restrains will be inefficient.

Firstly, the direction of innovation shall not totally deviate from reality. Policies like the "Green Sprouts Law", the "Balanced-delivery Law", the "Equal Tax Law" and the "Market Exchange Law" adopted by Wang Anshi in his revolution during the reign of Shenzong of Song Dynasty were all innovative and strategic. To Huang Renyu, a Chinese historian, Wang "attempted to manipulate national affairs through financial regulation and the width and depth of his revolution had never been talked about anywhere else", the revolution was trying to "commercialize fiscal levy extensively".

In our point of view, there was no shortage of targeted stimulus like "targeted reductions" in policies of Wang Anshi. For example, the "Green Sprouts Law" scheduled that "each year before the autumn harvest, when the last year's grain was already consumed but the new one not ripe yet, the local government had to give out money and grain as seeds and the money was recollected, including an interest rate of 2 per cent, in summer and in autumn, together with the tax, which was exactly targeted financial support to the "three rural issues". The "Hydraulic Works Law" encouraged the people to clear land so as to transform it into usable field and build dykes and dams for irrigating fields, which was also a standard according to which the government achievement of local officials would be assessed. In addition, it also provided that the local governments should give loans to help the farmers to solve their financial problems, which was just like the collection of capital based on the platform of local government debt since the breakout of the international financial crisis. The "Market Exchange Law" provided "founding a market exchange bureau in Kaifeng to purchase commodities not needed on the market for later sales", the thinking of policy-making behind which was identical to the modern macro-economic policy making featuring "the government underpins the market so as to ease the economic fluctuations". Despite his good-will, his policy innovation failed to produce expected results.

In less than a year after the start of the revolution, apart from the troubling disputes between the upper class members for and against the revolution, there were also "evil practices" in the implementation of the new policies (for example, some local governments forced farmers to borrow loans in the name of the "Green Sprouts Law"; some local governments forced the people to build infrastructure in the name of the "Hydraulic Works Law"). In the end, almost all the new policies were abolished. One of the reasons of the failure of Wang's revolution lies in the fact the advanced financial and commercial policies and means were far beyond the needs and ability of the backward administration and production sectors.

Secondly, the direction of innovation shall not deviate from laws of nature, economy and society. For a certain period of time, many scientists tried to discover the so-called "ether" or invent a perpetual motion machine which continually does useful work without requiring outside energy, both were denied by history for violating laws of the objective world. There are also traceable laws governing economic and social development and their violation may lead to divergent consequences instead of results of effective innovation. For instance, from the perspective of economics, the distributed energy resources featuring "energy to the people", 3D printing technology and other innovative energy production and usage may seem to be innovation short of scale merit. Large-scale investment without careful assessment may lead to "strategy misleading".

Thirdly, products of innovation shall benefit the public. In this respect, the traditional Chinese system has its advantages, yet it also means huge internalized cost for enterprises, scientists, engineers and other entities. In the future, we must pay attention to better combination of the individual interests of innovation entities and the public interests of society by making use of the market system.

All in all, innovation is an (if not the only) important means by which China is to stride over the "international labor division trap". Original work in certain fields or technology progress and innovation derived from introduced technology is, no doubt, important, yet the establishment of an institutional environment and ideological system is more important for only after that China can become a really innovative country.

Dilemma of Re-globalization

As discussed above, the ultra rapid economic growth of China benefited from the increased labor productivity brought about by the expansion of its market and the enhancement of its labor division and specialization. The expansion of its market was due to, for one thing, the market-augmenting strategy adopted by the Chinese government and, for another, the open international economic system. Without an open international economic system, the government would be unable to help access its domestic production elements, commodities and service to the global market.

However, in recent years, the global economic system is increasingly fragmented. The initial stage of the fragmentation could date back to 1997–1998 when the Asian Financial Crisis broke out while its taking shape did not happen until the break-out of the 2007 US Sub-Prime Financial Crisis. When the Asian Financial Crisis broke out, the IMF governance or the "Washington Consensus" mythology behind it was widely questioned and Asian countries thoroughly examined the international economic order and governance, recognizing that only by relying on targeted cooperation inside this area can the regional welfare be truly guaranteed, hence the beginning of the Asian financial cooperation process featuring the "Chiang Mai Initiative" and its multilateralization. Prior to that, the economic cooperation in Asia was basically imitation of and learning from such patterns as those of the European integration and Free Trade Area of Americas.

After the break-out of Asian Financial Crisis, all countries realized that, with USA and its European allies playing the dominant role, the security and stability of the markets in developed countries is certainly superior to the prosperity and progress in other countries. For instance, the American mainstream thought holds that "democratization of politics" and "economic liberalization" is the cornerstone of peace. The rigid requirements about privatization and liberalization in the "Washington Consensus" permeated both the propositions on development policies of Latin America and the preconditions put forward in the relief of the Asian Financial Crisis. According to John Williamson, the initiator of the "Consensus", former Vice President and chief economist of the World Bank, the "Consensus" was originally "the lowest common denominator of policy advice for Latin American countries addressed by the Washington-based institutions"[18] and these institutions include the US Department of Treasury, the Board of Governors of The Federal Reserve System, the IMF and the World Bank. Such institutional setup clearly suggests the "Consensus" is dominated by the American administration and implemented by international organizations. It is difficult for such global governance with the above setup as the core and standard to convey the intentions of other countries and therefore impossible to obtain the respect and recognition of other participants.

Mahathir Mohamad, former Prime Minister of Malaysia, pointed out in a pretty outspoken manner that he particularly hated the Western double standards, "their values are to be accepted as universal; Asian values are deemed irrelevant". Although the Asian Financial Crisis facilitated the awakening of the Asian consciousness, the emerging markets in Asia themselves do not have some sort of "Washington Consensus" with "economic liberalization" as the core or a program of action with a solid theoretical basis and specific actions to replace it in guiding the new international economic governance. For a long time, all countries were still busy with fixing the governance approach with the neoclassical economics as its basis.

[18] Williamson (2000).

The 2007 US Sub-Prime Crisis and the 2010 Europe's Sovereign-Debt Crisis considerably changed the traditional belief that emerging economies are always a weak link in crisis or origins of crises. Seeing the two-speed recovery at the wake of the crisis, other developed countries, which were still struggling bitterly, couldn't help but envying the "unique and good scenery" in those emerging economies with China as a representative. As a result, the legitimacy of the US and European governing theories was undermined. It's becoming increasingly difficult for the governance with neoclassical economics as its basis to reflect on the governance ability distribution in the international society and the changes of the aspirations it has been supporting. However, the new governance is not mature enough, which has become a major obstacle that hinders the efficiency of the global economic system from being enhanced. Under this background, new schemes such as the Regional Comprehensive Economic Partnership (RCEP), BRICS Cooperation Mechanism, Trans-Pacific Partnership Agreement (TPP) and "the Belt and Road" began to take shape and the global economic system tends to be more "fragmented".

Fragmentation is different from diversification. In a diversified global economic system, the various economic governance measures in different regions all had a core of neoliberal or neoclassical economic theory, which could be used as a standard or reference. In a fragmented global economic system, however, the model or theory that functions as the standard or reference is absent and no economic governance theory can be a common belief. Without efficient leadership in the international economic system, the global reform would be weak, regional and trans-regional economic cooperation would also face great uncertainty and the competition among different governance patterns would turn white-hot.

Then the developed countries began to push for the establishment of another wave of global rules. That process did not deny globalization, instead, it went forward along the road blazed by globalization while it had its own characteristics. Compared with the old rules, the new ones will be more strict, more uniform, more universal while more implicit in its impartiality. Looking back, this process is simply at an initial stage. Yet history shows us real revolutions would break out in silence while the people involved and their peer didn't even realize that they were make history.

In October 2009, George Soros, the founder of Open Society Institute and world-famous financier, delivered a series of speeches, which, in particular, spoke of the relationship between the financial crisis and the world and China.[19] To him, the prevailing global order is what he calls "a multilateral mechanism of international capitalism" featuring the US-led "Washington Consensus". Although the mechanism did not fully collapse but it has been greatly weakened, its inherent flaws have been revealed after the breakout of the financial crisis. It has been proved that the "international capitalism" has two major types inherent instability: lacking in sufficient global financial supervision and justice for "this mechanism is partial to the rich people and the rich countries compared to the poor people and the poor countries". What's worse, "international capitalism" is increasingly challenged by a viable alternative, namely, "state capitalism". As "the rise of China offers a fundamentally different form of

[19]Soros (2009).

economic organization than the current international financial system", China has become, in the eyes of Soros, a representative of the so-called "state capitalism" countries. According to Soros, the "state capitalism" in China has three characteristics as follows: one, its policy-making is often out of political considerations instead of pure business purposes; two, when dealing with countries that are rich in natural resources China only cares about the resources but not the nature of the regime or the interests of their people; three, China attaches importance to bilateral channels but less importance to the international multilateral system. China's long-term hesitation to join in the EITI has been cited by Soros as a typical example in question.

Then Soros pointed out that humankind was at the end of an era. The financial crisis will have great impacts on the relative positions of major countries and the whole world. "To put it bluntly, the United States stands to lose the most and China is poised to emerge as the greatest winner." From the global perspective the change of relative positions between the United States and China is the most significant and correspondingly other countries are also adjusting their strategies in accordance with the historical course. The world is facing a choice between two fundamentally different forms of organization. We may label them international capitalism and state capitalism. The former, represented by the United States, has broken down and the latter, represented by China, is in the ascendant. Soros argued, now that the "international capitalism" can hardly survive and the international system based on "international capitalism" is bound to cause conflicts between countries, the way to save the world is: a new multilateral system based on more solid principles, a new "Bretton Woods" system and an order in which supervision regulations must cover the whole world. "G20" must play a key role in the process of the establishment of new institutions. The process needs to be initiated by the United States, but China and other developing countries ought to participate in it as equals. China is set to emerge as the winner from the current turmoil. He said China should submit to this new system because, in order to continue rising, it must make itself acceptable to the rest of the world. According to Soros, China must learn to pay more attention to the opinion of the rest of the world for "other countries in the world will never subordinate individual freedom to the prosperity of China".

In October 2011, Hilary Clinton, former U.S. Secretary of State, published an article entitled "America's Pacific Century"[20] in *Foreign Policies*. She wrote: the future of politics will be decided in Asia. The United States will be right at the center of the action and lock in a substantially increased investment—diplomatic, economic, strategic, and otherwise—in the Asia-Pacific region. Harnessing Asia's growth and dynamism is central to American economic and strategic interests. One of the most prominent of these emerging partners is, of course, China. China represents one of the most challenging and consequential bilateral relationships the United States has ever had to manage. When talking about bilateral economic ties, Clinton bluntly named four requirements for China: (1) end unfair discrimination against U.S. and other foreign companies or against their innovative technologies; (2) remove preferences for domestic firms; (3) end measures that disadvantage or appropriate

[20]Clinton 2011.

foreign intellectual property and (4) allow its currency to appreciate more rapidly, both against the dollar and against the currencies of its other major trading partners."I laid out four attributes that I believe characterize healthy economic competition: open, free, transparent, and fair." She had many hopes for TPP, calling it "a benchmark for future agreements" and hoped it would "grow to serve as a platform for broader regional interaction and eventually a free trade area of the Asia-Pacific". The USA, she said, "will continue to embed our relationship with China in a broader regional framework of security alliances, economic networks, and social connections."

Five months earlier than the publication of Hilary's article, Robert Hormats, Under Secretary for Economic, Energy and Agricultural Affairs, published a signed article entitled "Ensuring a Sound Basis for Global Competition: Competitive Neutrality"[21] on the official blog of the U.S. Department of State. To Hormats, the core of future US foreign economic policy should be, above all, a political commitment to "competitive neutrality", that is, market competition not intervened by external factors, aiming to redesign existing international economic rules and regulations so as to guarantee the fair competition between state-owned enterprises and other enterprises. He added, over the past 20 years, especially after the breakout of the financial crisis, state-supported enterprises and sovereign wealth funds rushed into the market in large numbers and gradually won competitive advantages by relying on the state support. In particular, the state-supported enterprises in China have achieved extraordinary harvests. In his article, Hormats insisted waywardly that the intervention of the government twisted the market, arguing that kind of state capitalism not only placed those American companies without support from the government in an adverse position but also threatened the liberal capitalism. In response to what he saw the challenge of "Chinese model" to American competitiveness and the global system, Hormats indicated that the USA was working with other member states of the Organization of Economic Co- operation and Development in changing international trade and investment guidelines and management principles for state-owned enterprises through developing a so- called "competitive neutrality framework" so as to realize taxation neutrality, debt neutrality, regulatory neutrality and guarantee comparable commercial rates of return between state-supported firms and private companies, and the setting of prices that reflect actual costs. In order to obtain support from non-member states of OECD, the USA is also rather active in taking part in the United Nations Conference on Trade and Development. Additionally, it has written down a "competitive neutrality" provision in TPP.

In July 2011, Michael Spencer, a recipient of the 2001 Nobel Memorial Prize in Economic Sciences, published a long article entitled "The Impact of Globalization on Income and Employment" in *Foreign Affairs*.[22] He said, as the process by which markets integrate worldwide, globalization has a stunning impact. For most of the postwar period, U.S. policymakers assumed that growth and employment went hand in hand, and the U.S. economy's performance was largely determined by domestic consumption. Even by 2000 the impact of globalization on wealth distribution and

---

[21] Hormats (2011).

[22] Spence (2011).

employment had been rather mild as a whole. However, the globalization over the past ten years showed for the first time that growth and employment in the United States were starting to diverge. With the development of globalization, the position of emerging economies in the value chain was constantly on the rise and this kind of "global economic structure evolution" was becoming a continuous and irreversible change. Between 1990 and 2008, the number of employed workers in the United States grew from about 122 million to about 149 million. Of the roughly 27 million jobs created during that period, most were in non-tradable sector of the economy, to be specific, 10 million in the government and the health-care industry, about 40% of all newly created jobs. In contrast, the tradable sector of the economy only created 600,000 jobs during that period, about 2% of all new jobs. Among the tradable sectors of the economy, areas such as semi-conductors, pharmaceuticals and information technology services that the US had been dominant have been largely replaced by emerging economies. As a result, many job opportunities are lost. Spence pointed out that, the employment structure of the U.S. economy has been shifting away from the tradable sector, except for the upper end of the value-added chain, and the shift may be even faster in the future. Besides, the ability of the non-tradable sector of the US economy will also decline. In a word, the United States should brace itself for a long period of high unemployment.

Spence added that the key standard to measure the size of a company, industry, or economy is to determine its added value. Although the value added per employee increased steadily by an annual average of 0.7% from 1990 to 2008, specific growth rates in the two major sectors were rather different: whereas value added per employee in the tradable sector grew from $79,000 to $120,000, 52% up whereas in the non-tradable sector it grew from $72,000 to over $80,000, only 12% up. It is obvious the incomes of workers are closely correlated with value added per employee. Given almost all the created jobs were in the non-tradable sector of the economy, income distribution in the US became more uneven between the two sectors. Given that American multinational companies would "export jobs" in large numbers in pursuit of profits and workers at the upper-end in the tradable sector had more job opportunities while workers at the lower end had less job opportunities, the imbalance was becoming more and more serious. Before offering his solution, Spence made the point of criticizing two prevailing ideas: the prolonged and worsening unemployment and income distribution issue in the USA today was neither a cause of market failure nor a lack in openness in the global economy. The real reason, he argued, is rooted in "global economic structural evolution", or globalization. According to Spence, the ultimate way out of the dilemma for the United States was to increase the employment in the tradable sector of the economy. To that purpose, apart from expanding investment in education and infrastructure and reforming the tax structure, American policy-makers must also make their choices so as to actually protect the employment in the tradable sector in the United States. He especially warned that doing so might cause some loss in efficiency but has its worth and the Germans had long been doing so.

Several arguments being hyped abroad can be noted from the above review: one, the globalization process prior to the breakout of the financial crisis had a rather strong sense of impartiality in its impact, causing much damage to some countries while benefiting some countries a lot; two, China ranked the first place among the beneficiaries although India and other countries were also sometimes mentioned while the USA suffer the greatest loss; three, the rapid rise of emerging economies including China benefited enormously from the global political, economic and security systems offered by the USA, otherwise their rise would be out of the question; four, beneficiaries like China are content to a free rider but refuse to shoulder the responsibility of providing global or regional public goods; five, the secret of these beneficiaries' success in their economies lies in their adherence to a firm opportunist policy and blandly ignoring or simply turning a blind eye to international rules; six, due to the support from the state, Chinese state-owned enterprises have obtained competitive advantages, which, however, greatly undermined the principle of fairness; seven, at least part of the economic nightmare suffered by the USA and some other developed countries may be explained by the unfair competition and labor distribution caused by globalization; eight, at the wake of the financial crisis, the USA and other developed economies drew a lesson from their previous painful experience and decided not to continue tolerating the free-riding and opportunist behaviors of China and other emerging economies; nine, in order to get out of their previous passivity, the USA is or is going to work with other developed countries or even some developing countries to restrain China by making new international rules; ten, if China continues to conduct as it will, its road to rejuvenation will be blocked by the rejection of the outside world.

Judging by the above ten arguments, it can be noted that another round of global rule making led by the USA is taking shape soon. Apparently, the main target of this wave of attacks is China. Although it might be surging soon, there's no need for China to panic. China has the experience of successful encounter with external severe challenges and its will and determination of safeguarding the open global economic system remains unchanged. Compared with 10 years ago, the overall strength of China has made a huge leap. Moreover, the gaming theory also manifests that rules, as a double-edged sword, restrain others as well as those who try to restrain others.

Anxiety Over Ideological Conflicts

Apart from possible tension caused by institutional competition, China also faces another type of pressure imposed on by an anxious external environment. The ever greater pressure is mainly embodied in the so-called "China threat". This theoretical opposition against China could date back to the "Yellow Peril" in the latter half of the 19th Century and early 20th Century.

In 1873, Bakunin published his *Statism and Anarchy* at the age of 60. A year earlier, he had been expulsed from the First International by the Hague Congress because of his anarchism. However, in this masterpiece published rather late in his life, Bakunin hurried to propose to the Czar government, vigorously agitating for engaging with the huge threat from China. His excuse was that China would certainly move north and northwest because it was too crowded with a population of 400 million or 600 million. Millions of Chinese, he added, would not only occupy the whole Siberia and Central Asia but also go across the Ural River to the Volga River. To him, the Chinese were too terrifying, overpopulated yet incomparably stout and bellicose. As he suggested, the Czar government should "send all its troops to Siberia and Central Asia" and "lead all its people to conquer the East"[23]. Bakunin's ideas are considered to be one of the origins of the so-called "Yellow Peril".[24]

China (The Qing Dynasty) at that time and in a rather long time that followed was absolutely no substantial threat to the Russian Empire. In 1858, China was forced to sign the *Sino-Russian Treaty of Aihui* by the Czar government. Because of the treaty, China lost almost all the land to the north of the Heilongjiang River, about 600,000 km^2, to the Russian Empire and the land to the east of the Wusuli River, about 400,000 km^2, were to be jointly administrated by both the Russian Empire and the Qing Dynasty, a treaty that caused the largest loss of land in modern history of China. In 1860, the Russian Empire again forced the Qing government to sign the *Sino-Russian Convention of Beijing* under the excuse of helping in the mediation of the Second Opium War, officially confirmed the *Sino-Russian Treaty of Aihui* and transferred the land between the east of the Wusuli River and the sea (including Sakhalin and Vladivostok), about 1 million km^2, to the Russian Empire. In 1864, the Russian Empire forced the Qing government to sign the *Sino-Russian Northwest Boundary Definition Memorandum* and the land to the east and the south of the Balkhash Lake and south and north of Lake Zajsan (now Lake Zaysan), about 440,000 km^2, was transferred to the Russian Empire. The fact was China's strength never "changed suddenly" in the year when Bakunin published that book and the "bellicose" Chinese never posed real threat to Russians. Even in 1882 and 1883, ten years later, the Russian Empire was still able to seize vast territories of China through the *Sino-Russian Ili Treaty* and *the Sino-Russian Treaty on the Kobdo-Tarbaghatay Boundary.* Obviously Bakunin's assumption of the so-called "Yellow Peril" was meant to polish invasion by fabricated threats.

Apart from Russia, there were also a lot of believers of the "Yellow Peril" in the USA, the UK and Germany. In 1895, in his letter to Nicolas II, the last emperor of Russia, William II, the last emperor of Germany, said that he himself had drawn a "picture of Yellow Peril", which shows the European powers, represented by their own guardian gods, are gathered together by the archangel Michael from heaven to join hands in their fight against the invasion of Buddhists, heretics and barbarians and safeguard the Cross.[25] When remarking on the picture by "one of the most ridiculous people at our time", William II, the last German emperor in a scornful tone, Leo Tolstoy took the liberty of adding a figure of seated Confucius next to the

---

[23]Bakunin (1982).

[24]Lv (1979), p. 1.

[25]Lv (1979), p. 114.

Buddha, one of the rivals stared at by Michael and his men.[26] It is not hard to imagine a "Dragon", an image of China, was also in that picture, no matter it was next to the Buddha or Confucius. Another advocator of "Yellow Peril", A. Diosy, Fellow of the Royal Geographical Society and Vice Chairman of UK Japan Association Commission, made a thorough interpretation of the "picture of Yellow Peril" in his book, *The New Far East,* asserting with much certainty, that scourge (Sakyamuni) "was sitting on the back of a dragon, closing in through storm clouds and flicker of flames. That was unmistakably a dragon from the Far East".[27]

In order to better serve the purpose of exerting merciless prosecution in the name of "justice", it seemed to be somewhat not convincing in the beginning of 20th century, which saw the rapid development of science and technology, to identify "demons" simply by race or religion. To that purpose, some exponents of "Yellow Peril" tried recklessly introduce other "scientific" theories into their arguments so as to increase the rationality and rationale of the "Yellow Peril" theory. In October and November, 1876, a special commission founded by both the US House of Representatives and Senate carried out investigation into the Chinese immigrants issue in San Francisco. It was said the commission interviewed hundreds of people for their opinion about the issue. One interviewee cited from a "knowledgeable ethnographer", arguing any race with an average cranial capacity no more than 85 cubic inches is unable to build a free regime. The cranial capacity of the Chinese (and black people in America) was only 82 or 83 cubic inches, much less than that of modern Germans, Englishmen and British Americans, whose average cranial capacity was 90–92 cubic inches. Due to the shortage in cranial capacity, the Chinese would never be able to become freemen and "select in a rational and decent way the best and purest people to rule and manage them" and they would only take votes to be a tool for making money, thus threatening freedom and the progress of humankind. Allowing such inferior races to enter the USA would jeopardize freedom and the career of the free regime.[28]

Malthus's theory on population also became an important resort for those exponents of "Yellow Peril", the former arbitrarily asserted that population multiplies geometrically and food arithmetically and the latter "the reproduction of inferior races is faster than that of superior ones" and the yellow race and the black race would rapidly populate the tropical and subtropical areas in America the whole world so "there's no way to drive them away other than eradicating them by incredibly large genocide."[29]

Neither the "Yellow Peril" theory nor any other scientific theory relied on by those exponents of the theory can stand up to any scrutiny. What's more, there are evident contradictions among these arguments. Some hold that the "Yellow Peril" is

---

[26]Historically, the Yellow Peril referred to by William II was mainly the threat from Japan yet he included the Chinese in that threat. Leo Tolstoy remarked, "If Japan and China forget Sakyamuni and Confucius just like we forget Jesus Christ, they will soon master the art of killing people." Lv (1979), p. 128.

[27]Lv (1979), pp. 137–138.

[28]Lv (1979), pp. 53–55.

[29]Lv (1979), p. 91.

disastrous because the expansion of inferior races will squeeze the living space of superior races while others advocated that China "even doesn't need any genius to build any kind of bright future, it only takes some ordinary leaders who are willing to adopt those progressive measures of Europe while not breaking the customs, traditions and other stereotypes to build China into a country that no European powers dare to ignore. It will then have an army that is able to go across Asia by following a certain set of procedures and a navy that can take on any fleet the most powerful European country can send to the Chinese waters."[30] The belittling and "praiseful" comments here are both instrumental, meaning to make up excuses or fabricate a basis for carving up China and pillaging.

The modern version of the so-called "China Threat" emphasizes more explicitly the potential conflicts caused by ideology from two aspects:

For one thing, China is assumed to be threatening in light of differences in ideology and political institutions or even individuality of culture or civilization. Perpetual peace can be maintained among the western countries, they argue, is simply because they have "democracy". A well-known metaphor goes that "democratic" countries are all herbivores while "nondemocratic" countries carnivores. Therefore, to maintain peace, the carnivores must be turned into herbivores. To those exponents of "China Threat" that hold the above belief, the socialist political system of China means dictatorship and totalitarianism. A fundamental lesson the 20th century taught us is the democratic system and the totalitarian system can not coexist. Due to the differences between their purposes and thinking, conflicts between them will happen sooner or later, either in the form of a cold war or in the form of a hot war, and finally end with the victory of one side and the collapse of the other.[31] After the collapse of the USSR and the drastic changes of eastern Europe, China became the only large socialist country in the world. Under the impact of "the third wave of democratization", South Korea, the Philippines, Indonesia, Taiwan and other economies in East Asia all made much progress in terms of "democratization" while only China refused to change. Such firm rejection to the "democratic" system was literally hard to bear.[32] Some western scholars of Chinese studies asserted that China would collapse the way the USSR did or become a militaristic regime ruled by the military after the death of Deng Xiaoping.[33] However, all these predictions turned out wrong, leaving all those exponents of "China Threat" bitterly regretful. Moreover, some researchers came to explain the inescapability of confrontation in view of the individuality of culture and civilization. Alastair Iain Johnston argued that China's actual strategic culture in history was not the doctrine of Confucius and Mencius that China has been purporting but a cultural realism that pursues expansionism, which supports cross-border and preemptive attacks aimed at political destruction and annexation after military victories.[34]

---

[30] Lv (1979), p. 97.

[31] Gertz (2013).

[32] Storey and Yee (2002a).

[33] Gertz (2013).

[34] Johnston (1995), pp. 112–113.

For another, apart from the ideological conflicts caused by ideology or civilization, there's also another belief that the prosecution the West imposed on China in modern history caused a victim mentality in China[35], which will lead China to take its revenge against the West once it rises again. The Chinese government has been saying that it was the political encroachment, economic exploitation and military invasion of the western imperialists that deprived China of its pride as the "Middle Kingdom" in history and brought to modern China the "century-old national humiliation". This victim mentality, argued the exponents of "China Threat", made the Chinese people ready to accept schemes like that of Mao Zedong's "forever revolution" and wipe out their national humiliation the violent way so as to restore China's historical central position in the world.[36] Under such background, some international observers even interpreted Deng Xiaoping's proposition of "maintaining a low profile" as "concealing true intentions, bide its time before going on the offensive".[37] As a matter of fact, it was mistaken to be another Chinese saying, namely, "enduring hardships to plan retaliation" because the strategy of "keeping a low profile" doesn't have the implication of "hiding one's true intentions and bide one's time to retaliate".[38] Some researchers assume China's behavior based on the history of Western powers in their pursuit of hegemony. Paul Kennedy, a historian, pointed out that the rise of the British Empire, Germany and France in the 18th century and the 19th century and the ups and downs of the USA, Japan and USSR both indicated the rise of emerging powers is bound to cause global instability and the reconstruction of international political and economic orders.[39] Since it has become a ritual for western powers, why should we believe that China, who still has a vivid memory of its humiliation in the recent past, would repay injury with kindness and be exceptionally benevolent during its rejuvenation?

Without a plausible way to "drive out" suspicion out of mind, suspicion might become a self-fulfilling prophecy, dragging all parties of suspicion into a whirlpool of hostility or even mutual prosecution.

Thucydides Trap

Some people start from the realism prevailing in the West, arguing that international relations are determined by such human nature as selfishness, greed, and pursuing power and China is no exception; a rejuvenated China will definitely have conflicts with the existing power structure. Hans J. Morgenthau, an expert of international relations, argued that, families, institutions, countries or any other human organizations are all inclined to pursue dominance. In nature, international politics, as of

[35] Medeiros and Taylor Fravel (2003).

[36] Jian (2003).

[37] Lai (2010).

[38] Tang (2003).

[39] Kennedy (1987).

all politics, is of necessity power politics.[40] Besides, there isn't a world government to regulate behaviors of countries. As a result, all countries pursue power so as to realize their national interests. According to this theory, whether China will carry out reform in accordance with western democracy or abandon its own culture to be completely westernized as a latecomer to this power banquet, it will necessarily have an intention to obtain national interests from the neighborhood or the world through power expansion. They take the increasing tension in China's territorial disputes with its neighbors as evidence, indicating that China wants to change the status quo or the existing order by such means as military threats. Some observers also suggested China's purchase of advanced fighter planes, warships and submarines from Russia in recent years once again testifies that China is bellicose.[41] More drastically, the return of Hong Kong and Macau was also seen as aspiration for rebuilding and expanding the Chinese Empire, arguing this "Greater China", which may dominate the whole East Asia and appear to be a robust common market which will increase opportunities for trade and investment in the world may unavoidably threaten the business vitality and strategic stability in other regions of the world.[42]

This traditional pattern of "a strong country must seek hegemony" may enmesh China and the USA and even the whole world into the "Thucydides Trap". The famous historian Thucydides in ancient Greece pointed out that the reason why the war between Athens and Sparta finally became inescapable was the rise of Athens and the fear this rise instilled in Sparta. This situation in which " an emerging power must challenge the old one while the old one must respond to this challenge, thus making war inevitable" is referred to as "Thucydides Trap". Research shows that "since 1500, there are 15 cases in which an emerging power challenged the old one and 11 of them led to war. Germany is a best example. After unification, Germany replaced the UK to be the largest economy in Europe. Well, in 1914 and 1939, Germany's invasion and the UK's response led to two world wars. Similar cases also existed in Asia. Upon its rise, Japan wanted to challenge the order that had been established or to be established in Asia by the European colonists so as to replace it with an Asian order with Japan as the core. In the end, that led to a war in which Japan invaded other Asian countries in the name of anti-western powers."[43]

Not surprisingly, the increase of China's economic strength and overall national strength drew deep concerns of existing powers. Former President Barack Obama's chief Chinese specialist, Fred Thompson is well-known in the world of Chinese for his comments on the Sino-American relationship. He said, "China and the United States are engaged in a major gamble with each other on the rise of China today and in the future. China is gambling that Americans will give support and cooperation during its rise; the United States is gambling that a powerful China will share responsibility with the US instead of challenging the rights of the US in the international system in the decades to come. At present, both China and the US have a bet. Of course, where

---

[40] Hans (1973).

[41] Storey and Yee (2002b).

[42] Harding (1995), p. 33.

[43] Zheng (2012).

there's a bet there's a loser. Who is going to be the winner depends on the efforts and wisdom of the politicians and citizens of both countries."[44] Some scholars put forward a strategy called "offshore balance", suggesting the established major country work with its military allies neighboring China to provoke conflicts and contain China's development. Regarding that, Joseph Nye once remarked in a warning sense, "if you treat China as an enemy, you are certain to have an enemy."[45]

Faced with such a wave of containing China, Chinese leaders took the initiative to enhance trust, manage differences between China and the USA as well as other developed countries and elaborate on China's road of peaceful development, striving to win friendship and understanding of China's road around the world. During an interview with *The World Post*, Xi Jinping made it rather clear that "the theory that a strong country must seek hegemony does not apply for China", "looking back at our long history and cultural background, it's clear that seeking hegemony is not in our cultural genes. We must unite together against the Thucydides Trap, that is, devastating tension between emerging countries and developed countries or that between developed countries." China hopes such attitude and actions can alleviate the risk of enmeshing the world into the Thucydides Trap. However, that shall not solely depend on the efforts of China. China needs independence as well as peaceful development for they build on each other. To make this road a success, China must integrate and expand the common interests with established major countries especially the USA. Scholars and policy- makers of both sides must fully understand the strategic importance of these common interests. Just as Robert B. Zoellick, former United States Deputy Secretary of State and the 11th President of the World Bank, said, "It is absolutely necessary for both China and the USA to realize structural reforms and global rebalancing. Cooperation can increase hopes and possibility for success... The USA and China have economic and developmental concepts that can help other countries, namely, natural resource exploration, agriculture, greater manufacturing industry and supply chain, service sector, infrastructure or investment. The USA and China have common interests in terms of inclusive growth, good governance, transparency and anti-corruption, trade and avoiding the "prosperity-recession" cycle."[46]

References

Acemoglum, D. and J. A. Robinson. 2006. A. Economic backwardness in political perspective. *American Political Science Review*, 100(01): 115–131.

Alastair I. Johnston. 1995. *Cultural Realism: Strategic Culture and Grand Strategy in Chinese History* Princeton, NJ: Princeton University Press, pp. 112–113.

Bakunin. 1982. *Statism and Anarchy*. Trans. by Ma Xiangcong et al. Commercial Press, pp. 109–110.

[44]Interview with Sen. Fred Thompson, www.pbs.org/wgbh/pages/frontline/shows/china/interview s/thompson.html.

[45]Nye (2015).

[46]Zoellick (2014).

Bell, D. 1984. *The Coming Back of the Post-Industrial Society–A Venture in Social Forecasting*. Trans. by Gao Xian. The Commercial Press.
Cai, Fang. The only way to surmount "Middle-income Trap" is reform, *Reference News*, March 14, 2016.
Clinton, Hillary Rodham. 2011. America's Pacific Century. *Foreign Policy*. October 11.
Gertz, Bill. 2013. *The China Threat: How the People's Republic Targets America*. Regnery Publishing. p. 1.
Hai, Wen. Innovation and Education are key to China's transformation and upgrade, *Reference News*, April 5, 2016.
Hans, J. Morgenthau. 1973. *Politics Among Nations: The Struggle for Power and Peace* (Fifth Edition). New York: Alfred A. Knopf, p. 35.
Harding, Harry. 1995. The Concept of 'Greater China': Themes, Variations and Reservations, in David Shambaugh ed., *Greater China: The Next Superpower?*. New York: Oxford University Press, p. 33.
Hormats, Robert D. 2011. Ensuring a Sound Basis for Global Competition: Competitive Neutrality. DipNote. May 6. https://blogs.state.gov/stories/2011/05/06/ensuring-sound-basis-global-competition-competitive-neutrality.
Hu, Angang. "Middle-income Trap" is a false proposition to China, *Reference News*, March 18, 2016.
Huntington, S. P. 1989. *Political Order in Changing Societies*. Trans. by Wang Guanhua. SDX Joint Publishing Company.
Jian, Chen. 2003. A Response: How to Pursue a Critical History of Mao's Foreign Policy. *The China Journal* 49: 137–142.
Jia, Kang and Su Jingchun. China needs institutional innovation to break through the "bottleneck period". *Reference News*, March 23, 2016.
Kennedy, Paul. 1987. *The Rise and Fall of the Great Powers: Economic Change and Military Conflict from 1500 to 2000*. New York: Random House.
Kuznets, S. 1955. Economic growth and income inequality, *The American Economic Review*: 1–28.
Lai, David. 2010. *Coming of Chinese Hawk*. Carlisle, Pennsylvania: Strategic Studies Institute, pp. 1–3.
Li, Daokui. China is able to surmount "Middle-income Trap", *Reference News*, March 15, 2016.
Li, Yining. Only by Surmounting "Three High Mountains" Can We Avoid "Traps", *Reference News*, April 4, 2016.
Lin, Yifu. China has unique advantages to become a high-income country, *Reference News*, March 25, 2016.
Lv, Pu. 1979. *Historical Sources of Yellow Peril*, China Social Sciences Press.
Medeiros, Evan S. and M. Taylor Fravel. 2003. China's New Diplomacy. *Foreign Affairs*: 22–35.
Nye, Joseph. "Only China Can Contain China." *The Huffington Post*. Accessed on July 14, 2015. http://www.huffingtonpost.com/joseph-nye/china-contain-china_b_6845588.html.
Olson, M. 1963. Rapid growth as a destabilizing force. *The Journal of Economic History*, 23(04): 529–552.
Soros, George. The Way Forward, http://www.ftchinese.com/story/001029656, November 11, 2009.
Spence, A. Michael. 2011. The Impact of Globalization on Income and Employment. *Foreign Affairs*. July/August.
Storey, I. and H. Yee. 2002a. The China threat: perceptions, myths and reality (Routledge), p. 3.
Storey, I. and H. Yee. 2002b. *The China threat: perceptions, myths and reality.* Routledge, p. 4.
Sun, Guangzhen and Zhang Yuyan. 1997. Interest Groups and "Jia Yi's Law: A Preliminary Analytical Framework, *Economic Research Journal*, No. 6.
Tang, Shiping. 2003. *Shape an Ideal Security Environment for China*. China Social Sciences Press, p. 240.
Tocqueville, A.D. 1992. *The Old Regime and the Revolution*, Trans. by Feng Tang. The Commercial Press.

Williamson, J. 2000. "What should the World Bank think about the Washington Consensus?" *The World Bank Research Observer* 15 (2): 251–264.
Zhao, Dingxin. Will revolution happen in China today?. *21st Century*, December, 2012.
Zheng, Xinli. China has a great potential in becoming a high-income country, *Reference News*, April 7, 2016.
Zheng, Yongnian, China needs philosophical thinking over Sino-US relationship, *Lianhe Zaobao*, September 4, 2012.
Zoellick, Robert B. 2014. "U.S., China and Thucydides". *The National Interest*. Accessed on October 4. http://nationalinterest.org/article/us-china-thucydides-8642.

Chapter 5
Creating a Future of Long-Term Peace and Common Prosperity

It is essential for the practice and theory of peaceful development to go hand in hand. For any discipline, there are seven constituting elements: basic assumptions, concepts, range of facts, specific theories, problems, testing methods and values.[1] We adopt three basic assumptions concerning the research of long-term peace and common prosperity: first, personified states are subjects of international relations, and their logic of conducts is in line with the assumption of an "economic man", that is, a state takes the pursuit and maximization of its own interests as its object; second, a war of a world scale is unlikely to break out, for all major powers of world are possess nuclear weapons, and it is highly impossible for them to settle disputes by way of war; third, the international interdependence is enhanced and will be probably increasingly so, which makes an isolation policy cost more than ever. With the three assumptions, the gaming of international interests will mainly take the route of establishing international rules, safeguarding international order, and extending one's own interest with a view of others' interests. If the latter two assumptions hold true, China will be in a position to amend and perfect current international rules via peaceful means, and realize the Chinese dream of the great rejuvenation of the Chinese nation in the process of promoting long-term peace and common prosperity.

In order to have a clear exposition and analysis, new concepts, which are summarized and extracted from real-world practice, are needed for theoretical construction. For instance, concepts such as modernization of governance system and governance capability, a new model of Sino-US major-country relationship between China and the United States, human beings sharing a community of common destiny, and the Belt and Road Initiative are all concepts of originality and of the times.[2] On the basis of the three assumptions, the range of facts to be investigated with the traditional and new concepts includes the conducts of China and its interaction with international community, out of which specific theories will be developed and laws governing con-

[1] Zhang and Li (2008).

[2] Xi (2016).

Y. Zhang and W. Feng, *Peaceful Development Path in China*, China Insights,
https://doi.org/10.1007/978-981-13-1439-1_5

ducts will be explored. Theories represent nothing other than the inference relations between concepts. The present chapter will be focused on three classes of concepts concerning long-term world peace and common prosperity, i.e., the internally-oriented concepts of comprehensively deepening reform and modernization of state governance, the externally-oriented concepts of enhanced engagement in global governance, strengthening and extending regional security network and establishing a new model of major-country relations for world peace, and the interaction-oriented concept of the Belt and Road Initiative. Each subsection will explore and answer questions as to how to coordinate the internal and external factors and their interaction so as to realize the Chinese dream and integrate it with the dream of the world. These questions are still developing and receiving answers accordingly. Their final test will depend on further practical development or empirical-logical extension.

Peaceful development is rooted in the following values: what the Chinese people pursue is also what the people of other countries desire. Socialism with the Chinese characteristics is not "Chinese exceptionalism". Such core values of socialism as "prosperity, democracy, civilization, harmony, freedom, equality, justice, rule by law, patriotism, professionalism, integrity and kindness" are values accepted by most countries, and in line with the goals of human rights, equality, justice, freedom, social progress, livelihood, peace, security, common interests and economic development, as determined by "We the Peoples of the United Nations" in the UN Charter. To establish a harmonious world of long-term peace and common prosperity is a common wish shared by the people of all nations, and also the sublime goal along the path of peaceful development for China. However, the ways for the realization of these values can be diversified, and should comply with the history and reality of a nation. Modes of social and economic development should be compatible with development results. It is necessary to build mutual trust and recognition between different countries and civilizations, and to enhance the awareness of human beings sharing a community of common destiny, on which basis their cooperation can be promoted. Diversification, inclusiveness and cooperation serve as pillars for creating a new order of long-term peace and common prosperity.

Comprehensively Deepening Reform and Opening-Up

The reform and opening-up of China has entered deep waters. The Third Plenary Session of the 18th CPC Central Committee states that decisive results should be achieved in important areas and key links at the end of the "13th Five Year Plan". To such an end, it takes not only the spirit of bravely acting and boldly trying but also wisdom and determination.

The direct object of comprehensively deepening reform and opening-up is for the Chinese economy to achieve sustainable growth. We have explained in the Third Chapter that the source of economic growth lies in the improvement of labor productivity, which in turn depends on the level of division of labor and professionalism. Division of labor and professionalism benefits from the enlargement of market size. It is then advisable to look to market size and marketization for new points of economic growth.

First, it is essential, as required by the Third Plenary session of the 18th Central Committee of CPC, to put the idea of giving the decisive role of market a full play in resource allocation into practice. It is not up to the government but to the market to decide the strategic importance of an industry and to find out emerging industries. With regard to industry development, the government should only make "hypothesis", adopt an open attitude as to whether the "hypothesis" will pan out, allow the market to test it, never stick to its own opinion, and not be afraid of owning up to its mistakes and shouldering due responsibilities. To trust the market is to trust the people, and to protect the fairness and justice of the market is to provide encouragement and support to mass entrepreneurship and innovation.

The needs of the people should be guided rather than suppressed, and the role of government is to serve rather than demand obedience. Only with old mentality and stereotypes dispensed with can room be made for the needs of the people and the release of their talent. Admittedly, in many cases, mass innovation is ahead of state policy. State policy, laws and regulation should protect such grassroots efforts as long as they are conducive to promoting and liberating productivity, rather than blindly crash them in the name of illegality. And this is in the spirit of the Deng Xiaoping's legalizing the "household contract responsibility system".

Second, in addition to "deepening" reforming domestic elements and commodity market by way of marketization, deepening opening-up is also needed to enhance the ability to access global resources and market share. By way of enlarge outside market, domestic division of labor and professionalism can be promoted, realizing growth in new areas. According to the projection of the Asian Development Bank and the World Bank, infrastructure construction in the Asian-Pacific area will take at least 8 trillion dollars in the next decade. The Asian Infrastructure Invest Bank initiated by China can make up for the deficiency of fund in this respect. The investment at once helps improve the infrastructure of host countries and provides outlet to the surplus producing capacity in infrastructure construction of China, and thus helps maintain and enlarge China's advantage and employment in relevant industries.

Besides, the interconnection of infrastructures will integrate the labor force, resources and fund of host countries into the global market with China included, and enable them to benefit from globalization. Once the people obtain benefits, their concepts will change accordingly. The enhanced expectations and needs will demand these host countries to conduct institutional and conceptual reform and opening-up, to be more open to China, and to be more integrated into the modern world economy network. And this will serve as new impetus for China in obtaining new market and promoting growth.

Third, emphasis is laid on the role of technological advancement in creating new economic growth points. New technologies and their industrialized application always bring about emerging large-scale market. On the one hand, internal technological innovation needs to be enhanced; on the other, the relation between China and technologically advanced countries needs to be straightened out. The widening gap between them in terms of technology cannot go unchecked, and it may help to bridge the gap to make joint efforts with other developing countries to reestablish relevant international rules concerning intellectual property. The enormous economy volume of China can be a hotbed for the rapid industrialization and marketization of some new and high technology. Take high-speed rail for example. While it is quite hard for such a technology to go into business in small- and medium-sized countries, China succeeds in putting it into industrialized application and lowering the overall trade cost. Advantage scale like this should be attached more importance. We should select proper advanced technologies, and put them into use so as to generate powerful productivity with the benefits of the Chinese market, creating new economic growth points.

It should be noted that, though with sustainable growth as a goal, in the process of comprehensively deepening reform and opening-up, China ought to pay more attention to development quality rather than quantity. The Chinese economy has entered a "new normal", with a consensus reached with the effect of lowering or downplaying expected GDP growth rate. In 2015, more than 70% of provinces, districts and cities have lowered their expected GDP growth rate for 2015 or maintained the same rate as the last year. The province with the largest margin of decrease was Qinghai with its expected GDP growth rate lowered from 9.2% of 2014 to 8% for 2015. Shanghai led the country in canceling the expected GDP growth rate in its annual government work report. In another word, China needs a new "baton" to test the development results of the reform and opening-up policy.

As early as December, 2013, in the Notice on Improving Assessment of Leading Body and Leaders of Local Party Committees and Local Governments issued by the Organizing Department of the Central Committee of CPC, it has already been clearly stated that assessment of local organization should improved in terms of downplaying the role of GDP, and enhancing that of quality and profits and of sustainable development. The "new climate" seen in local two summits of this year can be understood as the practice of the overall plan by the central government according to new conditions and changes.

Under the "new normal" as reflected by these changes, the economic development of China is now undergoing a fundamental shift from quantity-oriented to quality-oriented. In terms of quantity or scale, China's GDP calculated by market exchange rate now ranks No. 2 in the world, and that adjusted by PPP has replaced the United States as the world No. 1. Against this background, it would be less meaningful to continue to lay emphasis on GDP growth rate. In fact, the "GDP first" concept may aggravate the excess of producing capacity in certain areas and industries, and may even lead to a general crisis. Short-term "full employment" which results from such a concept may also result in a potential risk for large-scale future unemployment or organized instabilities.

However, to downplay the role of GDP is not to give up GDP once for all, and still less to antagonize GDP growth against social and economic development. Even Shanghai, which leads the country in reform, stopping mentioning expected GDP growth rate in the government work report this year, still treats GDP as an important reference for assessing social and economic development. For example, it is stated in the Shanghai government work report that "the social overall expenditure for research and development accounts for more than 3.6% of the city's GDP", which can in a sense be viewed as a requirement on GDP growth.

From the perspective of long-term development, downplaying GDP growth rate is in line with the people's wishes and the general trend, because the indicator cannot reflect the people's expectations and wishes for a comprehensively improved livelihood, such as green environment, safe foods, better education, convenient transportation, healthy work and happy retirement years. On the other hand, while downplaying expected GDP growth rate, there should be a set of new standards to assess development quality and a corresponding assessment system in order to unify national policies and decrees and market behaviors, and to provide guidance to local governments in competition for the overall welfare of the people.

It is a lot harder to assess economy quality than quantity. Although unitary GDP growth may be subject to government intervention, being increased vicariously by government investment or even by glossing over economic data, it has the benefit of easy supervision over investment modes and data-faking. Once a more complicated assessment of economy quality is adopted, and all matters are judged on the data provided by the government, it would be easier to conceal facts from higher-level authorities and deceive the people, and cost more in inspection and examination, and it would be more difficult for the central government to hold local government accountable for their behaviors. Consequently, the new assessment system should aim at a new standard by integrating subjective and objective indicators, material and popular indicator, incorporating subject indicators based on the evaluation of the people, so as to make up for the difficulty in unified measurement due to regional differences.

But it is no hurry to enact such an indicator system. With certain basic principles clarified, local governments should be given a certain period of time to experiment, and to perfect and promote the system on the experience obtained. There will be a process from system transformation and finalization. It is a process of testing as well as of mobilizing. After going through the process, once the system is finalized, all local governments will find it easy to adjust themselves and ready adapt to the new system. Before this situation, GDP growth rate may still have some position in assessment.

Reform is always a self-reform. Revolutionary battles have already been launched in different fields. Economic system reform is an important aspect of the comprehensive deepening reform, the core of which is to well-handle the relation between government and market, requiring an improvement in both the transformation of governmental functions and the perfection of market mechanism. The goal for the year of 2014 of reducing by one third the number of matters requiring administrative examination and approval by the State Council departments has been accomplished ahead of time. By May, 2016, the right of administrative examination and approval for 618 matters, which account for 40% of the total number, has been delegated in 9 batches from the State Council departments to lower-level departments, and the requirement of administrative examination and approval for 491 of them has been canceled. Besides, 230 local projects designated by the central government have been canceled, 303 items of intermediate services have been cleared and normalized and 11,073 normative documents have been annulled. Following the example of the State Council, local governments at all levels have taken as an important indicator of the intensity of reform the number of matters with the requirement of administrative examination and approval canceled or downgraded, and the clearing up of power boundaries. All the 31 provinces of the country have published the power list for departments at the provincial level, 24 of them have published accountability list in addition, 17 of them have also announced the power list and the accountability list for departments at municipal and county levels, and some provinces have made active experiments with power list for town governments.[3]

Streamlining administration and delegating power to lower levels contain two aspects: one is to cancel some matters requiring examination and approval, and the other is to delegate the power of examination and approval for some matters to lower-level authorities. The logic for the former is that matters for the cost and profit of which those micro-decision-making subjects should take full or main responsibility (or matter without "external factors") ought to be decided by enterprises and market. But for matters whose benefits are obtained by the subjects and whose cost may easily be transferred to the public should be subject to strict examination and approval, and this is to prevent over-expansion of production for the sake of individual interests at the cost of the overall social value. Some business owners make huge profits from pollution-emitting production while the environment suffers, and a calculation finds out that pollution treatment costs much more than the contribution they have made in terms of tax payment, employment and economic growth. For such businesses, administrative examination and approval cannot be canceled.

The logic for delegating the power of examination and approval to lower-level authorities presupposes that governments at a lower level are more familiar with concrete situations, and that decisions made by better-informed departments can respond to local demands more appropriately and more timely. According to the logic, power delegation should be limited to a reasonable level, not simply to the lowest and put all the pressure on grassroots governments. Some matters depend on the comprehensiveness and wholeness of information, which lower-level authorities, though grasping a full command of details, cannot obtain a macro, accurate and wholistic understanding but view them on a higher level; some matters entail a scale effect, which must be realized with a wider range of practice so as to generate enough benefits; some matters demand cross-regional coordination, and power delegation to the lowest level may result in grassroots authorities' passing the buck. Moreover, better-informed lower-level authorizes exercising power without supervision may also conceal facts from higher-level authorities and deceive the people.

Three measures should be taken to prevent the "free fall" of streamlining administration and delegating power to lower levels. The first is to define power in accordance with responsibility. There can only be as much power as responsibility. More power with less responsibility may lead to power abuse, and more accountability with less power may impede work. Power should be defined according to different levels and governmental responsibilities of different departments.

[3]Luo and Luo (2016).

The second measure is to make power and responsibility public. Powers and responsibilities of governments at different levels should be made public to the people. The openness is not just to list the complicated items and articles on the government websites, and factually makes them inaccessible to the people with "mountain-like documents and sea-like regulations'. Non-technical openness of power and responsibility should be simple and clear, and for technical openness, there should be specialized departments providing timely and clear explanations to the people concerned.

The third measure is to strictly hold relevant party accountable. To define power in accordance with responsibility is about the ability of government, enabling governments at various levels to respond timely and effectively to local demands; to make power and responsibility public is about the possibility of supervision of government, enabling the public to make accurate judgments concerning the work of governments at various levels; to strictly hold relevant party accountable is about the strength of supervision, subjecting empowered and responsible departments failing to fulfill their responsibilities to severe punishment. If the third measure becomes a "soft restriction", all the efforts above will be in vain.

The reform of fiscal and tax system should concentrate on giving a full play to the role of finance in the modernization of state governance system and governance capability. To straighten out governance system and enhance governance capability at all levels, it is necessary, internally speaking, to reasonably divide the power of office and finance among different levels, and to establish a system where power of office is matched with expenditure responsibility; externally speaking, to improve the transparency of budgeting and its execution, and to exercise the supervising function of such organs as people's congress in a reasonable way. It is of particular importance to institutionalize the supervision of budgeting and its execution and make it operable. There is a long way to go in this respect.

The reform in currency and financial sphere has gone under way along the direction of marketization and orderly opening-up with the focus on improvement of risk prevention and control mechanism. The standing meeting of the State Council has approved the Measures of Implementing Deposit and Insurance System. The system will be conducive to the steady promotion of interest rate marketization and other relevant reforms. It is advisable to comprehensively consider the risks and reform demands in all the financial subfields, pay special attention to financial stability.

The reform of state-owned enterprises should be conducted with a clear idea. It is improper to go back to the old way of domestic merger in a sweeping manner on account of some unorderly competitions among large-size state-owned enterprises in international market. For the establishment of modern company system in state-owned enterprises, it is essential to trust market and depend on market competition to improve efficiency and increase consumer surplus. The proper way to drag state-owned enterprises out of difficulties is for decision-makers of the enterprises to rely on make market forces rather than administrative orders.

As for establishing an open economy system, China is facing more and more international pressure, and hence should have a standard as to what to do and what not to do. What shall and must be done should be done as soon as possible, and with a "reverse transmission mechanism" smoothened, outside pressure can be quickly transformed into bonus of institutional reform. To what shall not be done, China should not turn a blind eye but establish and explicitly express its principle, thus adopt an open manner of conduct of principle, and maintain an image of "transparent interaction" in international affairs.

Reform involves a power struggle of all sides. Reforms in democracy, livelihood, rule by law and ecology are not to be ignored. Decision-makers will hear voices from all sides, and they should have the determination of reform, focus on key problems and main contradictions, actively solving problems and putting their decisions into practice, and by no means should they be led by various ideas and interferences. Only by putting fundamental reforms into practice can reforms proceed in a clear and smooth manner.

Modernization of Governance System and Governance Capability

In many researches, governance is treated as a term related to government. Both words are derived from the ancient Greek κυβερνάω (which originally means taking the helm and then refers to the action of guiding, controlling and manipulating), and are overlapping in their references and gradually differentiated in terms of usages. [4]

In modern usage, *governance* enjoys a more diversified and wider range of reference and usage. It is not only applied to the field of state political activities, but also to such fields as business operations. In business operations, the word is in contrast with business management just as it is in contrast with government management (i.e., government) in state politics. Hence, it might be more precise to say that *governance* is a term in contrast with *management*. In a company, there is a distinction between company governance and business management, and in a country, there is a distinction between state governance and government, and globally, there is a distinction between internal (or regional) governance and "world government".

As for the distinction between company governance and business management, the latter focuses on the leadership, control and order of business-owners and their representatives, adopting top-down hierarchical bureaucratic system (or bureaucracy) as the concrete structure for management, while the former lays emphasis on the role and influence of shareholders in business operations. The range of shareholders is much wider than management-related business subjects, including internal subjects such as owners, managers and workers of a company as well as external subjects such as the company's debtors, consumers, raw material suppliers, competitors, and local communities. With the increasingly complicated situation of business operations, to take the interests of more subjects into account would be beneficial for a company to take advantage of market opportunities and ward off risks. Under particular conditions, external shareholders can even be turned into a part of the company. For

[4] Yu (2000).

example, suppliers or competitors may be merged with the company via vertical or lateral integration to form a new business entity of a larger scale.[5]

As for the distinction between state governance and government, rule or administration, the subjects of governance are not restricted to government departments, either. Government or rule implies activities supported by formal power or police forces so as to enforce the execution of policies made in due time. In contrast with government or rule, state governance has a fuller implication. It refers to an interactive process between top and bottom, where government departments, non-governmental organizations, and various private organizations, under the guidance of the same goal, deal with public affairs by way of cooperation, consultation and partnership. The power direction is multi-dimensional rather than simply from top to bottom. Social forces can have a more important role in governance. By way of normal channels, they can exert an influence on government in a bottom-up fashion.[6] Specifically, governance involves cooperation between political authorizes with civil society, between government departments and non-governmental organizations, and between public organizations and private organizations, including forced and voluntary cooperation. Cooperation at these different levels constitute a network of cooperation.

The recent emergence and popularity of the concept of governance in social sciences and the practice of policy-making is not without reason, but deeply rooted in current social and economic development. First, the complexity, uncertainty, openness and diversity of social and economic development demand the involvement of more subjects in the governance of different fields. In a relatively simply and closed environment, it is easy for higher authorities to collect information required to formulate plans and supervise the execution of the plans. The cost incurred by such a type of management or rule is relatively low, and it does not demand the objects managed or ruled and other subjects to play an important role in policy-making. As the environment becomes more complicated, uncertain and open, government authorities or managerial personnel, even with an enormous hierarchical bureaucratic system, cannot hope to collect and process the huge amount of information, and their policy-making cannot be based on comprehensive information; even if plans have been formulated, it is impossible for them to give full incentives and supervision to all the links in their implementation so as to ensure strict execution of the plans in a correct direction. In contrast with management or rule, governance can provide reliable and timely information source for policy-making in a complicated and uncertain environment, and in the meantime, provide mobilization and incentives for the execution of plans or designs. Governance covers more interest-related subjects. Their interests can be better reflected in goal setting by way of governance. For this reason, they are ready to share the information they possess for goal achievement rather than hide it.

The second background for the emergence of the concept of governance is the disillusionment of the "blind faith" in government and market, which gives rise to governance as a new mode of distribution of resources. After the Great Depression in the 1930s, Keynesianism featuring governmental intervention became popular, the

[5]Grossman and Oliver (1986).

[6]Chen (2007).

myth of which was debunked by the stagnation in the 1970s. The "malfunction of government" then turned into a focus of scholars and policy-makers. For those who believe in the role of market, malfunction or failure of government is nothing but understandable, because only a complete reliance on market mechanism can produce good order. However, when it comes to the 1990s, market mechanism also failed to function. Private interest-oriented business operation could not realize efficient distribution of resources, either, and the "malfunction of market" became even worse. Market fundamentalists tend to take the failure of market as an exception or an accident. Whenever market fails, they will call for further enhancement of the role of market rather than restrict it. More people, however, recognize that there are boundaries for both government and market. Beyond the boundaries, there are vast room for adjustment and regulation, which requires a third party besides government and market to maintain order.

In the face of the "malfunction of government" and the "malfunction of market", there emerge three views concerning governance. The first is about "combination", that is, governance should incorporate market mechanism into management or rule in order to achieve coordination according to market principles.[7] The second is "substitution", that is, governance is a substitute plan for government and market mechanism, which relies on third-party civil voluntary organizations to establish a network of coordination. The relations within the network are neither plans or imperatives, nor competitions of a market, but feature mutual benefit and mutual dependence.[8] The third is about "synthesis", that is, governance should resort to diversified forces and means instead of solely relying on a collective group (government) or on market, since the "malfunction of government" and the "malfunction of market" have changed the people's view about how to solve public problems. The view holds that neither government nor market nor third-party organizations are perfect, and that governance should take advantage of different methods and avoid their disadvantages, choosing the best leading mode in according with concrete situation and specific fields. In general, the success of governance requires the full play of the force of market, a powerful civil society, and an efficient and clean government so that a cooperative governance can be achieved by the participation of government, market, and civil organizations. Though government is not the only subject of governance, with the view to modernization, the central government shoulders the major responsibility for state governance and social transformation. And the central government will normally retain its right to open, close, adjust governance mechanisms, and the right to establish other mechanisms. [9]

The third background for the emergence of the concept of governance is that in the era of globalization, international actors out of their own interests demand the dissolution of the integrity of sovereignty of national countries in the name of the legitimacy of governance. On the one hand, globalization brings about a group of multinational corporations which are not bound by loyalty to any national country.

[7] Kazancigil and Huang (1999).
[8] Rhodes (1996).
[9] Jessop (1999).

These corporations and their collaborators in a host country out of the consideration of their own interests try to break open the doors of developing countries, and thus actively pursue the restriction of the right of administration for the host country government in the name of governance. On the other hand, the World Bank together with other international organizations, as specified by its Charter, shall not take into account non-economic factors, but driven by the United States and other Western countries,[10] it takes on the task of promoting "legitimacy, participation, pluralism, freedom of the press and human rights". In order to avoid the accusation of interfering in the internal affairs of other countries, the World Bank chooses to legalize and technicalize interference under the banner of "governance". As indicated by some researchers, the World Bank is first of all concerned with the technical field. And this revolves around the establishment of "development framework" and "capability construction". The former is related to the instrumental factor, one of the formal factors for the establishment of a legal system. A set of rules familiar to all, for example, is also concerned with the independence of judiciary power, laws, and basic elements such as equality, justice and freedom. The World Bank believes that it is helpful in facilitating the efficiency of legal exchange, ensuring the uniformity of laws, updating legal system, and training judiciary personnel. The latter is concerned with improving policies and "budgeting discipline", perfecting training and bureaucratic process, reforming civil services, cutting down overstaffing in particular, improving the coordination within the bureaucratic system, and establishing the distinction between official affairs and private affairs. Both the legal system and the bureaucratic system are predetermined to be western-style. These supporting reforms, however, are proposed as something politics-or-ideology-neutral, saying that "the system is essential for a modern country".[11]

To sum up, the emergence of governance is driven by the consideration of both interest and efficiency. In general, the transition from state rule or government to state governance is in line with the development trend of the modernization of human politics. In comparison with rule or government, governance has the following features and implications:

First, the subjects of state governance are more diversified, and so are the sources of authority. The traditional rule or government concentrates on the singular role of government. In addition to government, governance involves the wide participation of enterprises, social organizations and the common people, implying that the public power of the government become more inclusive.

Second, the objects of state governance are more comprehensive so that a more timely and accurate response can be made to the actual needs of the people's livelihood. While the boundary of rule may be for a government to retain its power and to

---

[10]The Regan government lodged a clear criticism to the effect that the World Bank contributed to the development of socialist countries at the cost of capitalism, pressuring the Bank to go back in line with the diplomatic goals of the US government, and requiring it to take advantage of the inherent leverage in large loan projects to bring the beneficiary country to the direction of market economy.

[11]Williams and Tom (1994).

protect the interests of the ruling class, governance turns the attention to the public sphere and to protecting and enhancing the people's livelihood and welfare.

Third, the actual practice of governance is more flexible. Regulations and orders of government, laws and regulations and non-obligatory contracts of market organization and social organization can all serve as the sources of authority. The realization of state governance will not be a simple top-down process. On the basis of governmental macro-planning, all types of parallel governance will be more beneficial to improving the vitality and enthusiasm of local, regional and non-governmental participants.

Generally speaking, the concept of governance reflects the spirit of governance in terms of responsibility for the people, participation of local authorities, market force, focus on common interests, and social approval, and hence in line with the progressiveness of the times. The concept is mainly concerned with the problems as to how to legally, efficiently and fairly operate the power of the country.

In the traditional government or rule, government departments represent the only power center of administrating state affairs and social affairs, and the core of state power system is the powerful central government. In a particular period, government continues to expand its administrating functions in fields such as politics, economy, culture and social development, with the administrating power centralized. In the meantime, the size of government is expanded as well, bringing along an increasing number of civil servants, and an expanding fiscal expenditure. In contrast with the expansion of size, the improvement in governmental efficiency and capability lags behind, and sometimes there is even a decline in efficiency and capability. The situation contradicts the expanding and diversified needs of the people.

State governance system demand a reform of the government, restructuring it, market organizations and social organizations, and the relation between the central government and local government, with the ultimate goal of improving the capability of public service and the level of managing public affairs. In a modernized state governance system, maintaining public order, providing public service and dealing with specific public affairs are not only responsibilities of government department, but also responsibilities of non-governmental organization, voluntary civil organizations and market organizations. As for the responsibilities solely belonging to government departments, there should be a more efficient and clear division of labor between the central government and local governments.

Certainly, though government departments are not the only power units in governance system, they still play an indispensable role in decision-making in affairs at both national and local levels, one which cannot be replaced by other organizations. Their task is not limited to a direct execution of power to influence the society and conduct management, but also includes mobilizing other governance subjects to participate in governance, coordinating the relation of all sides, and establishing reasonable modern state governance system. All these tasks make higher requirements of the modernized governance capability of a government.

Since the 1970s and the 1980s, the transformation of governance modes has featured the pursuit of "good governance", which becomes a notable international wave and trend. It can be seen, in the transforming process of state governance modes in both the East and the West, that regardless of the differences in the practice of reforming state governance, the pursuit of "good governance" is the same, whose substantial contents are to reform the range of functions and operating modes of traditional bureaucratic system, and to explore new systems to enhance government efficiency and service quality.

Governments of the Western countries are facing a series of internal problems such as increasing fiscal pressure, rigid bureaucratic system, and lowering government capability to respond to public demands and emergencies, and also a series of external challenges such as financial crisis, economic crisis, environmental crisis, resource crisis, internet safety, and geo-politics. In order to improve state competitiveness and ability of emergency management, adapt to the demands of social development, strengthen the legitimacy and efficiency of government, public departments of Western countries resort to major transformations of their organization patterns and incentive system, and thus bring about a movement of enhancing governance. In the several decades of transformation, Western countries have seen changes and adjustments not only in the contents, modes and methods of government, but also re-positioning in the mutual relation of public department, market organizations and social organizations. These adjustments and reforms perfect the governance system of Western countries, and enhance their governance to a certain degree.

Since the founding of New China, the mode of government has been undergoing transformation, from the mode of a universal government before the adoption of reform and opening-up policy, to transformative modes after. Before the reform and opening-up, China established a "universal government" based on planned economy, aiming at implementing the goals of government and administration by way of government's comprehensive control of social life. Under this mode of government, the relation between the governor and the governed was realized as that between the controller and the controlled, the function of market was narrowed and even canceled, social departments turned into unimportant bodies dependent on the government, and the government obtained an enormous range of functions and power, but operated with strikingly low efficiency. In order to deal with complicated and complex government affairs, the government had to rely on the refining of functions, which led to a giant governing subject consisting of more and more institutions. However, more often than not, there was more than one subject for a single affair, giving rise to the phenomenon of "thousand threads above, and a single needle below". After the reform and opening-up, along with globalization and domestic social and economic development, and the initial establishment of open economic system, market economy and democratic politics have become an irreversible trend for the social and economic development of China. Even so, the Chinese government and society are still in the process of transformation, with institutional establishments including state governance system being in the making and waiting for further improvement.

The modernization of state governance system and governance capability for China should be separated neither from the established experience of other countries, nor from the history of China. Objectively speaking, the political development of China in thousands of years, notwithstanding dynastic cycles, does not undergo fundamental change in terms of political system before New China. In about 100 years since the Revolution of 1911, the Chinese state and society altered fundamentally, but did not form a mature and complete government mode and state governance system. If accepted without criticism, these historical "heritages" may hinder the efforts to deepen the reform of state governance system and to facilitate the modernization of state governance capability; but if accepted with "creative transformation" and with criticism, they may contribute to the modernization of state governance system and governance capability. In sum, it is the historical mission of the CPC and the Chinese government under its leadership to learn and study the experience of the reform of state governance in the Western countries with a view to the history and realities of China, and to explore a route suiting the current political, economic and culture development of China to reform state governance system and build governance capability.

Modernization of state governance system and governance capability is a scientific proposition and strategic judgment made by the decision-makers of China drawing on Western governance theory of the modern times, especially of late 1980s and early 1990s, and on the basis of the lessons and experience of internal and international governance. The Decision on Major Issues Concerning Comprehensively Deepening Reforms rectified by the Third Plenary Session of the 18th CPC Central Committee rectified states that "the general purpose of deepening its all-round reform is to develop socialism with Chinese characteristics, to advance modernization in the State governance system and governance capability." Xi Jinping clearly points out that "a country's national governance system and governance capacity represent a concentrated embodiment of that country's systems and its capacity to enforce those systems. China's national governance system can be understood as a full set of closely linked and coordinated national systems through which the country is governed under the leadership of the Party. It consists of institutions, mechanisms, laws, and regulations with regard to economy, politics, culture, society, ecological progress, and Party building. China's national governance capacity refers to our capacity to administer various social affairs through the application of national systems. This includes promoting reform, development, and stability, handling domestic affairs, foreign affairs, and national defense, and governing the Party, the state, and the armed forces." This important explication provides a scientific demarcation to the connotation of state governance system and governance capability. To have a correct understanding and an accurate grasp the scientific connotation of the two concepts will serve as the basis of thought to advance the modernization of governance system and governance capability. Heads of government departments and researchers also come up with their understanding and interpretation of the modernization of state governance system and governance capability according to their expertise and from their perspectives. Jiang Bixin, the deputy president of the Supreme People's Court, points out that the modernization of state governance system and governance capability is to institutionalize, scientize, normalize and routinize state governance system so as to enable the country's leaders to employ the mentality of rule by law and laws and regulation to govern the country, which will turn the institutional advantages of the socialism with Chinese characteristics into the efficiency and effectiveness of state governance.[12] Yu Keping, the deputy director of Central Compilation and Translation Bureau, stresses that the modernization of a country's governance system can be measured by at least five standards: the first is the institutionalization and normalization of the execution of public power, which demands a complete system for governance by government, market and society to arrange and normalize public order; the second is democracy, that is, public governance and institutional arrangement should ensure that the sovereignty belongs to the people or that the people are the masters of their own country, and all public policies should reflect the will and the subject status of the people; the third is rule by law, that is, the constitution and laws should be considered the highest authority, everyone is equal before the law, and no organization or individual is allowed to possess powers beyond the law; the fourth is efficiency, that is, state governance system should effectively maintain social stability and social order, and be conducive to enhancing the administrative efficiency and economic interest; the fifth is coordination, that is modern state governance system operate as an organic rule system, all levels from the central government to local governments, from government to social governance, and all institutional arrangements should be coordinated as a unified whole, and they cannot be separated.[13] Xin Xiangyang, researcher with the Academy of Marxism, the Chinese Academy of Social Sciences, holds that state governance system is a system and mechanism established with a certain concept of governance so as to ensure the smooth operating of a country, and that state governance capability refers to the level and quality of a country to coordinate subjects of all fields and to handle their relations.[14]

The modernization of state governance system and governance capability is of profound theoretical and practical significance to the future political development, the realization of the cause of socialist construction and the national prosperity of China, and even to international order and the development of the concept of global governance.

In the first place, modernization of state governance system and governance capability is the latest development of the theory of governance. The development is not simply a deduction from one concept to another concept, but adopts the essence of western theories of governance with open-mindedness, draws on the experience and lessons of traditional governance of various countries, and combines the practice of the Chinese revolution and construction, particularly the practice of reform and opening-up, constituting a new paradigm of governance.

In the second, the gradual modernization of state governance system and governance capability will provide a safeguard to the political, economic and social reform of China. After thirty-year development, the reform of China is now entering deep waters. In addition to "crossing the river by feeling for the stones", the country is also in dire need of scientific theories and effective institutional designs based on them for guidance so that various development pitfalls (for example, the middle-income trap, international division of labor dilemma, and Thucydides's trap) can be avoided.

[12]Jiang (2013).

[13]Yu (2013).

[14]Xin (2014).

Finally, the modernization of state governance system and governance capability will contribute to the reform of international economic governance system and the formation of a new international order. The international financial crisis has broken the "myth" of the neoliberal concept of governance, and a new widely-accepted concept of governance is yet to come. International multilateral governance has reached a standstill or predicament, various types of regional, cross-regional mechanism have sprung up, and international governance moves along the tendency of "fragmentation". The exploration of state governance system and governance capability by the Chinese government and the Chinese people will enrich the "toolbox" of governance for humanities' striving for good governance, and will contribute to the formation of a new international economic order.

Actively Participating in Global Governance

Global governance refers to "the sum total of self-imposed international systems, rules and mechanisms established by a multi-centered international community consisting of states or economic bodies in order to deal with problems of a global nature; or for the lack of a world government, the process to overcome the malfunction of international politics and market by international participants via joint efforts."[15]Global governance is mainly concerned with the five aspects of equality, democracy, cooperation, responsibility and regulation.[16] It is clear that in an international community without a world government, China can only participate in global governance by way of advocating joint efforts to overcome the malfunction of international politics and market, and enhancing the improvement of relevant institutions. To this end, it is necessary for China to adhere to values common to humanity, and to propose some principles and set the example in sticking to them with the aim of normalizing its own behaviors and influencing others.

1. Participation in global governance should be in accordance with the goals of the UN Charter

The UN Charter is considered as the fundamental law of the United Nations. It establishes the goals, principles and organization setting for the UN, prescribes the responsibilities, rights and obligation of its member states, and lays the basic principles and methods to handle international relations and to keep world peace and security. It is an inescapable responsibility for each member state to comply with the UN Charter and to uphold the authority of the UN.

The Preamble of the UN Charter solemnly advocates "faith…in the equal rights… of nations large and small"; the first article establishes the goal of developing "friendly relations among nations based on respect for the principle of equal rights and self-determination of peoples"; the first section of Article 2 specifically stipulates that

---

[15]Zhang and Ren (2015).

[16]Zhang (2016).

"the Organization is based on the principle of the sovereign equality of all its Members," the seventh section states that "nothing contained in the present Charter shall authorize the United Nations to intervene in matters which are essentially within the domestic jurisdiction of any state"; and again Article 78 says that the relationship among Members of the United Nations "shall be based on respect for the principle of sovereign equality".

It can be seen that the UN Charter stresses national sovereignty and equal rights of different countries, listing it as the first among all principles and treating is as a fundamental organizing principle of the United Nations, from which other principles follow. The principle of equal sovereignty includes the following elements: first, all nations enjoy an equal legal status; second, all nations are fully entitled to the rights inherent in their sovereignty; third, all nations have the obligation to respect the dignity of other nations; fourth, a nation's territorial integrity and political independence is inviolable; fifth, all nations are entitled to choose and develop their political, social, economic and cultural system; sixth, all nations shall fully and honestly fulfill their international obligations and peacefully coexist with other nations. The recognition of equal sovereignty by all nations constitute the basis for mutual trust among nations.

It is a historical necessity that the UN Charter stresses the importance of the principle of equal sovereignty. Before the establishment of the principle, each trying to cheat the other and jungle law were common practice in international relations. Industrial revolution in particular brought some countries into the stage of modern capitalist production ahead of other. These capitalist countries enjoying early development, with their powerful guns and ships, practiced colonization and expansion in the vast area of Asia, Africa and Latin America by way of unfair treaties, carved up the world for interests with bloody means, and incorporated the labor and resources of backward countries into the colonial and semi-colonial system with themselves as the centre. In such a system, they held absolute suzerainty. They exercised their control by sending out officials or fostering local deputies, exploited local raw materials and labor by taking advantage of their suzerainty, and dumped manufactured goods into these places.

The conduct of the big bullying the small, and of the strong bullying the weak encouraged the practical logic of infidelity and striving exclusively for profit. In such an atmosphere, keeping integrity and sticking to international justice would incur damage, while obtaining profits with no scruples and against morality were respected. In the Paris Peace Conference of 1919, China as a party of the Allies who have won the First World War was required to transfer its sovereignty interests in Shandong Peninsula taken by Germany to Japan. The proposal lodged by China to retrieve its rights to Shandong was vetoed. The issue gave a full explication to the fact that in an international system lacking equality and mutual trust, the weak would fall into the miserable situation of being a prey to be carved up by big powers, even if it was on the winning side.

The two world wars, the Second in particular, awakened the national awareness of Asian, African and Latin American countries. Small and weak colonized or semi-colonized countries seized the opportunity to take actions to retrieve their rights, when the power of capitalist countries was on the decrease. To annul unfair treaties was the major appeal of these colonial and semi-colonial countries. The UN Charter establishes equal sovereignty and thus provides a institutional confirmation and encouragement for these countries to strive for equal status, and lays a solid foundation for the normal post-war international relations and international order.

China was a country which suffered severely and harshly from the invasion of big powers especially Japan in modern times. The nation staged a hard and long struggle against unfair treat by the invaders, and obtained a hard-won victory. By the turn of the century, China fell victim again to the Charter-trampling conducts of some countries and organizations in the Embassy Bombing Incident. Because of the indelible memory of the hardships caused by the invasion wars and the domineering behaviors of the imperialist countries, China will continue its tireless pursuit of peace and equality with more determined stance and uphold the authority of the principle of sovereignty equality as established by the UN Charter.

2. Participation in global governance should be based on the five principles of peaceful coexistence

The five principles of peaceful coexistence are the basic principles in normal international relations, exchange and cooperation, which are proposed by the Chinese government and jointly advocated by the Indian and Burmese governments. In 60 years, the five principles of "mutual respect for sovereignty and territorial integrity, mutual non-aggression, non-interference in each other's internal affairs, equality and mutual benefit, and peaceful coexistence" serve not only as the basis for China's independent foreign policy of peace, but are also accepted by most countries of the world, turning into important rules for international relations.

Since their first written presentation in a formal international document, the five principles of peaceful coexistence manifest the meaning and expectation to enhance mutual trust in international community on the basis of equality in a general sense. On April 29, 1954, the five principles of peaceful coexistence were formally written into the preface to the Agreement between the China and India on Trade and Intercourse between the Tibet Region of China and India. On June 28 of the same year, a joint communique issued by both the Chinese and the Indian premier stated, "the premiers of both countries reaffirm these principles (i.e., the five principles of peaceful coexistence), and believe that these principles should be applied to the relations between them and countries of Asia and the world. If these principles are applied not only to the relations among nations, but also to general international relations, they will serve as the basis for peace and security. Then what is currently feature and doubt will be replaced by trust."

Mutual respect for sovereignty and territorial integrity is the premise and basis for equality and mutual trust. Sovereignty and territorial integrity are core interests of a nation. There can be no mutual trust if core interests are not respected. Only with respect for each other's core concerns can be conditions established for equal treatment and peace. Mutual respect implies unswervingly safeguarding one's own sovereignty and territorial integrity without impinging on the core interests of other countries. Comrade Xi Jinping addressed it, "while pursuing peaceful development, we will never sacrifice our legitimate rights and interests or China's core interests. No foreign country should expect China to trade off its core interests or swallow bitter fruit that undermines China's sovereignty, security or development interests. China is pursuing peaceful development, and so are other countries. This is the sure way for all the countries in the world to seek common development and peaceful coexistence. … China will never seek development at the expense of any other country's interests, nor will it shift its problems onto others. We will actively pursue peaceful and common development, uphold the multilateral trade system and participate in global economic governance."[17]

Mutual non-aggression and non-interference in each other's internal affairs are the basic demands of peaceful coexistence, equality and mutual trust. Historically, aggression and interference are always "privileges" of power politics and hegemonism. The five principles of peaceful coexistence and the independent foreign policy of peace proposed and practiced by China are China's promises of never pursuing hegemony and expansion to the world. Never pursuing hegemony is in line with both the strategic thoughts of China and the basic state policy. The country does not pursue hegemony now, and will not pursue hegemony when it becomes powerful in the future. The ideal for China is to establish an equal, fair and reasonable world. To achieve the ideal, leaders of New China since Mao Zedong consistently adhere to the basic policy of never pursuing hegemony, which is a message to the world and also a norm restraining itself. Although China does not pursue hegemony and participate in hegemonic competition, it will not tolerate hegemonic conducts in international community. In the face of unfair and unjust power politics, China will not turn a blind eye and retire into its own world. China will always serve as a staunch force in fighting against aggression and interference and in maintaining world peace.

The principle of mutual benefit sets a higher demand of equality and mutual trust, and also serves as a positive guarantee to the sustainability of peaceful coexistence. On the basis of equality and mutual trust, different countries can learn from other's strong points to offset their weakness, draw on the lessons of others and make common progress; the people of all countries can share the results of world economic, scientific and technological, social and cultural development. These shared interests can improve the overall benefits of peaceful coexistence, for which reason the people will value even more the international environment of equal treatment and peaceful coexistence, stay alert to forces which may do harm to such an environment, and break the plot of domestic interest groups, which seek profits by exploiting other countries and kidnapping national policy-making.

3. To advance global governance should pay attention to the diversity of civilizations and the inclusiveness of economic growth

Inclusiveness and mutual learning are the basic principles in handling international relations under the contemporary conditions. Recognition of and respect for the diversity of civilizations provide the premise and impetus for inclusiveness and mutual learning. Civilization (*wenming*) in Chinese originally means *bright culture* and *flourished education*, and now refers to a social condition of humanity which

---

[17] Xi (2013).

breaks out of backwardness and barbarism, reaching a higher level of development and culture. The English word *civilization* is derived from Latin *civilis*, which has the reference of the process of "urbanizing" and "citizenship", then comes to refer to "division of labor" and "cooperation", that is, a situation in which people live harmoniously in a "social community", and also an advanced stage of social and cultural development and the process of achieving such as a stage. There is no evidence in the history of the Western world and the East showing that a single path exists to achieve the stage of flourished education or advanced harmonious situation, no way to determine a single mode of division of labor or cooperation for building civilization, and no valid argument to prove that there is an ultimate condition to which all civilizations will move.

From the evolution of civilization, civilizations always reflect and suit their own geographical environment, climatic and phenological conditions, resources and special products. As a matter of fact, the major civilizations of the world strongly assume geographical features of their birth places. The Mesopotamian civilization originated in Tigris and Euphrates, hence the name two-river civilization; the ancient Egyptian civilization had its origin in the Niles; there was the Indian civilization along the Indus in sub-continental South Asia; the east Mediterranean enjoyed the Aegean civilization; and the Yellow River and the Yangtze River provided the cradle for the Chinese civilization. Up till now, there are more than 200 countries and regions in the world with a population of 6 billion divided into over 2,500 nationalities speaking more than 6,000 languages, converting to many religious beliefs such as Christianity, Catholicism, Islam, Buddhism and Taoism. The colorful world is created jointly by the people of different colors, languages and cultural backgrounds. The Convention on the Protection and Promotion of the Diversity of Cultural Expressions rectified by the United Nations Education, Science and Culture Organization (UNESCO) on October 21, 2005 affirms in the very beginning that "cultural diversity is a defining characteristic of humanity", and points out that the significance of cultural diversity lies in the fact that "cultural diversity creates a rich and varied world, which increases the range of choices and nurtures human capacities and values, and therefore is a mainspring for sustainable development for communities, peoples and nations."

To achieve inclusiveness and mutual learning and to actually "turn the diversity of our world and difference among countries into dynamism and driving force for development",[18] it requires respect for the diversity of civilizations in addition to recognizing it. But it is nothing easy. In the long history of humanity, discrimination against alien groups and genocides never stop. The genocide of Hitler, the "melting pot" of the United States, the "Russification" by the Soviet Union, the apartheid in South Africa, the "integration" in Mexico, and the "Macedonianization" of Bulgaria are memories engraved in the minds of the present generation of mankind. Some theories expounding the confrontation and conflicts of civilizations are also based on the diversity or differences of civilizations. More severe consequences would be caused by only recognizing differences without tolerating and respecting diversity than just ignoring differences.

[18] Xi (2013).

For inclusiveness and mutual learning, we need an aesthetic perspective to look at the diversity of civilizations. Unlike material wealth which represents the sum total of things that can be accurately measured and compared, a civilization also includes incommensurable spiritual elements. These elements should not be viewed as obstacles for communication or reasons for confrontation. On the contrary, an appreciation of these elements may bring new insights and consolation, and instigate tremendous creativity. Karl Marx once posed such a question, "you admire the delightful variety, the inexhaustible riches of nature. You do not demand that the rose should smell like the violet, but must the greatest riches of all, the spirit, exist in only *one* variety?"[19] Xi Jinping also point out, "culture exchange needs not only mutual understanding and respect, but also overcoming prejudices and misunderstandings. Cultural diversity is an objective fact of humanity, and also a fundamental feature of the modern world. The differences in ideology, social system, and development mode shall not hinder the exchange between civilizations and lead to confrontation. We should actively protect the diversity of civilizations, promote dialogues between different civilizations, learn from each other rather than confronting each other, and make the world more colorful."[20]

The diversity of development paths and the corresponding social systems provides the sources for the diversity of civilizations. To respect the diversity of civilization is first of all to respect the independence of each society, which bears all the contents of a civilization, in choosing its own system and development path, and to recognize its basic right to self-determination. "Only the wearer shoes knows if they fit or not. Only the people can best tell if the development path they have chosen for their country suits or not."[21]

Some countries, however, relying on the economic and technological advantages obtained from colonialism, aggressively export their political modes, cultural concepts and development path under the banner of "human rights", "freedom" and "democracy", "transplant their experience" to other countries and regions while disregarding their concrete condition. They stigmatize and demonize development modes different from theirs, "let go of those who comply with their methods, and punish those who do not". Their domineering attitudes do not only pose a major threat to the national culture and spirit of other countries, but also a potential major threat to the sovereignty and political security of other countries. To this situation, Deng Xiaoping made the follow insightful remarks, "... they often infringe upon the sovereignty of poor, weak countries of the Third World. Their talk about human rights, freedom and democracy is only designed to safeguard the interests of the strong, rich countries, which take advantage of their strength to bully weak countries, and which pursue hegemony and practice power politics."[22] Besides, some countries wantonly interfere in other countries' internal affairs and even wage war for their interests, disregarding the diversity and complexity of historical traditions, ethnic relations and social envi-

---

[19]Marx (1995).

[20]Xi (2009).

[21]Xi (2013).

[22]Deng (1993).

ronment of other countries. In the long history of mankind, the development path of the imperial states which attempted to encroach upon other countries and nations and even to eradicate them by power always became narrowed, and gradually moved to decline and final demise. The Ottoman Empire which crossed Asia, Africa and Europe and the Mongolian Empire which swept across Europe all inevitably fell into decline.

China advocates the diversity of development path since ancient times, stressing that "gentlemen seek harmony but not uniformity". The chapter of the mean in *the Book of Rites* (*Li Ji*) has it that "in dealing with others, goodness should be praised and inability should be pitied, and it is the way of appeasing them", meaning that on occasions of international communication, we should sing highly of the good will and conduct of others and consider and handle their deficiencies rationally so that distant countries and nations will live in peace. If all states especially big powers can understand the development path of other countries out of good will, adopt a rational attitude towards differences or "deficiencies", objectively analyze the causes thereof, and peacefully bridge these differences, a long-lasting world peace can be achieved. There is another ancient parable of China which warns that even if it is out of good will that one's will is imposed on others, a tragedy may still follow. The story in *Zhuangzi* goes like this: the Emperor of the South Sea is known as Change. The Emperor of the North Sea is called Dramatic; the Emperor of the Centre is called Chaos. Change and Dramatic met every so often in the region of Chaos. Chaos always treated them kindly and virtuously. Change and Dramatic said, "Everyone has seven orifices so they can see, hear, eat and breathe. Chaos does not have these. Let us bore some holes into him." Each day they bored a hole into Chaos, but on the seventh day Chaos died. In world of incomplete information, the apple of one's eye can be others' poison. For one to interfere in others' business and do things on their behalf may realize its own "high standards" in appearance, but actually violate the objective laws of social development for local areas and thus result in severe consequences. With respect to the big problems concerning the rise and fall of a nation and the welfare of the people, the limitedness of human rationality must be acknowledged, a vigilant eye must be kept on intellectual and moral conceit, and the development path chosen by the local people must be respected.

Undoubtedly, China has gone on a socialist path suiting Chinese characteristics. As we have discussed above, there is a view in the West to the effect that Western countries practicing "democratic system" are herbivorous, and countries practicing other systems are carnivorous, whose existence itself poses a threat to the former, and the threat can only be eliminated by promoting "democracy" and staging "color revolution", by turning carnivorous animals into herbivorous animals. The metaphor highlights the differences among development paths or systems, but exchanges the concept of "difference" by "rivalry". The Chinese path does not pose a threat to other countries. First, the basic experience of the Chinese system or path is to combine external experience and theories with the Chinese characteristics and practice. China bears no ill will against any country with the Western countries included, adopting their experience and practice with a positive and open attitude with restricting itself by ideological differences. Second, in the process of exploring a development path suiting its conditions, China has met with setbacks and suffered from foreign interferences. "Do unto others as you would be done by." China will not impose the kind of sufferings and hardships it has went through on other countries or regions. Third, the Chinese path is still in progress by trial and error, cannot be said to be perfect. Although some countries show strong interest in the Chinese path and experience, while helping these countries, China never does things beyond its scope of power, never seeks to turn its development path into a role model. Rather, China adopts a very prudent attitude towards the expansion of its experience, and encourages these countries to explore their own path. Xi Jinping in a speech made in Tanzania said, "there is no one-size-fits-all development model in the world. The diversity of civilizations and development models should be respected by all. China will continue to firmly support African countries in their quest for development paths that suit their national conditions and increase exchanges of experience in governance with African countries. This will enable us to draw on each other's time-honored civilizations and development practices, and better promote the common development and prosperity of China and Africa."[23]

The idea of "inclusiveness and mutual learning" is proposed on the basis of traditional Chinese wisdom and a characterization of current practice of international relation. Inclusiveness means the ability to accommodate differences. "Things are generated with materials, but identical materials do not generate new things." That is, new things can only come into being by the harmonious interaction of different things. The underlying key is to learn from each other. The countries of the world enjoy different conditions and varied restrictions. If looking at the world with a stereotype of "whoever does not belong to us is a barbarian", one would be extremely arrogant, complacent and conservative, if not being constantly involved in energy-depleting conflicts. One can only accumulate experience and lessons so as to achieve steady development by modestly learning from the advantages of other countries and avoid making mistakes they have made.

The inclusiveness as in "inclusive growth" is identical with that in "inclusiveness and mutual learning". The former focuses on that aspect of growth which may benefit all countries, regions and people. As a new concept of economic development, inclusive growth is oriented towards the values of equality, justice, sharing and compatibility. What is advocated by the concept is equal rights, just rules, achievement sharing and interest compatibility. To summarize, inclusive growth is at least related to the three following dimensions:

First, inclusive growth should taken man as the foundation, benefiting everyone. Over the past 20 years, the world in economic globalization has realized fairly rapid development, while the income gap between the rich nations and the poor is widening. Within many countries, the same is true of the gap between high-income and low-income groups. The widening gap gives rise to a series of contradictions. Recently, some scholars have listed income distribution inequality at global level as one of the biggest threats to humanity in the future years, and more and more men of insight all

---

[23]Xi (2013).

over the world have treated enhancing the inclusiveness of development as a basic strategy to meet the major challenges confronting humanity.

Second, growth is the cause for each country and even for each individual. Even though by inclusive growth, people normally refer to the first dimension above, the responsibilities taken by each country and each individual should not be ignored. The general improvement of welfare is a goal of social progress, and this can only be achieved by the hard work of each and every one in the country. There are differences about the endowment and starting points among nations, and for individuals, there are also differences in ability and opportunity. All these differences may lead to the difference in economic growth rate, and in the amount of income. But it is no reason to exempt the responsibility of each country and each individual for their own growth. They are supposed to make due contributions rather than share the achievement of economic growth by waiting for assistance or charity.

Third, inclusiveness should be united with growth. Inclusiveness is manifested in development achievements justly shared and job opportunities fairly obtained, which should not hinder growth. The improvement of the overall human welfare has only one source, that is, economic development. Without economic development, common prosperity would be waters without sources and trees without roots. In this sense, growth has a priority over inclusiveness. For a relatively backward country in the process of fast industrialization and urbanization, the public have even stronger expectations for quickly improving their livelihood by way of economic development, and such a country should special attention to growth. On the other hand, when inclusiveness could not be fully guaranteed, the conditions and basis for development would collapse, because without social harmony and stability, economic development would not be sustainable. Here inclusive growth presents itself as a specific concept: the relation between inclusiveness and development is not an "either/or". We should make efforts to harmoniously unify economic development and common prosperity. When designing institutions in order to promote economic development, a consideration should be given to inequality; and when designing institutions with equality as the top priority, the design should pay special attention not to damage efficiency.

Inclusiveness and mutual learning can contribute to the inclusive growth of world economy and achieving common prosperity of the world. If quality in rights, opportunity and rules is to be achieved, the spirit of inclusiveness and mutual learning in international relations must be upheld. For example, giving a special concern and treatment to the right to exist and develop for developing countries; assisting developing countries and underdeveloped regions in enhancing their ability of self developing, enabling them to share the achievements of economic globalization; adhering to fair competition in international economy and trade, advocating liberalization of trade and investment, and objecting against trade protectionism of any type, to establish an open and just trade and investment environment for the development of all countries and regions, and for the recovery of world economy. All these practices, to developing countries especially underdeveloped regions, are to "teach one how to fish" rather than "just give one fish", ultimately contributing to enhancing the overall level of world economy.

4. To promote global governance should advocate the awareness of human beings sharing a community of common destiny.

Community is a concept originating in sociology, referring to human collectivity formed on the basis of blood ties, geography and culture. People within a community share common values and traditions, which reflect their shared feelings, beliefs and consciousness of collectivity, binding the homogenous individuals together. One basic function of a community is to provide a degree of certainty and security for the lives of its members, who maintain a close social relation of mutual dependence, mutual trust and mutual assistance.

The concept of community as in "human beings sharing a community of common destiny" transcends its sociological sense. First, it transcends the limited range of blood ties, geography and culture, treating human beings as a collectivity sharing common interests and cause and providing mutual assistance. Such a community follows as a result of the evolution and deepening of economic globalization. Driven by technological advancement, capital, labor, resources, land, knowledge and beliefs of the world start to transcend geographical boundaries, and come to be deeply integrated into a limitless global network. Underlying the process is the globalization of a series of institutions and rules. In general, globalization enhances work efficiency and improves people's livelihood, and in the meantime, human behaviors and destiny are increasingly subject to the adjustment and control of the global governing system. The Asian financial crisis of 1997, the American subprime crisis of 2007 and the subsequent European sovereign debt crisis of 2010 all show that there are institutional deficiencies in current globalization. Some countries and regions start to adopt measures of financial and trade protectionism, multi-lateral cooperation gets into trouble, and a trend of anti-globalization is on the rise. However, the Chinese leader firmly stated, "despite the impact of the financial crisis which has changed to a certain degree the situation of economic growth of the world, the general trend of deepening globalization does not change. The Chinese government holds that should future international financial crisis occur, governments of all countries are supposed to take their responsibility for advancing economic globalization in the direction of balanced, all-beneficial and all-winning development...We are strongly against and firmly resist protectionism of all types, upholding a fair, free and open system of global trade and investment."[24] Only with an acute sense and an accurate understanding of the general trend of the world development can the historical necessity of a new starting point for globalization be grasped in the face of major setbacks, and can a concept of human beings sharing a community of common destiny be proposed so as to lay a solid foundation of concept and feeling for globalization at material level and institutional level.

Second, the concept of human beings sharing a community of common destiny is to solve or to deal with uncertainty and security problems common to all members of human society rather than limited to a certain group of people. These problems follow from the continual surge of international problems and a lack of coordination by something positive like a world government. International problems are closely

[24] Xi (2010).

related to globalization. In the first place, globalization brings international problems about, and then these problems push the people to a perilous situation and call for attention to and reflections of globalization. Along with the deepening of globalization, problems such as population, food supply, climate change and environment pollution, depletion of unrecyclable resources, drug dealing and organized crimes, terrorism and the turmoil of international monetary and financial system become worse. However, the lack of a world government or the anarchism of international community decreases the efficiency of cooperation of all countries to deal with these problems. The profits incurred by solving international problems will be shared by the entire humanity, but the cost generated is to be borne by one country or one nation. From a narrow-minded perspective of nationalism and statism, the imbalance between cost and benefit will lower the effectiveness of global governance. If all countries look at the matter in this way and refuse assuming their major-country responsibilities, the international cooperation oriented to the solution of international problems will even collapse. To advocate the concept of human beings sharing a community of common destiny is aimed at putting the entire humanity in a position of facing these problems together. People of all nations, religions and cultures meeting shared challenges together will put their stereotypes aside, treat each other with honesty, make their due efforts, and finally dissolve risks.

Third, a community of common destiny for humanity is not the present world arrived at and being enjoyed, but a world we are strongly aspiring to inhabit and hope to possess. The birth and establishment of such a concept will provide a credible rational and emotional basis for all countries to move toward cooperation and mutual benefits. However, it should be noted that there is a large gap between the current world and the ideal community of common destiny for humanity. To bridge the gap requires joint efforts of all countries and particularly credible actions on the part of major countries, playing a pioneering and exemplar role.

It is China's responsibility and the right time to advocate the concept of human beings sharing a community of common destiny. The traditional Chinese thoughts feature cosmopolitanism (the *Tianxia* Doctrine) and uphold the spirit of responsibility. *The Family Analects of Confucius* records the following story. The King of Chu State once travelled outside, and lost his bow. His servants suggested going back to find it, but the King said there was no need, for it would be the people of Chu who found the bow. On the anecdote, Confucius commented that the King of Chu has not a mind broad enough. He could respond by just saying that "a person lost the bow, and a person got it", and there was no need mentioning the Chu State he belonged to. It is necessary to uphold the spirit of "not mentioning Chu" to advocate and establish a community of common destiny for humanity so as to promote economic globalization in the direction of balanced, all-beneficial and all-winning development, and to solve international problems. In practice, China has already taken some actions with a view to the concept, which provide credible evidence for China's proposal. During the Asian financial crisis of 1997, China, under enormous internal and external economic pressure, kept its promise not to devalue its currency, RMB, in the meantime provided financial assistance to neighboring countries like Thailand which was severely hit by the crisis, got through difficulties together with

East Asian countries, and won worldwide praise of the international community. Currently, developed countries among the major countries of the world are showing initial and yet unstable signs of economic recovery, the development of other emerging economies is facing many unfavorable factors, and uncertainty of world economy is on the rise. The critical situation requires strengthened international coordination and cooperation for all countries to go through these difficulties. China wishes to advocate with other countries the awareness of a community of common destiny for humanity, and to make contributions to stabilizing world economy.

In the spirit of a community of common destiny for humanity, China proposes the basic principle of "wide consultation, joint construction and shared benefits" for its participation in global governance. In a community of common destiny for humanity, no single country can have the final say, and international affairs should be managed by all countries through consultation.[25] Wide consultation refers to the consultation by all participants in establishing the basic principles, key areas, rules and mechanisms, and development planning for global governance so as to reach consensus; joint construction refers to the reform and innovation of global governance system by taking advantage of the strong points and potentials of all parties; shared benefits refer to the sharing of achievements and interests of global governance by all participant. The idea of "wide consultation, joint construction and shared benefits" upholds drawing on the wisdom of all participants, giving full play to the strong points of each participant, each making efforts according to its ability, and all sharing the achievements. The idea fully reflects the openness and inclusiveness of China's participation in global governance, which is in line with the development trend of the democratization of international relations. To practice this idea, a full play should be given to the initiative and activeness of all actors especially that of the developing countries, everyone's concerns and demands of should be heeded, all just interests should be protected, and all participants should be enabled to benefit from a good global governance.[26]

5. To promote global governance requires joint responsibilities and the fulfillment of major-country responsibilities.

China will stick to the same principle of "common but differentiated responsibilities" in its cooperation with every cooperator such as the United States, the neighboring countries, and other cooperators. Participants should take due responsibilities and bear common international responsibilities. Due to the differences in rights, power and strong points among countries, their responsibilities should be differentiated. The principle of "common but differentiated responsibilities" is not only conducive to the equality and justice in the distribution of responsibilities, but also to the effectiveness of cooperation which leads to the realization of mutual benefit.

Common responsibilities do not mean equal responsibilities. The distribution of responsibilities should be conducted according to the principle of "common but differentiated". That is to say, on the one hand, all members of international community,

---

[25]Xi (2013).

[26]Zhang (2016).

big or small, powerful or weak, should bear responsibilities of making due contributions to solving international problems according to their ability; on the other, the range, scale, mode and time limit of these responsibilities should be differentiated according to the ability and feature of each member in accordance with the principles of international law. The principle of "common but differentiated responsibilities" is not a principle of shirking responsibilities, but one of enhancing the equality and efficiency of responsibilities and solving problems. Fundamentally speaking, the principle manifests the ideas of the balance between rights and responsibilities, and the combination of equality with efficiency.

The equal and just distribution of international responsibilities cannot be separated from rights. "That rights should be matched with responsibilities" is a widely acknowledged principle of international law. In the current international political and economic system, the establishment of all rules and mechanisms is dominated by developed economies, and countries of established interests as represented by the United States are the major beneficiaries of these rules and mechanisms, while emerging and developing economies cannot receive equal treatment, and they cannot exert the kind of influence matching their power. Although China has become the second biggest economy of the world in 2010, its discourse power and right of speech in international affairs lag far behind developed economies such as the United States. Under the circumstance, if China simply take the same responsibilities as other developed countries, it is not only unfair and unreasonable to China, but also against widely acknowledge principles of internal law, which may serve as a source of inequality and instability.

The equal and just distribution of international responsibilities cannot be separated from concrete process. Take environment and climate change as an example. The distribution of relevant responsibilities should be conducted in accordance with the principle of "whoever consumes pays". The industrialization of developed countries was realized on the basis of long-term consumption of the resources of the earth and severe pollution of the environment, which is a major cause for today's global environmental problems. Even now, developed countries such as the United States are consuming a major portion of the common resources shared by human beings. According to the BP Statistical Review of World Energy 2016 and the calculation of the World Bank, the United State with a population taking up 4.4% of the world consumed 19.7% of oil of the world in 2015, 4.5 times of per capita oil consumption of the world, while China's per capita oil consumption only accounted for 15.4% of that of the United States. Accordingly, developed countries such as the United States should bear more responsibilities rather than practice "egalitarianism" in the distribution of responsibilities.

In addition, the distribution of international responsibilities cannot be separated from the principle of efficiency. The reasonable distribution of international responsibilities among countries is an important reflection of the principle of efficiency. The distribution should take into account the advantages of different countries in different fields, giving a full play their respective strong points and roles. With respect to settling bilateral, regional and international problems, China and the United States each has its own strong points. In order to effectively settle problems confronting them both, the two countries should lead the efforts in their respective fields of expertise, making more contributions. China is a country whose growth rate ranks among the top in the world, has the largest amount of foreign reserve with the biggest trade surplus, and holds the largest amount of the US treasury securities. The United States is the biggest power of the world, possessing incomparable power in economy, military force and science and technology. In many major international problems, the function of the United States is indispensable, which cannot be replaced by other countries.

China has a long history of "combining interests and justice", "valuing justice more than interests", and "giving up interests to obtain justice", and the traditional idea of interests and justice has been incorporated in the concept and practice of China's foreign policy. President Xi Jinping proposes that diplomatic work should stick to the correct view of interests and justice, which will lead the Chinese diplomacy to new stage of activeness, development and expansion. He points out: justice reflects one of our views, it is the view of Party members, and of socialist country. Some people in the world live fairly well, some do not, it is not a good sign. True joy and happiness is the joy of all and the happiness of all. We hope that the world can develop together, particularly we hope that developing countries can step up their development. Interests demand the adherence to the principle of "mutual benefit". We should realize a win-win situation rather the situation where I win and you lose. We are obligated to provide assistance to poor countries according to our ability, and sometimes we should even value justice more than interests, and give up interests to obtain justice, but never pay attention only to interests and be preoccupies with interests.

To adhere to the correct view of interests and justice is a solemn promise on the part of China to the international community. It means that China will never be a "free rider" who enjoys everything and doing nothing in the international system. Rather it will actively participate in international affairs starting from righteous cause of world peace and development, sticking to its roles of a practitioner of peaceful development, a promoter of common development, a protector of multi-lateral trade system, and a participant of global economic governance, making more contribution to advancing the process of humanity. If a tree stands over the forest, the wind will hit it. Recently, China is increasingly charged of "irresponsibility". The correct view of interests and justice is a best response to such charges. Xi Jinping's important thought of sticking to the correct view of interests and justice in diplomatic work further enriches the core values of China in foreign affairs. The thought is not only significant in guiding diplomatic work of the new times, revealing the moral aspect of the Chinese dream, but also adds to the treasury of values shared by humanity.

To adhere to the correct view of interests and justice demands a corresponding action strategy. The strategy should neither ignore foreign affairs, nor require China to bear unlimited responsibilities to the international community, but enable the country to take actions flexibly and sustainably to achieve the unity between interests and justice. The strategy can be characterized by "diffusing pressure", "proper responsibility", "inclusive development", "gradual reform", "rational response" and "support of public opinion".

The first is "diffusing pressure". China has an enormous economic volume, which develops at a very fast speed. This has given shock to the established international order and posed as a threat to the interests of countries of vested interests such as the United States, turning China into a major object to defend against for them. China is now under a lot of pressure, which mainly comes from international rules. There is in international community a loud call for China to accept the current international rules. "Diffusing pressure" means that China will adopt the policy of "cooperation", and lay more emphasis on "the collective rise of emerging economies and developing countries", into which the rejuvenation of China is incorporated. Specific measures include strengthening the cooperation of "BRICS countries", continuing to enrich the contents of BRICS cooperation by introducing new cooperative modes or new fields such as currency and finance, food safety and resources supply, promoting the institutionalization of the mechanism of the BRICS platform, and expanding it to BRICS Plus in a proper time to include others. Countries of first choice for BRICS Plus can be emerging economies within G20 (which is E11 with South Korea included).

Besides, the measures also include strengthening the cooperation among member nations of the Shanghai Cooperation Organization, and promoting the negotiations for the "Free Trade Zone" of China, Japan and South Korea.

The second is "proper responsibilities". For an emerging major country like China, it is not only necessary but also a must to bear international responsibilities according to its own ability. There are three principles concerning bearing international responsibilities: first, responsibilities must match with rights; second, bearing responsibility must be in line with national conditions and according one's own ability; third, the relations between short-term interests and long-term interests and between local interests and collective interests must be well addressed. In today's world, developed countries headed by the United States dominate the process of establishing international rules, and most of these rules are not neutral, but in the meantime, it should be noted that one important feature of rules or regulations is that they restrict the behaviors of one's own as well others'.

The third is "inclusive development". Peaceful development serves as a very good concept of diplomatic strategy, playing a positive and important role in establishing a favorable international environment for China's development. But today and in the future, it is not enough stress the peaceful and non-threatening nature of China's development. Its inclusiveness should also be emphasized, that is, the development of China is surely to bring benefits to the world, and all countries can obtain opportunities for welfare improvement from China's development. To stress the international inclusiveness of China's development is also an important part of China's international responsibilities. The development of China has an aspect of externality, which can be positive and negative. In comparison with "peaceful development", China will pay more attention to "positive externality", and does its best to limit "negative externality". The fourth is "gradual reform". China is in a position of acceptor with regard to the current international rules and systems. When we become powerful, some demands will probably be made to pursue the change of some rules and systems. High expectations are held in this respect, but I believe that there is still a long way to go. It is not only realistic but also unnecessary to fundamentally alter the unreasonable international order or rule, or more precisely, international order or rules more favorable to countries of vest interests. What we need to do and can do in the next decade is to take advantage of opportunities and combine with other major emerging economies to gradually make local changes to the non-neutral international rules currently adopted, aiming at the effect of "converging water drops into a river".

The fifth is "rational response". China is new on the road to the great national rejuvenation, and moving ever closer to this historical process. One important condition for the promising tendency is a peaceful external environment. The biggest threat to the China's rejuvenation is war, especially wars involving China and wars between China and its neighboring countries. Currently and in a certain period of time ahead, China will pay a special attention to the "intensity" in its efforts to safeguard its land and sea sovereignty, "aiming at perfection". In the meantime, China should take account of the harm of extreme nationalism, and be wary of the risk of falling into the pitfall of arms race.

The last is "support of public opinion". A good "story" is needed to establish an environment for expounding and upholding the theory of "peaceful development" and "inclusive development". The story should show that the national rejuvenation of China and the improvement of the welfare of the entire humanity supplement each other so that the development and rise of China can be accepted and acknowledged by the international community.

Strengthening and Extending Regional Security Network in the Spirit of "the Big Serving the Small"

The Sino-US relation is the pillar of the world stability, but a sustainable stable Sino-US relation cannot be established by the compliance or obedience of one side. From the perspective of China, a stable relation with its neighboring countries is the basis for the country to sit at the table with the Unites States to negotiate with words rather than guns.

Historically, China's foreign policy concerning its regional environment has made a detour. Only with a clear understanding of the logic of its evolution can its previous functions and present limitations be grasped, and can a reasonable future choice be made. In plain words, since the founding of New China, its foreign policy and strategy concerning the regional environment have undergone several models such as "one-sided" policy, "output" policy and "drawing back" policy, and now are meeting the demands and challenges of "going out".

Right before the founding of New China, in articled entitled On the People's Democratic Dictatorship published in *People's Daily*, Mao Zedong proposed the "one-sided" foreign policy, which means that China would swing to the side of socialist camp headed by the Soviet Union in international and foreign affairs. Though the "one-sided" policy was not without controversy, the substantial contents following from the policy and their consequences are indisputable: China acknowledged Soviet Union's position of "Big Brother", in matters concerning foreign relation consulted the Soviet Communist Party,[27] in trade "opted for doing business first with the Soviet Union and countries of new democratism, and selling products to Western countries only in case of surplus",[28] and the Soviet Union provided for China comprehensive support and assistance in security, economy, science and technology, and city management. These facts show that China then had only "one side", but no "regional environment", and when a "regional environment" could be proposed and discussed, it was only that China was part of the "regional environment" of the Soviet Union.

From the late 1950s to the early 1960s, the Sino-Soviet relation broke up due to a series of disputes. One of them is that the Soviet Union believed that "the forces of peace have so grown that there is a real possibility of averting wars", while China considered the idea as a revisionist conduct of making concessions to the United States. According to Mao Zedong, "so long as imperialism exists there will always be soil for aggressive wars"[29] After the breakup of the Sino-Soviet relation, the foreign policy of China changed to "extending relations with the Third World countries and facilitating revolution in the Third World", which was partially to offset the influence of the Soviet Union and to win the competition with it. From 1963 to late 1965, China spent a huge amount of money and a lot of materials on these countries, exchanging assistance for their opposition against the Soviet Union and for their support of China.[30] Before the Cultural Revolution, "revolution output" manifested a major aspect of political correctness. Countries like Cambodia, Burma, India, Nepal, Sri Lanka, Kenya and Algeria were all under the pressure of China's "output" of revolutions.[31] This strategy of "output" represented an effort of China to establish a certain regional environment. However, the attempted was unrealistic in terms of the power of China at that time and of the judgment of international political situation. Instead of the expected situation that "raising one's arm to call for action and numerous would respond and act", China was isolated in the international community. "Friends" becomes fewer, and "enemies" became more vicious.

The failure in "revolution output" to the Third World and the severe conflicts along the Sino-Soviet border determined China to revert to practical politics and foreign politics, including joining the United Nations and improving relations with the United State. Notably, after the Cultural Revolution, the diplomacy of China has gradually assumed the character of independence. As Foreign Minister Huang Hua told UN General Secretary in late August 1982, "China will never cling to any superpower. China will never play the 'US card' against the Soviet Union, nor the 'Soviet Card' against the United States. We will also not allow anyone to play the 'Chinese

[27]For example, Chen Yun has consulted Kovalev for advice as to whether to do business with the capitalists of Hong Kong. See Shen (2009).

[28]Ibid.

[29]Whiting (2008).

[30]Robinson (2008).

[31]Ibid., p. 241.

car.'"[32] In the meantime, China's policy concerning its regional environment was also adjusted, started to establish more comprehensive relations with neighboring countries rather than support the opposition party within these countries according to ideological standards.

After the reform and opening-up, China began to declare and practice a self-disciplined policy concerning its regional environment. The policy was based on the deep reflections on the previous strategy of "revolutionary diplomacy", with its core being that China would not pose a threat to the security of the regional environment and not pursue the establishment of a "sphere of influence" in the neighboring regions. In consideration of the radical forces relevant to China, which constituted the major cause of instability in the regional areas, the long-term assertion and practice of this self-disciplined "drawing back" policy achieved fairly good results. It did not only dispel the doubts (if not enmity) of neighboring countries about China, but also created a safe environment for the regional economic development. What is the most remarkable may be that members of the Association of Southeast Asian Nations, which was originally established to prevent communist expansion, have finally become the regional partners of China the cooperation with whom is the deepest with the fastest development speed and the biggest results.

The report of the 16th Party Congress makes a highly condensed generalization and summarization of the diplomatic work since the reform and opening-up,[33] pointing out that "we will continue to cement our friendly ties with our neighbors and persist in building a good-neighborly relationship and partnership with them. We will step up regional cooperation and bring our exchanges and cooperation with our regional countries to a new height." The reports of the 17th and the 18th Party Congress similarly stress the "friendship and partnership with our neighbors", and expressly make is a guideline for foreign policy.

If China is the major source of security concerns of the regional areas, then the above promises will make some obvious contributions to stabilizing regional security. In 30 years of reform and opening-up, China has won a high degree of credibility for its self-disciplined promises by way of the long-held peaceful foreign policy and wide and numerous relations of trade and investment with neighboring countries. Under this situation, to re-assert the self-discipline nature of our conduct is not only unhelpful to enhance regional security and stability, but may also encourage opportunist activities of some regions or countries and damage the regional security and stability of China.[34] In another word, the source of actual or potential regional threats to security has shifted from China itself, but China mistakenly holds onto the old strategic view concerning the regional environment and the imagination that "China's self-discipline is a gesture enough to express good will and bring about

[32]Pollack (2008).

[33]Wang (2003).

[34]On December 21, 2010, in a symposium on *China's Regional Security Environment Review: 2010* released by the Asian-Pacific Study Centre of the Chinese Academy of Social Sciences, Zhou Fangyin discussed the situation in his speech, "Express Our Determination to Uphold Our Interests in a Substantial Manner".

stability". It follows that in the face of actual and emergent factors of instability in the regional environment, China is unable to deal with the situation for the lack of a reserve of adequate strategies.

Since entering into the new century, more and more scholars learn that China is in need of strategy of a "big regional environment" with several concrete proposals made. One viewpoint holds that a "big regional environment" represents a geographical extension of the traditional regional environment. For example, the "double-circle strategy" of a "big regional environment" will take "China as the centre, and the 20 countries immediately adjacent to China" as the first circle, and the Asian countries immediately adjacent to those countries in the first circle as the second.[35] Another idea is to consider a "big regional environment" as an integrated whole of the four areas of Northeast Asia, Southeast Asia, South Asia and Central Asia, incorporating interrelations as well as differentiations, and as possessing the possibility to extend eastward and westward, with "the West including West Asia and the Middle East, North and East Africa and areas of the Indian Ocean, and the East including areas of Oceania".[36] In an era of low technological level, the geographical regional environment may be identical with areas at the edge of the radiation of economic and cultural influence of the central region. Consequently, to define a regional area in geographical terms is also justified by economic, political and cultural consideration. However, in the current era of fast development of high technologies, advanced telecommunications and transportations, it will not be appropriate to understand regional environment purely by geographical terms. Obviously, to limit and define a "big regional environment" as a geographical extension of neighboring areas will greatly lower the analyzing value of a "big regional environment" as a new theoretical concept.

The second view point is to take major countries and "countries or forces have a relation of major concerns and interests with China" as the extension of China's regional environment. For example, to take the relations of China with non-bordering countries and regions like Russia, Europe, the United States and Japan as an integral part of the relation in the "big regional environment",[37] or to take source countries and regions of resources and energy (for example, the Middles East and Central Asia), which are of extreme importance to China[38], or countries and regions of high geographical strategic value to China (for example, Australia)[39] as a part of China's "big regional environment". The viewpoint does not differentiate the "importance of China to them" from the "importance of them to China", and thus cannot clearly present the nucleus-periphery structure implied by the concept of regional environment. More importantly, the first idea ignores the differences in the methods of

[35]Shen (2009).

[36]Chen (2006).

[37]Ruan, Zongze. To model a "big regional environment" favorable to the development of China. http://www.cssm.gov.cn/view.php?id=6071.

[38]Yan (2006).

[39]Zhang and Huang (2007).

China's to handle relations with major countries and with traditional neighboring countries. In the actual practice, it may lead to a strategic turmoil.

The third viewpoint holds that a "big regional environment" is an open concept without boundaries. Both "distant relatives" and "close neighbors" are in China's regional environment, and should be treated as such.[40] The viewpoint advocates an outlook of the Chinese development from a global perspective. To China who grows to be world major power and plays an increasingly important role, the concept of a static regional environment is subject to constant revision and may ultimately be discarded. This definition of "big regional environment", while emphasizing its "bigness", actually dissolves "regional environment" itself.

The above ideas concerning big regional environment are highly inspiring, but also reflect the importance and complexity of the concept, not to mention a strategy built upon it. In fact, we may look at such a strategy from a pragmatist point of view. Such a strategy is necessary because it may solve problems that cannot possibly be solved with a traditional strategy of regional environment. In another word, under the current international situation especially the regional situation of China, there is a "lack of strategy" or "strategy inappropriateness", calling for a strategy with a view to a big regional environment. From the review above, we can see that the problem such a strategy tries to solve is: what should China do when its regional strategy of self-discipline cannot meet the demand of regional security?

To answer the question, it is necessary to understand the political and economic background against which the effects of the traditional regional strategy continue to diminish in the 30 years of reform and opening-up. Though the guideline for the Chinese foreign policy puts "regional environment on top priority", the "priority" is still listed a level lower than a "major country as the key". In the reports of the 16th and the 17th Party Congress, the discussion of regional relations of China comes after its relations with developed country. Essentially, the 30-year development has been achieved by cooperation with developed countries, or in Mencius's words, by way of "the small serving the big". In economy, China's export-oriented development highly relies on developed countries, which justifies the above-said ordering of discussions in political documents. In 2009, the sum total of importation and exportation with major countries such as the United States, Japan, South Korea, Germany and Australia still accounts for 40% of that with the world (in 1999, it was close to 50%), and 13.5% with the United States alone.

Against this background, China can obtain enough strategic freedom to strengthen economic relations with neighboring countries, and need not worry about the opposition or checking from extra-regional major countries, so long as China does not pursue a "dominating role" in military and political affairs in its regional area. This is what is called "only the wise man knows to be the small and serve the big". In the 1990s, Comrade Deng Xiaoping gave an excellent characterization and summarization of this wisdom, that is, "to keep a low profile". China has handled its relations

---

[40] Lu, Zhongwei. The situation of differentiation and combination of forces in China's "big regional environment". http://www.cssm.gov.cn/view.php?id=6070.

with major powers according to this creed, and achieved tremendous progress in economic growth and strengthening economic relations with neighboring countries.

In recent years, along with the increase of the comprehensive state power of China, China's international influence increases likewise, which leads to the narrowing of its strategic elbow room. It is quite understandable that for a poor man, it is enough to convince others that he will not take risks, and others will let him alone in his low profile, hard work and silent prospering. But once he becomes rich, possessing powers, fact horses and elegant clothes, neighbors will wish him to build bridges and amend roads, and to provide assistance to the poor and education, that is to be a kind and charitable rich person. If he sticks to his old way, remaining silent in dealings with others, keeping his feelings to himself, and showing smiles of good will which might look mysterious to others, it will lead to doubts as to the legality of his fortune, or as to his real intentions. The same is true of a country. With the achievements in hands, China's self-discipline of doing no evil does not convince neighboring small countries, and in addition, makes other major countries suspect or even believe that lying behind China's self-disciplinary strategy is are aggressive plans. The situation results in a din of "China threat theories" and "China responsibility theories".

In the final analysis, there is a strategic deficiency in the mentality of "the big serving the small". In comparison with developed countries, or from the perspective of per capita economy or of underdeveloped regions in China, the country will be a small and backward country in a long term. But in comparison with medium-and-small-size economies, or from the perspective of total economy or of the frontier eastern coastal regions of reform and opening-up, the country is already a leviathan, and still undergoes fast development. Therefore, in addition to "never being the leader", and never conducting cooperation with major countries in a challenging manner, China should propose a clarified and credible (that is, suitable to the interests and ability of China) guideline in the spirit of "the big serving the small". Only the benevolent man knows to be big and serve the small. According to the *Analects of Confucius*, benevolence is to discipline oneself and restore rituals. Rituals refer to order, rules of conduct, that is, institutional arrangement, and "disciplining oneself" can be understood as "setting an example to comply with rituals, and taking responsibilities and making sacrifices when necessary". To discipline oneself and restore rituals is to initiate and establish an order or institutional arrangement, and to practice state conduct in accordance with this order or arrangement, the effects of which are to extend such rituals or order so as to enable every country benefit from conducts complying with them. This concept of benevolence is apparently different from the "major-country generosity" when dealing with small countries, which results in unprincipled compromise, appeasement and concessions.

To declare a big regional strategy built on the concept of "the big serving the small" is another way to take international responsibilities. If the responsibilities of China are not defined and asserted according to its actual power, first, the country cannot provide stable expectations for its conduct to other countries, increasing the difficulty in dealing with international affairs; second, it will give other countries an excuse to impose upon China "limitless responsibilities"; third, China will lack preparations of policies and materials facing emergent changes in regional affairs. China will not be bound up and fall into a passive situation by practically and realistically bearing responsibilities, of which others may expect China and China is capable, rather as Thomas Schelling said, "more freedom can be obtained by binding up one's own hands."[41]

Thus, one ideal way is to define and assert China's big regional strategy based on its responsibilities. First, it is concerned with China's geographical periphery, that is, bordering and neighboring countries and regions of China. Their prosperity may not be beneficial to China, but they surely will damage the interests of China if falling into turmoil and chaos. To delimit geographical periphery is due to the responsibilities that come from mutual dependence and assistance. Second, it is concerned with China's physical surrounding. Comparing economic relations with the codependency of organic bodies, physical surrounding would refer to countries and regions which show imbalanced high dependence on China. To physical surrounding, China does not pursue the expansion of the imbalanced dependence, but attempts to strengthen the political and economic exchanges among them, and to protect the security and mutual dependence in the whole region, and finally realizes a dependence on a common market and common production system with China as an important part. The third is concerned with psychological surrounding. To delimit it is due to the responsibilities that come from the recognition of soft powers such as the Chinese culture, development modes and living style by other countries and regions. It should be pointed out that psychological surrounding does not imply that China will dominate other cultures by its own. On the contrary, the roots of the Chinese thoughts are to take a static stance to appease distant people, and to attract other countries and region to establish a regional culture benefiting all participants, i.e., what is mentioned above as rituals as in "disciplining oneself and restoring rituals". In a word, geographical, physical and psychological surroundings constitute our understanding of big regional environment. With these concepts in mind, a big regional strategy can be established to respond to problems which cannot possibly be solved with the traditional regional strategy.

To sum up, big regional strategy can have the following simple description: it will, by way of international cooperation, develop geographical surrounding into physical surrounding, and physical surrounding into psychological surrounding. Obviously, the physical surrounding here is not restricted to geographical surrounding. It should be made clear that from the perspective of a higher-level strategy, big regional strategy is a means rather than an in itself. It does not require China to build a new long-term "centre-periphery" structure in order to counter other systems. On the contrary, China takes it as a route to a "harmonious world".

Specifically, development should be placed at the centre of building a regional security network. Quite different from Europe and North America where developed countries are concentrated, most of the neighboring countries of China are still underdeveloped or developing. It remains a formidable task for them to eliminate poverty and improve the livelihood of the people, which can only achievement by development and economic growth. Poverty is the source of instability. When poverty

[41] Feng and He (2005).

becomes normal, exploitation becomes way of surviving, and workers become the objects of exploitation, people's mind will corrupt and social order will collapse. And then security problem will remain unsolved, which in turn dampens people's enthusiasm for production, leading to an even poorer society.

To jump out of this vicious cycle requires internal efforts as well as external cooperation and support. It takes institutional arrangement for a sustainable regional security outlook to enjoy popular understanding and play its part. The institutional arrangement which is related to these efforts and support is manifested in the following respects. First, it needs a platform or channel to integrate into international market so that resources and labor of underdeveloped or developing regions can be integrated into the global division of production network, and commodities and service produced can be integrated into regional or international market. This sets demands over the integration of regional economy of relevant countries. The diversity of development levels within Asian countries provides a possibility for low-income countries to integrate into international market by degrees according to a certain gradient. Emerging economies with a development level being somewhere between underdeveloped countries and developed countries can serve as a ladder for this catching-up development.

Second, it should establish a financing mechanism suitable to the Asian areas, proving fund-raising support for development. The financial arrangements in the present Bretton Woods system contain a set of inflexible additional conditions, which largely ignore local situations and lower the availability of fund and its effectiveness, and thus cannot fully meet the demands of the development of Asian countries. The Asian Infrastructure Invest Bank (AIIB) initiated by China can make up for the deficiencies of the present financial system.

Investment concentrated in infrastructure enjoys three advantages. First, it may, by way of infrastructure investment, break the "curse of resources" confronting underdeveloped countries. The improvement of infrastructure is beneficial for underdeveloped regions to integrate into global market at a low cost, activate their domestic production and investment capability rather than stay at the stage of selling resources and increasing consumption. Second, it may take the advantage of shifting production capability of emerging economies like China, and help them solve the problem of surplus capability of production. Third, it may help bind together the interests of major countries in and outside the area, enhance their interdependence and mutual trust, and create a more stable international environment. Infrastructure construction takes a huge amount of money and a long cycle. With the AIIB participating in Asian construction projects, once initiated, parties involved may suffer severe damages from the breakup of their cooperation relations, which prospect may conversely strengthen the will of them to work with one heart and joint efforts. It implies that investment in Asian infrastructure is also investment in regional security and trust.

Third, a standing working mechanism should be instituted to conduct information exchange and policy coordination concerning the "security issues in development" and "development issues for security". Asian countries feature diversity. They are different in size, wealth and power, and differ in numerous ways in historical and cultural traditions and social systems. Again their security interests and demands can be diversified. Territorial disputes and conflicts that exist between some countries within the regions have the tendency to become sharp. Then it is necessary to establish a flexible and effective working mechanism to manage risks, enhance trust and dispel doubts. The Conference on Interaction and Confidence-Building Measures in Asia (CICA) provides a platform for high-level exchange and decision-making concerning major security problems for Asian development.

Lastly, a sustainable regional security network needs the understanding and support of countries out of the region. Fundamentally, sustainable regional security is new model of security outlook featuring inclusive development. It is not an absolution security aiming at the elimination of some threats and potential risks. It pays more attention to the assessment of security cost, and will not wantonly engage in military actions to exclude threats without regard to cost. What it pursues is a "negative peace". The bottom line is to ensure that security concerns will not hinder regional development and cooperation, rather will facilitate development. The view and these efforts of security are active, but not radical, and are beneficial to the harmony of the world.

Establishing a New Model of Major-Country Relations and Peacefully Establishing a Constitution for the World

In 2012, Academia Sinica of Taiwan held an exposition featuring the theme of "Hu Shi and Chiang Kai-shek" with a thought-provoking subtitle, "men of different principles may work together". It is said in the *Analects of Confucius* that "men of different principles should not work together", that is, if people have different ideals and views, it is unnecessary for them to do any business together. The subtitle, which characterized the relation between Hu Shi and Chiang Kai-shek, was opposite to this doctrine. Jiang was a strongman in the Republic of China, and leader of the Nationalist Party of China (NPC, or the Kuomintang). Sun Zhongshan had a comment on him, "he is sturdy and hated vulgarity too much, that is why he cannot get along". Dai Jitao, Jiang's sworn brother, said "the staunchness of my brother's self is incomparable. However, he tends to lose temper over trivial matters, and never makes any efforts to restrain himself." When in Taiwan, Jiang's words were absolutely authoritative, and his behaviors were like an autocrat. Hu Shi was a well-known liberal intellectual. Coming right back from the United States to his motherland, he started to criticize NPC. When in Taiwan, he was in charge of Academia Sinica during Jiang's administration, having a 30-year-long struggle with Jiang. They were by no means friends "with nothing hidden from each other", and more often than not had different ideas. Once Jiang visited Academia Sinica in persona and made a speech to show his respect. In the speech, Jiang said that Academia Sinica should take "rejuvenation of national culture" as one of its tasks. Hu Shi, taking this as a violation against the principle of "academic independence", refuted Jiang's talk on the site. Jiang was so angry that he wrote in his diary that this was the second most insulting experience he had in his life, and that he lost sleep, needing sleeping pills. Though Hu Shi and Chiang Kai-shek had different views and ideas, they could inform each other on major issues and even hold the same view. This shows that men of different principles may also work together. In fact, in the face of major problems concerning all parties, it is only by the working together of parties of different principles that a solution acceptable to all can be found.

The maxim is also applied to the Sino-US relation. China and the United States are different. One is the biggest developing country, adhering to socialism with Chinese characteristics, and the other is the biggest developed country, adhering to capitalism. Both of them are important members of a globalized international economic system, whose behaviors will influence the system and be influenced by the system. The situation requires that in order to maintain the stability of international economic system, both sides should consult each other and must do so on many issues. Someone says that China has implement a hundred-year "strategic deception" program to convince the United States that the American "democracy" can be exported to China, and in exchange, the United States provide China "enormous" support in finance and technology.[42] The so-called "enormous" support is actually fair trade without any cheating. As for the so-called "strategic deception", one can simply read the *Selected Works of Deng Xiaoping* to know that China consistently declare that it will adhere to its socialist path. The mutual support between China and the United States shows that countries of different nature can conduct wide cooperation. Actually, China and the United States can not only conduct bilateral cooperation benefiting both sides, but also cooperation benefiting various sides, even cooperation in multi-laterally establishing rules and institutions for basic international economic governance and international rule construction.

The world economy is now entering a new period of instability. The crisis was the past, but the recession is not over, which may lead to new crisis, plunging the recovering world economy from valley to abyss. Because of the recent reverse of fund flow due to policy exist, emerging economic show signs of a new financial crisis. In a highly globalized world, the abruptness of financial crisis and intense infectiousness place developed economies as well as emerging economies under risk at nearly the same time. To be an isolated paradise is just a willful thinking. Against this background, China as the biggest emerging economy and the United States as the biggest developed economy are supposed to work hand in hand, enhancing policy coordination and preventing and managing disasters together. In this respect, China and the United States have reached some consensus in their joint efforts to deal with the Asian financial crisis and the international financial crisis caused by subprime crisis. The two countries, as the two major economies of the world, should lead the world in doing more in line with the trend to contribute to the world and the offspring in addition to their win-win cooperation in dealing with crises and challenges, to "create a peaceful environment for future generations", and to realized the transition from positive peace to negative peace. The 40-year-long development of Sino-US relations proves that the interests shared by the two countries are much more than

[42]Pillsbury (2015), pp. 7–8.

their divides. A series of constructive cooperative mechanisms have been established between them in many fields. Since the 1980s, the two countries have established more than 60 dialogue mechanisms, in fields such as politics, economy, military affairs, education, science and technology, anti-terrorism, nuclear non-proliferation, and international and regional affairs. In political, the two countries have issued several joint statements, clarifying the direction for Sino-US relations. In economy and trade, they have established many mechanisms for dialogue and communication. Besides the Sino-US Strategic and Economic Dialogue and its precursor the Sino-US Strategic Economic Dialogue, there are other mechanisms such as the Sino-U.S. Joint Economic Committee established in 1979, and the Sino-US Joint Commission on Commerce and Trade established in 1983. In military affairs, the two countries have established such mechanisms of dialogue as the Sino-US maritime military security consultation mechanism, and the mechanism of defense consultation and meeting between the two defense ministries, and have had good cooperation in areas such as military archives and humanitarian aid and disaster mitigation. In cultural exchanges and local cooperation, the two countries have signed such documents of cooperation as the Sino-US Agreement on Cultural Cooperation, the Sino-US Agreement on Educational Cooperation, and the Sino-US Agreement on Intergovernmental Cooperation of Science and Technology, and established such mechanisms as the Sino-US Joint Commission Meeting on Science and Technology Cooperation, the China-US Cultural Forum, the China-US High-Level Consultation on People-to-People Exchange, China-U.S. Governors Forum, and the China-US City-Level Economic Cooperation Conference.

All these established mechanisms have laid a solid foundation for the building of a "new model of major-country relationship between China and the United States". A new model of major-country relations is not only to maintain peace between the coasts of the Pacific Ocean in a negative sense, but also to create cooperative areas with more productivity, promoting interests for both sides and building a peaceful and prosperous environment in a globalized era. This demands that cooperative mechanisms incorporate more arrangements which bind interests created by both sides together, in addition to measures to manage conflicts. China and the United States should by way of dialogue do research of and make judgments about the trend of economic and social development, which is of real importance to the fundamental welfare of the people of the two countries and of the world, and coordinate their actions in a direction of seeking profits and evading damages. Specifically, a new model of major-country relationship between China and the United States should step up efforts in the following four respects:

First, dialogues should develop into actions. Dialogues are never the end, neither the promulgation of the results achieved by dialogues. The results should be put into actions by both countries. Empty talk harms the nation, practical action helps it thrive. The cooperative results reached by the two sides should be examined and assessed in time, and their "enforceability" should be examined in the spirit of practicality. Those results, which exceed capability or are inappropriate, should be singled out and excluded, and those enforceable results should be enforced with more efforts. The executing process should be open, and the actions of relevant functional department should be subject to the supervision and demands of the public opinion of both countries and of the world.

Second, exchanges should develop into integration. Many of the established mechanisms between China and the United States stay at the level of information exchange, and both countries need a blueprint for a higher-level structural integration. For example, in economy, it is highly possible that China and the United States establish a new order of economic cooperation in the economy-adjusting process undergoing in both countries. For the United States, the primary task for the time being is to recover economy, stabilize growth, and create new jobs. China is now dedicated to a shift of its development mode, which will bring new drive force for the recovery of US economy. The urbanization of China and the implementation of national income doubling program will generate an enormous opportunity of investment and consumption demands, opening a wide space for future US export to and investment in China. The Chinese enterprises will continue to practice the "going out" strategy. More and more enterprises coming from China will make an investment in the United States and open factories there, which will contribute to the employment of the United States. Up till the end of 2012, the investment in the United States that comes from China has created more than 30,000 jobs. It is estimated that by 2020, a total sum of 200,000–400,000 jobs will be created. Still more jobs will be created by the import from China, with the business of clothes and toys alone setting up close to 600,000 jobs. The two countries need more mechanisms including bilateral investment agreement to ensure their integration.

Third, mutual trust should develop into mutual understanding. As one of the most important bilateral relations in the world, China and the United States should not only realize mutual trust, but also seek mutual understanding. Mutual understanding implies not only that both sides will trust the intension and capability of each other, but also that both sides will understand each other, and consider each other's difficulties in their shoes, achieving "empathetic understanding". The silver rule of Christianity says "do unto others as you would be done by", which provides a way to handle general bilateral relations. But for a new model of major-country relationship between China and the United States, the silver rule may not be enough. Besides the cool rational principle of "eye for eye, tooth for tooth", it may be helpful to accept the warm and respectful golden rule coming from Confucius, "don't do to others what you don't want others do to you". The incompleteness of reason and contract determines that it is not possible for China and the United States to include and normalize all conducts of both countries by a contrast exhausting all possibilities. In areas where no rules and regulations are set up, an attitude of "patience and kindness" should be adopted to bridge divides.

Forth, the two-country perspective should develop into a global perspective. The world cannot ignore a message jointly made by China and the United States. Therefore, the two countries should make an objective and clear-minded judgment about the tendency of the world, and create positive energy for the welfare of the people of the two countries and of the world. One important aspect is the judgment about the economic globalization. Currently, globalization suffers from setbacks in world trade rules, climate rules and in international financial order. It is a worrying tendency. It should be noted that the current setback results from endogenetic deficiencies such as the over-emphasis of "liberalization" before the crisis. Value chain trade, and regional and cross-regional production network have altered the structure of globalization, and yet a set of global rules suitable to the new structure waits to be established. This requires China and the United States to transcend the problems of the two countries, and propose new view, concepts and rules from the perspective of the world and of humanity so as to create a new globalizing process with more inclusiveness and harmony.

Admittedly, no idealized optimism should be entertained concerning the future Sino-US relations, where both sides get along well with each other like glue. It should be recognized that between China and the United States, the two important economies in the world economic system, there is a competition, and that the competition may become even more intensified in the future, just like that between the US and Japan, and between the US and Europe. We can imagine that in certain regions and fields, China, the United States and other major economies may fiercely compete with each other for market, resources, fund, rules and recognition.

In fact, such competition has already emerged at both macro-level and micro-level. For example, at a US-African Summit held in Washington, in August, 2014, with dozens of African leaders attending, president Obama announced that American enterprises would make an investment of 14 billion US dollars in African projects of construction, clean energy, banking, and information technology. Two months before the summit, in his first visit to Africa as premier of China, Li Keqiang helped bring about more than $10-billion-worth projects of African infrastructure construction by Chinese enterprises. Some American media claimed that Obama attempted to challenge China as Africa's biggest trade partner. Since 2009, China has remained the biggest trade partner of Africa in five consecutive years, and is also an important development and cooperation partner and source of investment. Africa in its turn serves as China's important source of import, the second biggest market of contract construction, and new investment destination. The United States feels that the country neglects or misses the development of Africa in the past years, and is need of "make-up efforts" and "catching up with China" in this respect. At macro-level, the Sino-US relation and foreign policies of both countries seem to struggle with each other, while at micro-level, the gaming between the two assumes a more belligerent color. The US Department of Commerce, in August, 2014, announced to levy an initial tariff at the rate of 20% to 40% on photovoltaic products manufactured by mainland China and Taiwan, and the State Ad ministration of Industry and Commerce of China opened an investigation case in the suspected monopolizing conduct of Microsoft Corp. Some express concerns that if the Sino-US relations are too tight at macro-level, economic and trade exchanges at micro-level will severely suffer. Conversely, if frictions at micro-level are not effectively managed and controlled, the overall situation of Sino-US relations will be damaged by escalating "revenges and counter-revenges".

It may not be a bad thing for both sides to compete for their respective interests. Adam Smith said a long time ago, "it is not from the benevolence of the butcher, the brewer, or the baker that we expect our dinner, but from their regard to their own interest." They compete for their respective interests, and while they obtain profits, consumers also benefit from this competition by obtaining products and services of better high price/performance ratio. The competition between China and the United States in Africa is exactly the case. Their investments benefit from the fast development of Africa, and Africa can get more low-cost funds. In fact, in these fields, opportunities for cooperation between the two countries can be found in their competition. For example, China has invited the United States to participate in large infrastructure construction projects life dam construction in Africa, and share fund pressures and security costs.

Competition may lead to common prosperity with one premise, that is, competition should restricted by certain rules, which will make clear the bottom line of the other side to the effect that "something can be done, but something cannot". A new model of major-country relationship between China and the United States proposed by China is aimed at establishing a constitution for the competition between major countries, excluding by means of rules modes of competition that may cause collective elimination so that the result of competition is directed towards enhancing efficiency, creating dividend of peace and common prosperity. So long as all parties hold the will to establish a new model of major-country relation and evade the old way of confrontation, competition among them will be productive, and a global competitive co-prosperity[43] can be expected.

Donald John Trump was elected the new President of the United States on November 8, 2016. Like the Brexit referendum, the result failed nearly all predictions of major media and researchers so that someone described the high-frequency of low-frequency incidents with the words that "the swan lake of 2016 was crammed up with black swans." When the result fell out of the expectations or wishes of mainstream classes, it is not proper to dismiss it as abnormal.[44] Rather the viewpoint by which mainstream classes look at the world should be examined to see whether there is a systematic mistake. Zbigniew Kazimierz Brzezinski pointed out in *Strategic Vision: America and the Crisis of Global Power* that there is the emergence of "awakening of populations until recently politically passive or repressed".[45] Karl Polany in his book the *Great Transformation: the Political and Economic Origins of Our Time* has already proposed the idea that societies are constituted by two opposing movements: the laissez-fair movement and protective movement. When laissez-fair economy widens the gap between the rich and the poor, causes environmental deterioration and moral degradation, which seem intolerable to the silent majority, a society will swing back to the protective movement.[46] This means that the current mainstream

---

[43]Some scholars hold that the goal of establishing a new model of major-country relationship between China and the United States is competitive coexistence. We believe that a further step should be taken, that is, competitive co-prosperity. See Shambaugh (2013).

[44]As a matter of fact, mainstream media started to use words like "crazy" and "deceitful" to describe the election between Trump and Hillary Clinton the election. Doyle McManus. Clinton and Trump will be held to different debate standards, but that's OK. *Los Angeles Times*, September 25, 2016. http://www.latimes.com/opinion/op-ed/la-oe-mcmanus-trump-clinton-debate-challenges-20160925-snap-story.html.

[45]Brzezinski (2013).

[46]Polany (2001).

classes of the world may underestimate the expectations of "the repressed groups" to seek "protection" and their efforts to such an effect. If such a protection goes extreme, it may be taken advantage of by populism and place the world in an abyss of mutual exclusion and confrontation.

It is not without grounds that on many occasions like the G20 Hangzhou Summit and the BRICS Goa Summit, President Xi Jinping warned that "protectionism and inward-looking trends are on the rise" and that "there is an undercurrent of anti-globalization". If the president-elect of the United States sticks to racism, populism and protectionism advocated in his campaign, a new model of major-country relationship between China and the United States may suffer severe setbacks. But the first interaction between President Xi and president-elect Trump was a good opening for the future. On November 9, President Xi made a congratulating call to Trump on his winning the presidential election. Though President Xi did not directly mention a new model of major-country relationship between China and the United States in the call, he stressed a relation of "non-conflict, non-confrontation, mutual respect, cooperation and mutual benefit", saying clearly that "cooperation is the only correct choice for the Sino-US relationship".[47] Trump responded that he has reached a clear consensus with President Xi on mutual respect.[48] It can be said that a new model of major-country relationship between China and the United States has the flexibility and potential to enable the two countries to move to competitive co-prosperity.

The Belt and Road Initiative

In September, 2013, President Xi Jinping made a proposal to build the Silk Road Economic Belt during his visit to Kazakhstan. In the next month, he made another proposal to jointly build the 21st-Century Maritime Silk Road during his visit to Southeast Asia. The two proposals attracted intense international attention. From September, 2013 to October, 2014, out of the 13 foreign visits of Chinese leaders, 11 include the introduction and expectation of the Belt and Road. In October, 2013, Premier Li Keqiang, during his visit to Brunei, included jointly building the 21st-Century Maritime Silk Road in his seven-point proposal on the framework of China-ASEAN cooperation for the next ten years. In November of the same year, Li Keqiang visited Romania and Uzbekistan. The former is considered as an extension of the Silk Road Economic Belt from Central Asia to Middle and Eastern Europe. When in Uzbekistan, he clearly stressed that all members of the Shanghai Cooperation Organization are on the Silk Road Economic Belt, and hoped that transportation facilitation could serve as a breakthrough point for cooperation. During the Sochi Winter Olympics in

[47]Xi Jinping made a congratulating call to Trump on his winning the presidential election of the United States. Xinhua News Agency, November 9, 2016. http://news.xinhuanet.com/world/2016-11/09/c_1119882357.htm.

[48]Reuters. China President Xi Jinping Tells Donald Trump the 2 Countries Must Cooperate. *Fortune*. November 14, 2016. http://fortune.com/2016/11/14/china-president-xi-jinping-donald-trump-cooperation/.

February, 2014, President Xi Jinping and Russian President Vladimir Putin reached consensus on the issue of interconnecting Russian Trans-Eurasian Rail with the Silk Road Economic Belt and the Maritime Silk Road. In the next month of the same year, in his visit to Holland, France, Germany and Belgium, President Xi said that the idea of Silk Road should enriched with a new meaning, and the Asian and European markets should be better connected so as to benefit all the people along the belt. In June, when Premier Li visited Greece, the Greek Premier expressed the intention of Greece to become the portal and hub for Chinese products to enter into Europe, and to strengthen maritime cooperation with China to jointly promote the construction of the 21st-Century Maritime Silk Road. In July, during President Xi's visit to South Korea, the host proposed the idea of Silk Road Fast Line, which might be connected with the Belt and Road, and both sides intended to extend the space for cooperation. In August, President Xi exchanges ideas on jointly building the Silk Road Economic Belt with the Mongolian leaders during his visit there, and Mongolia said that the country was discussing and actively implementing the Silk Road Economic Belt Initiative. In September, President Xi visited Tajikistan, Maldives, Sri Lanka and India. President Xi said that the Economic Belt was now entering into the stage of practical cooperation, and hoped that China and Tajikistan could take this opportunity to promote deepening reform. He highly praised Maldives as an important transition point on the ancient maritime Silk Road. He expressed the wish to jointly promote with Sri Lanka the rejuvenation of the 21st-Century Maritime Silk Road. He also expressed wishes to conduct an in-depth discussion with India about the Silk Road Economic Belt and the 21st-Century Maritime Silk Road Initiative, jointly leading the sustainable growth of Asia. In March, 2015, President Xi attended Boao Forum for Asia and made a speech in which he introduced the progress of the Belt and Road Initiative, and welcomed all parties to participate in this grand undertaking. During the Forum, the National Development and Reform Commission, Foreign Ministry and Ministry of Commerce jointly issued the Vision and Proposed Actions Outlined on Jointly Building Silk Road Economic Belt and 21st-Century Maritime Silk Road. On June 22, 2016, President Xi, in his speech at the Legislative House of the Highest Conference of Uzbekistan, summarized the results of the Belt and Road Initiative in the three years since its birth. More than 70 countries and international organizations have actively participated in building the Belt and Road, China has formulated and issued the Vision and Proposed Actions Outlined on Jointly Building the Belt and Road, and signed cooperation agreement on jointly building the Belt and Road with over 30 countries. China has signed cooperation agreement on production capacity with 20 countries, and jointly set up 46 extra-regional cooperative districts with 17 countries along the Belt and Road. The accumulated investment of Chinese enterprises amounts to more than 14 billion US dollars, and has created 60,000 jobs for relevant places. China annually sponsors 10,000 students from countries the Belt and Road to study or do research in China. In 2015, the bilateral volume of trade between China and countries participating in the Belt and Road exceeded 1 trillion US dollars, taking up 25% of the overall foreign trade of China. The direct investment of Chinese enterprises in the 49 countries along the Belt and Road approximated 15 billion US dollars, seeing an increase by 18% on a year- on-year basis. Investment from countries participating in the Belt and Road in China exceeded 8.2 billion US dollars, seeing an increase by 25% on a year-on-year basis. The Belt and Road has mostly completed the planning stage and is taking steps of conc rete implementation and sustainable development.[49] By August of the same year when the Chinese central government convened a work conference on promoting the Belt and Road Initiative, the number of countries and international organizations which actively participate in the Initiative has risen to more than 100, some influential landmark projects are gradually actualized and relevant constructions develop from nothing and extend from point to surface, whose progress and results exceed expectations.[50]

The Belt and Road is an initiative and plan of international cooperation first advocated by China. It is dedicated to safeguarding the international free trade system and the open world economy, aiming at promoting the orderly and free flow of economic elements, improving the efficiency of the distribution of resources, deepening market integration, advancing economic policy coordination of countries along the two routes for them to conduct a regional cooperation of a wider range, with a higher quality and at a deeper level, to jointly build an open, inclusive, balanced, all-benefiting regional framework of economic cooperation, to closely integration countries of Asia, Europe and Africa in a new mode, and thus to move to a new historical level by way mutual benefit and cooperation. The Initiative manifests China's active participation in international affairs and taking responsibilities suitable to major country. With the Belt and Road Initiative issued, the international community shows great concerns about what China will do with it, about whether China will "start a separate kitchen", that is, whether China will establish a new international order so as to contend for the leadership of international affairs. In fact, viewed from the perspective of the principles concerning the building of the Belt and Road, the Initiative is a practical and technical plan to make up for the undersupply of public products such as international infrastructure facilities and funds. It strictly complies with the goals and principles of the UN Charter, takes an open and inclusive attitude, adopts internationally accepted rules, and emphasizes cultural and people-to-people exchanges and harmonious coexistence. As for AIIB prospective founding members, China as the major initiator did not restrict the institution, but rather continued to keep it open to countries willing to participate. Right before the end of the window period for prospective founding members, China suddenly received the applications for accession from many countries such as the Great Britain, France and Germany. The total number of countries (and regions) which apply for accession to AIIB as prospective founding members rises from the original over 20–57.

Viewed from the perspective of the domestic mobilization of the Belt and Road Initiative, it is also mainly a construction plan. Take the Silk Road Economic Belt as an example. Upon the Initiative, relevant provinces of China have actively arranged supporting projects of investments and expositions. In 2014, the province of Shaanxi proposed to "create a new starting point for the Silk Road Economic Belt, advance the highland of inland development and opening-up", the Xinjiang Uygur Autonomous

[49] Xi (2016).

[50] Xi (2016).

Region proposed to "advance comprehensive opening-up with building the core area of the Silk Road Economic Belt as the center", the province of Gansu proposed to "place the Gansu part construction of the Silk Road Economic Belt on the top priority... work hard to turn a Gansu into a golden part of the Silk Road Economic Belt", and the Ningxia Hui Autonomous Region proposed to "develop Ningxia into a strategic supporting point of the Silk Road Economic Belt". Government work reports of other western provinces and municipalities which attended the work conference on promoting the Belt and Road Initiative, such as Chongqing, Qinghai, Yunnan and Sichuan, also responded to the strategy of the Silk Road Economic Belt, and listed it as one of the priorities of their government work. Besides, some other provinces, which did not attend the work conference convened by the State Development and Reform Commission and the Foreign Ministry, expressed wishes to be connected to, participate in and integrate into the Silk Road Economic Belt, and claimed to grasp, even race to grasp the opportunity of the national efforts to build the Silk Road Economic Belt. These provinces and municipalities constitute the domestic basis of China to implement and facilitate the strategy of the Silk Road Economic Belt.

In 2015, local government showed even more enthusiasm for the Belt and Road Initiative. Governments of more than 20 provinces and municipalities include the Belt and Road into their work reports, and even some of those which are considered as non-core area still take an active attitude. Most local governments see the Belt and Road as a major opportunity of the country to expand opening-up. It can be seen from the visions or plans outlined in the government reports of these places that local governments mainly intend to connect to the Belt and Road by infrastructure construction and implementation of large-scale projects. Western regions lay emphasis on the construction of transportation network of roads, railways, waterways and parts, while eastern regions stress the planning and arrangement of seaports, water channels and facilities for oceanic shipping. Along with large-scale investments in infrastructure construction, local governments hope to select and reserve a set of major investment projects and hold high-level expositions so as to build their places into a hub, center, highland, golden part or strategic supporting point.

Viewed from the perspective of the attitudes of countries along the two routes, intra-regional major countries generally support the Belt and Road Initiative. For example, Kairat Sarybay, the Foreign Minister of Kazakhstan, pointed out that the Silk Road Economic Belt advocated by China is line with Kazakhstan President Nazarbayev's New Silk Road Project, which is beneficial to Kazakhstan to realize its goal of becoming the hub of Central Asia's trade, logistics and commercial business. Kazakhstan is ready to actively participate in this huge project covering cooperation fields of economy, trade, investment and culture.[51] Rashid Alimov, Tajikistan Ambassador to China, held that the realization of the Belt and Road Initiative will surely provide new possibilities to the economic development of Central Asian countries, and will be conducive to strengthening the relation between Central Asian countries and Europe. With the Silk Road Economic Belt, Central Asian countries will not

[51]Daniyar (2014).

only find a sea gate, but also integrate into the international financial and trade flow system. Tajikistan is willing to participate in building the Silk Road Economic Belt. Kubanychbek Dzhusaev, Kyrghyzstan counselor to China, held that the Silk Road Economic Belt represented a serious generalization of the development experience of China, especially the experience since the reform and opening-up. China presents the experience to the world, and it is worthy of research and discussions on the part of all sides. The further development and prosperity of China will undoubtedly bring new opportunities to the development of Central Asia. The most urgent problem for the time being is whether the Initiative can be accepted and really understood by all sides. Their understanding and support of the Initiative will benefit them all.[52]

Countries of the Middle East also welcome the Initiative of China. Aluwaisheg Abdel Aziz, director of the Department of Comprehensive Economic Affairs with the Secretariat of the Gulf Cooperation Council, said that members of the Gulf Cooperation Council welcome the Initiative of China, and some members have already made announcement to actively participate in building the Belt and Road. Aziz noted the investment of China in and its loan cooperation with countries like Turkmenistan, Kazakhstan, Uzbekistan, Kyrghyzstan and Belorussia, believing that such cooperation will form a new economic and political alliance between China and other Asian areas including the Middle East. However, Aziz thought that China should make a better explication about the nature and prospect of such cooperation, making it clear as to how to implement the Silk Road Economic Belt with its prospective cooperative partners. Generally, Aziz held an understanding and supportive attitude towards the Chinese mode of foreign cooperation. In the past decade, China's investment and loan in fields like energy and infrastructure construction in Africa have occasionally been criticized or censured, but compared with the conducts of the westerners, China's measures generally received positive comments from African people. Aziz said that the Gulf Cooperation Council wanted to play a more active role in building the Belt and Road than simply being a receiver of investment and products.[53] Iran also wishes to be a more important petroleum export country to China when the territorial Silk Road opening to the West is built up. Currently, Iranian petroleum and natural gas channels connect to Pakistan. In future framework of the Belt and Road, China and Iran may construct energy channels connecting to China through negotiations.[54]

Middle and Eastern Europe have also expressed positive attitude towards the Silk Road Economic Belt. Dr. Justyna Szczudlik-Tatar with the Polish International Studies Center thought that the strategy of the Silk Road Economic Belt provides a new opportunity of the close cooperation between provinces of West China with European countries, especially those of the Middle and Eastern Europe. The cooperation initiative in transportation and energy between China and the 16 countries of the Middle and Eastern Europe show that the region also constitutes an important of the Silk Road Economic Belt. Besides, Szczudlik-Tatar also made suggestions that Poland should put the focus of its cooperation policy with China on western

[52]Chen and Tang (2014).

[53]Abdel Aziz Aluwaisheg (2014).

[54]Jiang (2014).

regions of China, and take Lanzhou New Area as a bridgehead to conduct economic cooperation between Poland and China.[55]

Generally speaking, the peaceful and constructive intention of China's the Belt and Road Initiative has gained recognition and understanding from most intra-regional countries, which hold a comparatively positive attitude. However, it does not mean that risks concerning the Belt and Road Initiative could be ignored. Some call the Belt and Road Initiative to a Chinese Marshall Plan. But as a matter of fact, the strategy of China is quite different from the Marshall Plan of the United States, with the former oriented to underdeveloped countries, and the latter to European countries. It is thus more difficult and more significant for China to implement the "going out" policy. The Marshall Plan was aimed at the rebuilding and rejuvenation of Europe. The word rejuvenation implies that Europe had enjoyed a prosperity, which was destroyed by war, and its will to return to prosperity would be strong. Economic growth is driven by demands, and demands in economy are the desire to possess paying capability. The Second World War broke the paying capability of Europe, but did not eliminate their desire. What was to be rebuilt was also this capability, which was relatively easy.

What China faces are many assistance-seeking underdeveloped or developing countries, whose infrastructure is in dire need of construction. They are quite different in terms of desire. For example, India has a long way to go to make up for the backwardness in infrastructure. According to Kissinger, Indian religion and culture call for patience and an abstinence of desires, which may cause more difficulties in persuading them to remove old facilities and build better infrastructure. For another example, there is a kind of tree called baobab in Africa. Its leaves can serve as vegetables, fruits as staple food, and the juice of the fruit can be drunk as beverage. A tree fulfills all the needs of sustaining human body. While the Chinese people continue to strive for a prosperous life after solving the problem of food and clothing, with the hot weather there and the easy living provided by nature itself, the driving force for them to develop is not enough. In a large measure, the strategy of foreign cooperation and assistance of China is not only to build up paying capability, but also to meet the challenges of building up desires (and institutions). It is a more difficult and more significant task to make underdeveloped countries appreciate the benefits of globalization and provide them opportunities to integrate into globalization.

Essentially, the key to the Belt and Road lies in the modernization of governance system and governance capability, which is, internally, to realize the modernization of state governance system and governance capability, and externally, to promote the modernization of international governance system and governance capability. With the main line in mind, the Belt and Road is not another starting point to drive economic growth by extensive investment. It is not to stop building new roads, projects and business districts, but to build them in a modernized governance system and market mechanism. If the mode or direction is wrong, regardless of the scale and amount of investment, the economy of China will go back to the old unsustainable path. If local governments implement projects of the Belt and Road in the old routine of obtaining

[55] Justyna (2013), pp. 6–8.

land by superordinate granting, preferential treatment in tax and investment subsidies, it is only harder to realize the modernization of governance system and governance capability. Now it seems that the enormous demands of investment generated by driving growth will turn into a surplus of production capability in the foreseeable future, the management of which will cost even more. A logical conflict and internal tension can be formed between the domestic part and the international part (where advantageous surplus production capability can be transferred) of the Belt and Road. If efforts can be made by domestic and foreign governments at various levels to improve governance concept, instrument and means so as to enhance governance system and governance capability, good projects suitable to industry upgrading will surely surface from the waves of mass entrepreneurship and innovation, which will facilitate the power of the place or the country. In this way, domestic governance and international governance will promote each other, and the global governance system will be improved.

References

Abdel Aziz Aluwaisheg, "China's New Silk Road Initiatives: A GCC Perspective", Arab News, January 17, 2014, http://www.highbeam.com/doc/1G1-357344793.html.

Brzezinski, Zbigniew Kazimierz. 2013. *Strategic Vision: America and the Crisis of Global Power*. New York: Basic Books, p. 31.

Chen, Guangsheng. 2007. *Towards Good Governance*. Zhejiang University Press, pp. 124–125.

Chen, Xiangyang. July 17, 2006. Establish a strategy of a "big surrounding environment" as soon as possible. *News Weekend*.

Chen, Yurong and Tang Zhongchao. 2014. Summary of the International Symposium on the Silk Road Economic Belt in the Context of Economic Globalization. *China International Studies*, No. 1.

Daniyar Mukhtarov, "Kazakhstan Considers Its Participation in Silk Road Economic Belt Project", Trend, January 10, 2014, http://en.trend.az/casia/kazakhstan/2228894.html.

Deng, Xiaoping. 1993. We must adhere to socialism and prevent peaceful evolution. *Selected Works of Deng Xiaoping Vol. III*. People's Press.

Feng, Weijiang and He Fan. 2005. A game theory confronting reality in the face: a commentary on the thoughts of Thomas Schelling, 2005 Nobel Prize laureate in economy. *International Economic Review*, November to December.

Grossman, Sanford J. and Oliver D. Hart. 1986. The cost and benefits of ownership: a theory of vertical and lateral integration. *Journal of Political Economy* 94: 691–719.

Jessop, Bob. 1999. The emergence of governance and its risk of failure: a case study of economic development. Trans. by Qi wu. *International Social Science Journal*, 01: 31–48.

Jiang, Bixin. 2013. Advance the modernization of state governance system and governance capability. *Guangming Daily*, November 15, 2013.

Jiang, Yuqiong. 2014. Regional cooperation of infrastructure construction and energy will string together the "new Silk Road". *Shanghai Securities News*, May 29, 2014, F05.

Justyna Szczudlik-Tatar, "China's New Silk Road Diplomacy", PISM Policy Paper No. 34. (82), 2013, pp. 6–8. https://www.pism.pl/files/?id_plik=15818.

Kazancigil, Ali and Huang Jisu. 1999. Governance and science: a market mode of social governance and knowledge production. *International Social Science Journal*, 01: 69–79.

Luo, Zhengguang and Luo Yufan. 2016. From Administrative Streamlining to Institutional Corruption Prevention: A Review on the Progress of China in Administrative Examination and Approval Reform. August 10, 2016. http://news.xinhuanet.com/politics/2016-08/10/c_1119367078.htm.

Marx, Karl. 1995. Comments on the latest Prussian censorship instruction. *Works of Marx and Engles vol I*. People's Press.

Pillsbury, Michael. *The hundred-year marathon: China's secret strategy to replace America as the global superpower*. Henry Holt and Company, 2015. pp. 7–8.

Polany, Karl. 2001. *Great Transformation: the Political and Economic Origins of Our Time*. Boston: Beacon Press, pp. 138–139.

Pollack, Jonathan D. 2008. The opening to America. In *The Cambridge History of China vol. 15: Revolutions within the Chinese Revolution*, ed. by R. MacFarquhar and J. K. Fairbank. Cambridge: Cambridge University Press, pp. 467–468.

Rhodes, R.A.W. 1996. The new governance: governing without government. *Political Studies* 44: 652–667.

Robinson, Thomas. 2008. China confronts the Soviet Union: warfare and diplomacy on China's inner Asian frontiers. In *The Cambridge History of China vol. 15: Revolutions within the Chinese Revolution*, ed. by R. MacFarquhar and J. K. Fairbank. Cambridge: Cambridge University Press, p. 228.

Shambaugh, D. L. 2013. *Tangled Titans: The United States and China*. Rowman & Littlefield, p. 4.

Shen, Zhihua. 2009. From Xi Baipo to Moscow: Mao Zedong declared to lean one-sidedly to the Soviet Uinon. *Journal of Chinese Communist Party History Studies*, No. 4.

Shen, Dingli. 2009. Double-circle strategy of the surrounding diplomacy of China. *Contemporary Asia-Pacific Studies*, No. 1.

Wang, Yi. 2003. To be good and partners with our neighbors. *Qiushi* No.4.

Whiting, Allen S. 2008. The Sino-Soviet split. In *The Cambridge History of China vol. 14: the Emergence of Revolutionary China*, ed. by R. MacFarquhar and J. K. Fairbank. Cambridge: Cambridge University Press, p. 482.

Williams, David and Tom Young. 1994. Governance, the World Bank and liberal theory. *Political Studies* 42: 84–100.

Xi, Jinping. 2016. Speech at the Symposium on Philosophy and Social Sciences. May 18, 2016. http://news.xinhuanet.com/politics/2016-05/18/c_1118891128.htm.

Xi, Jinping. April 7, 2013. Working together toward a better future for Asia and the world: keynote speech by Xi Jinping at the Boao Forum for Asia Annual Conference 2013. *People's Daily*, April 8, 2013.

Xi, Jinping. August 17, 2016. Advance the Belt and Road Initiative to benefit people along routes.

Xi, Jinping. February 25, 2010. Speech at the opening ceremony of the 2010 International Forum on Economic Globalization and Trade Unions. *People's Daily*, February 26, 2010.

Xi, Jinping. January 28, 2013. Speech at the third group study session of the Political Bureau of the 18th CPC Central Committee. *People's Daily*, January 30, 2013.

Xi, Jinping. June 22, 2016. Jointly build a great new Silk Road: Speech at the Legislative House of the Highest Conference of Uzbekistan. Xinhua Net. June 22, 2016. http://news.xinhuanet.com/world/2016-06/23/c_1119094900.htm.

Xi, Jinping. March 24, 2013. Follow the trend of the times and promote global peace and development: speech at the Moscow State Institute of International Relations. *People's Daily*, March 24, 2013.

Xi, Jinping. March 25, 2013. Bė trustworthy friends and sincere partners forever: speech at the Julius Nyerere International Convention Center in Dar es Salaam, Tanzania. *People's Daily*, March 26, 2013.

Xi, Jinping. March 27, 2013. Work hand in hand for common development: a keynote speech at the Fifth BRICS Leaders Meeting. *Xinhua net*, March 27, 2013. http://news.xinhuanet.com/world/2013-03/27/c_124511954.htm.

Xi, Jinping. October 13, 2009. Strengthen cultural exchange and promote world peace: speech at the opening ceremony of the 61th Frankfurt International Book Fair. *People's Daily,* October 14, 2009.

Xin, Xiangyang. 2014. Three basic questions on advancing state governance system and governance capability. *Theoretical Investigation* 02: 27–31.

Yan, Zhonglin. 2006. Energy strategy of China in a "big regional environment" with the Middle East and Central Asia. *Journal of Harbin Institute of Technology* (Social Sciences Edition).

Yu, Keping. 2000. *Governance and Good Governance*. Social Sciences Academic Press, p. 1.

Yu, Keping. 2013. Basic standard to measure the modernization of state governance system. *Beijing Daily*, December 9, 2013.

Zhang, Yuyan. 2016. Global governance: a Chinese perspective. *World Economics and Politics* 9: 5.

Zhang, Yuyan. 2016. 2016. Global governance: a Chinese perspective. *World Economics and Politics* 9: 8.

Zhang, Lu and Huang Ji. 2007. Australia in China's regional strategy: a new exploration of the strategic concept of "big regional environment" and diplomatic planning. *Contemporary International Relations*, No. 2.

Zhang, Yuyan and Li Zenggang. 2008. *International Economy and Politics*. Shanghai: Shanghai People's Press, p. 31.

Zhang, Yuyan and Ren Lin. 2015. Global governance: a framework for theoretical analysis. *Quarterly Journal of International Politics* 3: 1–29.

Concluding Remarks: The Legend of Ping-Pong

In 1890, it might be due to the poor weather, or the limited field space, that several British officers in India played tennis on the table. Though interesting, the tennis ball looked too heavy and the racket was too big for the table. They changed to hollow rubber ball and wooden racket later, the books which served as a dividing line of the table were replaced by a net, and a set of rules were established by modeling on that of tennis. The popularity of table-tennis should pay special gratitude to the Americans. It was the curious Americans who standardized the equipments of table-tennis in the early 20th century and put them into quantity production. And it was also because American manufacturer registered ping-pong, the sound of the ball hitting the table, as the trademark for the sport that table-tennis acquired the name, ping-pong. In the end of 1904, a Mr. Wang, owner of a stationary shop on Sima Road, Shanghai, bought 10 sets of ping-pong equipments to do performance in the shop, which started the journey of ping-pong in China, growing from scratch, from few participants to many, from weak strength to powerful. In 1926, the First International Table Tennis Invitation Tournament was held in Berlin, Germany. In the year next, the International Table Tennis Federation (ITTF) was established, and the Berlin Invitation Tournament was recognized retroactively as the First World Table Tennis Championships (WTTC). Since 1957, the World Table Tennis Championships started to be held every second year instead of every year. Currently, the ITTF is a major world sport organization with nearly 190 members. In 1988, table-tennis was listed as an Olympic Games event.

In the first few decades since the birth of table tennis, players mainly used wooden racket without any covering, with slow hitting velocity, power and spin, and only two hitting techniques were used, that is, drive and block. Later on, the British invented a racket covered with cylindrical pimpled rubber with elasticity and frictional force increased, which gave rise to the defensive technique of underspin chop. In the Men's Team Final of the Tenth World Table Tennis Championships, both sides sent out players of comparable ability using this technique so that less than half of the match lasted 6 hours. The invention of sandwich rubber racket in

Y. Zhang and W. Feng, *Peaceful Development Path in China*, China Insights,
https://doi.org/10.1007/978-981-13-1439-1

the 1950s by the Austrian changed this slightly tedious and boring style of ping-pong match. The Japanese players first applied this kind of racket, which could strike out balls of high velocity and strong spin. They invented the playing style of "backcourt long drive", and obtained brilliant achievements with "loop drive" in the World Table Tennis Championships, ending the dominance of Europeans in the game and starting a 10-year glory. But the good time is always short. Since the returning countryman Rong Guotuan won the first championship in the WTTC in 1959, the Chinese people with their style of "short court fast attack" featuring "speed, accuracy, relentlessness and flexibility" dominated the ping-pong world for 20 years, and in the early 1980s, they swept the WTTC bringing home all the seven championships. During the period, Europeans, especially the Hungarians and the Swedish, rallied their forces and made great efforts in the field, and invented a playing style combining fast attack and loop drive. The ping-pong world was entering an era of fierce competition in the 1990s and the early 21st Century.

The overall level of table tennis is advanced along with the improvement of playing style, innovation of tactics and training, as well as technological innovation of rackets. The improvement of the quality of sponge and rubber, the increase in their varieties, and the application of new types of glue all contribute to the development of table-tennis. The fast development, however, brings problems of its own. The ball moves at a faster speed with a more intense spin so that it is hard to predict the trajectory of a moving ball, thus decreasing the number of rounds by a large degree. The competitiveness and the aesthetic value of the game suffer a lot. Upon China's taking all the championships home, proposals were already made to change rules of table-tennis match, for examples, enlarging the ball size, heightening the table net and changing match systems. In the ITTF Convention of 1999 during the 45th WTTC, the "large ball reform" was put on the agenda, which stated a series of reforms in table-tennis rules. The "large ball reform" bill was approved the next year at a non-conventional meeting—the ITTF Special Meeting and International Congress held in Kuala Lumpur. Ever since, table tennis balls, whose diameter has been enlarged by 2 millimeters and whose flying speed has been lowered, enter the stage of the ping-pong world, and the previous 21-point match system has been replaced by a more competitive 11-point system. Since 2008, organic glue, which can enhance the elasticity of sponge and improve hitting speed, has been replaced by more neutral non-organic glue. In the meantime, hiding service, which increases the difficulty of return of service, has been banned.

History is inspiring. We can obtain the following inspirations and discoveries from the development history of table-tennis. First, demands are the mother of creation, and creation is not out of nothing, but always grows out of existing things, as table-tennis grows out of tennis. Second, the popularity of a game or a product is closely related to standardized production or mass participation. The quantity production of table-tennis equipments by the Americans lowered the cost and enabled the sport to become popular. Third, each generation produces its own outstanding talents, which lead the world for several decades. The first 60 years of the ping-pong world is rather like those of the modern history. The Great Britain opened the road, other European countries and the United States followed suit and Japan caught up. Fourth, the fundamental reason for the change of dominating power is the technological progress concerning "fighting weapons" and the innovation of tactics and strategy under the guidance of advanced concept. The revolution of playing styles of table-tennis can serve as an illustrating example. Fifth, game rules have an influence on results, and a change in rules may bring a change in results. In another word, most rules are non-neutral. This is the reason why some people tried their best to promote the "big ball reform". Sixth, even the smartest rule-maker cannot clearly see who will benefit the most from the current non-neutral rules. The British invented table-tennis and the German held the first international tournament. They did not do this to let the Chinese dominate the game.

For late-comers in a game to catch up, it is sufficient and necessary for them to vigorously introduce advanced technology and high-end talents, and actively participate in international competition. From the end of 1950s to the end of the 1970s, among all the sports in which China participated, table-tennis was the most international and most open. This is the seventh inspiration. Population scale, popularity or the accumulation of human resources sooner or later will play a decisive role in determining the result. The ping-pong tables that can be found in every primary and secondary school of China and countless number of ping-pong fans build up a large and solid ladder for athletes to climb the peak. This can be seen as the eighth discovery. For nearly 100 years, China learned from Western countries and tried to catch up with and even surpass them in competitive sports. Among them ping-pong is a game most worthy of bragging about for China. Here is a serious question: Why ping-pong rather than football, basketball or volleyball? Besides physical conditions, we can see that different from collective sports, ping-pong is individual with victories and losses attributed to a player himself, which can give a full play to incentive system. This is also true of badminton, billiards, tennis, swimming, and diving. This is the ninth inspiration. Finally, despite the fierce competition in rule establishing among states, there are still common interests, for the prosperity of table-tennis is the common wish of all players. If all parties, for their own shorted self-interests, make table-tennis lose aesthetic value and interestingness, the result is that all of them will be knocked out.

Regarding common interests and interest conflicts, more than half a century ago, the American economist Thomas Schelling discussed a simple and profound experiment. In the experiment, two subjects divide 100 dollars. They are asked to write down the amount that they want to obtain. If two numbers are added up to less than 100, each gets the amount that he has written down. If the sum is more than 100, each gets nothing. The result of the experiment is that most pairs of subjects adopted a cooperative attitude and wrote down a number less than 50. It is an important result, showing that human behaviors are characterized by the coexistence of common interests and interest conflicts.

In the experiment, two subjects must cooperate with each other to obtain benefits, and in the meantime their game is zero-sum, because the extra money one may get is the money one may lose. This is a normal situation facing humanity, and also a reality in the process of the rejuvenation of China.[1] Only with the relation between common interests and interest conflicts well handled, opportunities for common development created, and conflicts in the division of interests well managed can the world play proceed peacefully, orderly and sustainably. Certainly, to manage and control division of interests does not mean that all interests can be conceded or exchanged. "China does not covet the rights and interests of other countries, nor does it envy their development, but it will never give up its own legitimate rights and interests. We Chinese people do not believe in fallacies, but we are not afraid of them; we do not make trouble, but we are not afraid of it. No country should entertain the fantasy that China will barter away its core national interests or allow its sovereignty, security, and development interests to be infringed upon."[2]

In retrospect, to the Chinese people, the history of table-tennis, in which there are numerous sweet memories and boundless expectations for the future, can be said to be a legend. Perhaps, this history itself has reflected the economic development of China, epitomizing the development of China along a peaceful path to realize catching up and surpassing and the national rejuvenation. It is just like the happenings of the ping-pong world since the end of the 1960s. China is full of determination and confidence. Certainly, the final realization of all this is conditional, and the conditions lie, clearly and obscurely, visibly and invisibly, in the inspirations found in the development history of table-tennis.

---

[1]Zhang, Yuyan. 2016. Global governance: coexistence of human common interests and conflicts. *Exploration and Free Views*, No. 5.

[2]Xi, Jinping. July 1, 2016. Speech at a ceremony marking the 95th anniversary of the founding of the Communist Party of China. *People's Daily*, July 2, 2016.

References

Chinese References

Arbatov, G. A. 1998. *The Soviet Politics: Inside Information*. Trans. by Xu Kui et al. Xinhua Press.
Bakunin. 1982. *Statism and Anarchy*. Trans. by Ma Xiangcong et al. Commercial Press.
Bell, D. 1984. *The Coming Back of the Post-Industrial Society–A Venture in Social Forecasting*. Trans. by Gao Xian. The Commercial Press.
Brzezinski, Z. K. 2013. *Strategic Vision: America and the Crisis of Global Power*. New York: Basic Books.
Buchanan, J. 1988. *Liberty, Market and State*. Trans. by Wu Liangjian, Sang Wu and Zeng Huo. Beijing: Beijing College of Economics Press.
Cai, Fang. The only way to surmount "Middle-income Trap" is reform, *Reference News*, March 14, 2016.
Chen, Yan. 1996. *Maritime Silk Road and China-Foreign Cultural Exchanges*. Beijing: Peking University Press.
Chen, Guangsheng. 2007. *Towards Good Governance*. Zhejiang University Press.
Chen, Xiangyang. Establish a strategy of a "big surrounding environment" as soon as possible. *News Weekend*. July 17, 2006.
Chen, Yurong and Tang Zhongchao. 2014. Summary of the International Symposium on the Silk Road Economic Belt in the Context of Economic Globalization. *China International Studies*, No. 1, 126–132.
Commons, J. R. 1998. *Institutional Economics*. Commercial Press.
CPC History Research Center of the CPC Central Committee. 2011. *A History of the Communist Party of China, Vol. 2*. CPC History Press.
CPC Literature Research Center of the CPC Central Committee. 1996. *Poems of Mao Zedong*. CPC Literature Press.
CPC Literature Research Center of the CPC Central Committee. 1997. *A Chronicle of Zhou Enlai Vol. II*. CPC Literature Press.
CPC Literature Research Center of the CPC Central Committee. 2004. *A Chronicle of Deng Xiaoping: 1975–1997, Vol. I*. CPC Literature Press
Defoe, D. 2002. *Robison Crusoe*. Trans. by Ma Jing. Guangxi Nationalities Publishing House.
Deng, Xiaoping. 1993. *Selected Works of Deng Xiaoping Vol. III*. People's Press.
Deng, Xiaoping. 1994. *Selected Works of Deng Xiaoping Vol. I*. People's Press.
Deng, Xiaoping. 1994. *Selected Works of Deng Xiaoping Vol. II*. People's Press.
Engles, F. V. 1972. *The Origin of the Family, Private Property and the State*. People's Press.

Y. Zhang and W. Feng, *Peaceful Development Path in China*, China Insights,
https://doi.org/10.1007/978-981-13-1439-1

Evans, R. 1996. *Deng Xiaoping*. Trans. by Wu Shihong. Shanghai People's Press.

Fairbank, J. 1985. *The Cambridge History of China: The Late Ch'ing, 1800–1911*. Trans. by Institute of History Studies, Chinese Academy of Social Sciences. China Social Sciences Press.

Feng, Weijiang and He Fan. 2005. A game theory confronting reality in the face: a commentary on the thoughts of Thomas Schelling, 2005 Nobel Prize laureate in economy. *International Economic Review*, November to December.

Fukuyama, F. 2012. *The Origins of Political Order*. Farrar, Straus and Giroux.

Gao, Cheng. 2012. On institutional hegemony in the new empire system and governance pathway. *Teaching and Research*, No. 5.

Gordon, H. Chang. 2014. *Friends and Enemies: The United States, China, and the Soviet Union 1948–1972*. Trans. by Gu Ning et al. Central Compilation & Translation Press.

Greenspan, A. 2013. *The Age of Turbulence: Adventures in a New World*, Yu, J. Trans. CITIC Press.

Hai, Wen. Innovation and Education are key to China's transformation and upgrade, *Reference News*, April 5, 2016.

Hans, J. Morgenthau. 1973. *Politics Among Nations: The Struggle for Power and Peace* (Fifth Edition). New York: Alfred A. Knopf.

Hardt, M. and A. Negri. 2005. *Empire-the Political Order of Globalization*, Trans. by Yang Jianguo, et al. Jiangsu People's Press.

Hayek, F. A. 1997. *The Road to Serfdom*. Trans. by Wang Mingyi and Feng Xingyuan. Beijing: China Social Sciences Press.

He, Xin. 2002. *Long: Mythology and Truth*. Current Affairs Press.

He, Fan, Feng Weijiang and Xu Jin. 2013. Challenges of global governance and the strategies of China. *World Economics and Politics*, 7.

Hobbes, T. 2004. *On the Citizen*. Trans. by Ying Xing and Feng Keli. Guizhou People's Press.

Hong, Xingzu. 1983. *Additions and Annotations to the Songs of the South*. Zhonghua Book Company.

Hu, Huawei. 2004. Fiction and reality: Folklore, history memory and "archeology of knowledge" of social history. *Jiangsu Social Sciences*, No. 6, pp. 162–166.

Hu, Angang. "Middle-income Trap" is a false proposition to China, *Reference News*, March 18, 2016.

Huntington, S. P. 1989. *Political Order in Changing Societies*. Trans. by Wang Guanhua. SDX Joint Publishing Company.

Information Office of the State Council of China. 1991. *Human Rights in China*. November, 1991. http://www.scio.gov.cn/zfbps/ndhf/1991/Document/308017/308017.htm.

Information Office of the State Council of China. 2011. *China's Peaceful Development*. September, 2011. http://politics.people.com.cn/GB/1026/15598619.html.

Jessop, Bob. 1999. The emergence of governance and its risk of failure: a case study of economic development. Trans. by Qi Wu. *International Social Science Journal*, 01: 31–48.

Jia, Kang and Su Jingchun. China needs institutional innovation to break through the "bottleneck period". *Reference News*, March 23, 2016.

Jiang, Bixin. 2013. Advance the modernization of state governance system and governance capability. *Guangming Daily*, November 15, 2013.

Kazancigil, Ali and Huang Jisu. 1999. Governance and science: a market mode of social governance and knowledge production. *International Social Science Journal*, 01: 69–79.

Keohane, R. O. 2001. *After Hegemony: Cooperation and Discord in the World Political Economy*. Shanghai People's Press.

Li, Daokui. China is able to surmount "Middle-income Trap", *Reference News*, March 15, 2016.

Li, Yining. Only by Surmounting "Three High Mountains" Can We Avoid "Traps", *Reference News*, April 4, 2016.

Licbcrthal, K. 2010. *Governing China*. Trans. by Hu Guocheng and Zhao Mei. China Social Sciences Press.

Lin, Yifu, Cai Fang and Li Zhou. 1999. *The China Miracle: Development Strategy and Economic Reform*. Shanghai People's Press.
Lin, Yifu. China has unique advantages to become a high-income country, *Reference News*, March 25, 2016.
Liu, Shijin. 2011. Why China's identity as a "developing country" is problematic? *Qiushi*, No. 11, pp. 33–36.
Liu, Peilin. 2014. China regaining world No. 1: A historical lesson. *China Economic Times*. October 16th, 2014.
Lu, Nanquan. 2007. *A History of Economic Reform in the Soviet Union*. People's Press.
Lu, Zhongwei. The situation of differentiation and combination of forces in China's "big regional environment". http://www.cssm.gov.cn/view.php?id=6070.
Luo, Zhengguang and Luo Yufan. 2016. From Administrative Streamlining to Institutional Corruption Prevention: A Review on the Progress of China in Administrative Examination and Approval Reform. August 10, 2016. http://news.xinhuanet.com/politics/2016-08/10/c_1119367078.htm.
Lv, Pu. 1979. *Historical Sources of Yellow Peril*, China Social Sciences Press.
MacFarquhar, R. and J. K. Fairbank. 2008. *The Cambridge History of China vol. 14: the Emergence of Revolutionary China*. Cambridge: Cambridge University Press.
MacFarquhar, R. and J. K. Fairbank. 2008. *The Cambridge History of China vol. 15: Revolutions within the Chinese Revolution*. Cambridge: Cambridge University Press.
Maddison, A. 2006. *The World Economy: A Millennial Perspective*. OECD.
Mao, Zedong. 1994. *Selected Works of Mao Zedong on Diplomacy*, Beijing: Central Party Literature Press, Beijing: World Knowledge Press.
Marx, K. 1995. Comments on the latest Prussian censorship instruction. *Works of Marx and Engles vol I*. People's Press.
Mises, L. V. 1995. *Liberalism in the Classical Tradition*. Trans. by Han Guangming, et al. China Social Sciences Press.
North, D. 1984. *Structure and Change in Economic History*. Trans. by Chen Yu and Luo Huaping. Shanghai: Shanghai People's Press.
Odom, W. E. 2000. *The Collapse of the Soviet Military*. Trans. by Wang Zhenxi. Xinhua Press.
Olson, M. L. 2005. *Power and Prosperity*. Trans. by Su Changhe. Shanghai People's Press.
Pigou, A. C. 1920. *The Economics of Welfare*. London: Macmillan, 183.
Polany, Karl. 2001. *Great Transformation: the Political and Economic Origins of Our Time*. Boston: Beacon Press.
Qian, Mingci. 2007. *Mythologies and Legends of Ancient China*. Commercial Press.
Qin Yaqing. 1999. *Hegemony System and International Conflict: Acts of Support of the US in International Armed Conflicts*. Shanghai People's Press.
Ricardo, D. 1962. *Principles of Political Economy and Taxation*. Trans. by Guo Dali and Wang Yanan. The Commercial Press.
Ruan, Zongze. To model a "big regional environment" favorable to the development of China. http://www.cssm.gov.cn/view.php?id=6071.
Shen, Zhihua. 2002. *Selected Historical Archives of the Soviet Union, Vol. 23*. Social Sciences Academic Press.
Shen, Dingli. 2009. Double-circle strategy of the surrounding diplomacy of China. *Contemporary Asia-Pacific Studies*, No. 1.
Shen, Zhihua. 2009. From Xi Baipo to Moscow: Mao Zedong declared to lean one-sidedly to the Soviet Uinon. *Journal of Chinese Communist Party History Studies*, No. 4.
Sheng, Hong. 2000. The birth of Long: a political-economic story. *Du Shu* 12.
Smith, A. 1972. *An Inquiry into the Nature and Causes of the Wealth of Nations*. Trans. by Guo Dali and Wang Yanan. Commercial Press.
Soros, George. The Way Forward, http://www.ftchinese.com/story/001029656, November 11, 2009.
Stavrianos, L. 2005. *A Global History*. Trans. by Dong Shuhui et al. Peking University Press.

Sulayman. 1937. *Sulayman's Travels in the East*. Trans. by Liu Bannong. Zhonghua Book Company.
Sun, Guangzhen and Zhang Yuyan. 1997. Interest Groups and "Jia Yi's Law: A Preliminary Analytical Framework, *Economic Research Journal*, No. 6.
Tang, Shiping. 2003. *Shape an Ideal Security Environment for China*. China Social Sciences Press.
Tocqueville, A. D. 1992. *The Old Regime and the Revolution*, Trans. by Feng Tang. The Commercial Press.
Vogel, E. F. 2013. *Deng Xiaoping and the Transformation of China*. Trans. by Feng Keli. SDX Joint Publishing Company.
Williamson, Oliver and Scott Masten. 2008. *The Economics of Transaction Costs*. Trans. by Li Zijie et al. Being: People's Press.
Williamson, Oliver and Scott Masten. 2008. *The Economics of Transaction Costs*. Trans. by Li Zijie et al. Being: People's Press.
Wittfogel, A. K. 1957. *Oriental Despotism*. Yale University Press.
Wang, Yi. 2003. To be good and partners with our neighbors. *Qiushi* No. 4.
Wang, Tao. 2014. The theoretical work meeting of 1979. *Party History and Literature*, (13): 36–42.
Wen, Jiabao. 2008. The Chinese are fully able to feed themselves. *Farmer's Friend*, No. 9.
Xi, Jinping. 2013. Follow the trend of the times and promote global peace and development: speech at the Moscow State Institute of International Relations. *People's Daily*, March 24, 2013.
Xi, Jinping. 2013. Work hand in hand for common development: a keynote speech at the Fifth BRICS Leaders Meeting. *Xinhua net*, March 27, 2013. http://news.xinhuanet.com/world/2013-03/27/c_124511954.htm.
Xi, Jinping. 2014. *The Governance of China*, Foreign Languages Press.
Xi, Jinping. 2014. Promoting the Construction of (Shanghai) Free Trade Zone, Strengthening and Innovating Social Governance of Megalopolis. *People's Daily*, March 6, 2014.
Xi, Jinping. 2015. Advance the spirit of Bandung and promote cooperation and mutual benefits: Speech at the Conference of Asian-African Leaders. April 22, 2015. http://news.xinhuanet.com/politics/2015-04/22/c_1115057390.htm.
Xi, Jinping. 2016. Firm up Confidence and Seek Common Development, Remarks at the Plenary Session of the Eighth BRICS Summit, October 16th, 2016. http://news.xinhuanet.com/2016-10/16/c_1119727543.htm.
Xi, Jinping. 2016. Advance the Belt and Road Initiative to benefit people along routes. Xihua Net, August 17, 2016. http://news.xinhuanet.com/politics/2016-08/17/c_1119408654.htm.
Xi, Jinping. 2016. Jointly build a great new Silk Road: Speech at the Legislative House of the Highest Conference of Uzbekistan. Xinhua Net. June 22, 2016. http://news.xinhuanet.com/world/2016-06/23/c_1119094900.htm.
Xi, Jinping. 2016. Speech Marking the CPC's 95th Founding Anniversary. *People's Daily*, July 2, 2016.
Xi, Jinping. 2016. Speech at the Symposium on Philosophy and Social Sciences. May 18, 2016. http://news.xinhuanet.com/politics/2016-05/18/c_1118891128.htm.
Xi, Jinping. 2016. A New Starting Point for China's Development, A New Blueprint for Global Growths: speech at B20 summit opening ceremony, September 3, 2016. http://cpc.people.com.cn/n1/2016/0905/c64094-28690521.html.
Xi, Jinping. April 7, 2013. Working together toward a better future for Asia and the world: keynote speech by Xi Jinping at the Boao Forum for Asia Annual Conference 2013. *People's Daily*, April 8, 2013.
Xi, Jinping. February 25, 2010. Speech at the opening ceremony of the 2010 International Forum on Economic Globalization and Trade Unions. *People's Daily*, February 26, 2010.
Xi, Jinping. January 28, 2013. Speech at the third group study session of the Political Bureau of the 18th CPC Central Committee. *People's Daily*, January 30, 2013.

Xi Jinping made a congratulating call to Trump on his winning the presidential election of the United States. Xinhua News Agency, November 9, 2016. http://news.xinhuanet.com/world/2016-11/09/c_1119882357.htm.
Xi, Jinping. March 25, 2013. Be trustworthy friends and sincere partners forever: speech at the Julius Nyerere International Convention Center in Dar es Salaam, Tanzania. *People's Daily*, March 26, 2013.
Xi, Jinping. October 13, 2009. Strengthen cultural exchange and promote world peace: speech at the opening ceremony of the 61th Frankfurt International Book Fair. *People's Daily*, October 14, 2009.
Xin, Xiangyang. 2014. Three basic questions on advancing state governance system and governance capability. *Theoretical Investigation* 02: 27–31.
Yan, Zhonglin. 2006. Energy strategy of China in a "big regional environment" with the Middle East and Central Asia. *Journal of Harbin Institute of Technology* (Social Sciences Edition).
Young, A. 1928. Increasing returns and economic progress. *The Economic Journal* 38: 527–542.
Yu, Keping. 2000. *Governance and Good Governance*. Social Sciences Academic Press.
Yu, Keping. 2013. Basic standard to measure the modernization of state governance system. *Beijing Daily*, December 9, 2013.
Yu, Yixuan. 2013. On China's identity as a developing country, *Fudan International Studies Review*.
Zhang, Yuyan. 2003. The influence of war on economy. *International Economic Review*, No. 2, 11–13.
Zhang, Yuyan. 2003. Double-headed snake, spider and dragon. *Du Shu* 8.
Zhang, Shuhua. 2010. Mrs. Thatcher on the downfall of the Soviet Union. *Red Flag Files*, No. 11, 36–37.
Zhang, Yuyan. 2013. Global governance: Balance between common interests and conflicting interests. *IPER Observations*, No. 1322.
Zhang, Yuyan. 2014. Periods of important strategic opportunities: exogenous and endogenous. *World Economics and Politic*s, No. 1.
Zhang, Yuyan. 2016. Global governance: coexistence of human common interests and conflicts. *Exploration and Free Views*, No. 5
Zhang, Yuyan. 2016. Global governance: a Chinese perspective. *World Economics and Politics* 9: 5.
Zhang Shuhua and Wang Wen'e. 2010. A research on the authenticity of Mrs. Thatcher's 1991 Huston Speech. *Red Flag Files*, No. 23.
Zhang, Yuyan, 2013. Setting up foreign strategies of China based on its national interests. *Contemporary International Relations*, 10.
Zhang, Yuyan and Gao Cheng. 2004. *American Bullion and the Rise of the Western World*. Citic Press Group.
Zhang, Lu and Huang Ji. 2007. Australia in China's regional strategy: a new exploration of the strategic concept of "big regional environment" and diplomatic planning. *Contemporary International Relations*, No. 2.
Zhang, Yuyan and Li Zenggang. 2008. *International Economy and Politics*. Shanghai: Shanghai People's Press.
Zhang, Yuyan and Ren Lin. 2015. Global governance: a framework for theoretical analysis. *Quarterly Journal of International Politics* 3: 1–29.
Zhao, Dingxin. Will revolution happen in China today?. *21st Century*, December, 2012.
Zheng, Xinli. China has a great potential in becoming a high-income country, *Reference News*, April 7, 2016.
Zheng, Yongnian, China needs philosophical thinking over Sino-US relationship, *Lianhe Zaobao*, September 4, 2012.

English References

A Michael Spence, "The Impact of Globalization on Income and Employment", *Foreign Affairs*, July/August, 2011.
A Doak Barnett, "After Deng, What? Will China follow the USSR?", *China Quarterly*, 1992.
Abdel Aziz Aluwaisheg, "China's New Silk Road Initiatives: A GCC Perspective", *Arab News*, January 17, 2014, http://www.highbeam.com/doc/1G1-357344793.html.
Acemoglu D, Robison J.A., "Economic backwardness in political perspective", *American Political Science Review*, 100 (01), 2006.
Alastair I Johnston, *Cultural Realism: Strategic Culture and Grand Strategy in Chinese History*, Princeton, NJ: Princeton University Press, 1995.
Andrew Scobell, *China and Strategy Culture*, Honolulu: University Press of the Pacific, 2002.
Ariel H Ko, "Not for Political Domination: China's Foreign Economic Policy towards Vietnam, Singapore, and Malaysia in the Open Era", http://theses.gla.ac.uk/2235/.
Arvind Subramanian and Martin Kessler, "China's Currency Rises in the US Backyard", *Financial Times*, October 21, 2006.
Charles R Morris, *We Were Pirates, too: China is Stealing Our Trade Secrets just as We Stole Britain's.* December 16, 2012, http://www.postgazette.com/stories/opinion/perspectives/we-were-pirates-too-china-is-stealing-our-trade-secrets-just-as-we-stole-britains-666529/#ixzz-2aCgncdrg.
Clarke, R, "China's cyberassault on America", *Wall Street Journal*, June 15, 2011.
Dan Blumenthal and Joseph Lin, "Oil Obsession: Energy Appetite Fuels Beijing's Plans to Protect Vital Sea Lines", *Armed Forces Journal*, June, 2006.
Daniyar Mukhtarov, "Kazakhstan Considers Its Participation in Silk Road Economic Belt Project", Trend, January 10, 2014, http://en.trend.az/casia/kazakhstan/2228894.html.
David C. Gompert, Astrid Cevallos, Cristina L. Garafola, *War with China Thinking Through the Unthinkable*, Published by the RAND Corporation, Santa Monica, Calif., 2016. http://www.rand.org/content/dam/rand/pubs/research_reports/RR1100/RR1140/RAND_RR1140.pdf.
D. Hormats, "Ensuring a Sound Basis for Global Competition: Competitive Neutrality", *DipNote*, May 6, 2011, https://blogs.state.gov/stories/2011/05/06/ensuring-sound-basis-global-competition-competitive-neutrality.
Derek M. Scissors, *Will China's economy be #1 by Dec.31? (And does it matter?)*, 1st May, 2014. http://www.aei.org/article/economics/international-economy/will-chinas-economy-be-1-by-dec-31-and-does-it-matter.
Douglas, J.K., Nelson, M.B., & Schwartz, K., *Fueling the Dragon's flame: How China's energy demands affect its relationships in the Middle East*, US-China Economic and Security Review Commission, 2006.
Doyle McManus. Clinton and Trump will be held to different debate standards, but that's OK", *Los Angeles Times*. September 25, 2016.
Dreher, Axel, and Nathan M. Jensen, "Independent Actor or Agent? An Empirical Analysis of the Impact of U.S. Interests on International Monetary Fund Conditions", *The Journal of Law and Economics*, 50 (1), 2007.
E. Medalla, and J.D. Balboa, "The Impact of ASEAN China FTA Early Harvest Program: the Case of the Philippines with Focus on Short run Effects on the Agriculture Sector", Research Paper Series, 2007, http://ideas.repec.org/b/phd/rpseri/rps_2007-01.html.
Etzioni, A, "Accommodating China", *Survival: Global Politics and Strategy*, 2 (55), 2013.
Fleck, Robert K., and Christopher Kilby, "World Bank Independence: A Model and Statistical Analysis of US Influence", *Review of Development Economics*, 10 (2), 2006.
Francis B, *Gummere*, Beowulf, Wildside Press LLC, 2008.
Gallagher, K., & Porzecanski, R., *The Dragon in the Room: China and the Future of Latin American Industrialization*, Stanford University Press, 2010.

Gertz, Bill, *The China Threat: How the People's Republic Targets America*, Regnery Publishing, 2013.
Gomez, M.A., *Awaken the Cyber Dragon: China's Cyber Strategy and Its Impact on ASEAN*, 2013.
Guthrie, D., *China and Globalization: The Social, Economic and Political Transformation of Chinese Society*, Routledge, 2012.
Hans, J. Morgenthau, *Politics Among Nations: The Struggle for Power and Peace (Fifth Edition)*, New York: Alfred A. Knopf, 1973.
Harry Harding, "The Concept of 'Greater China': Themes, Variations and Reservations", in David Shambaugh (ed.), *Greater China: The Next Superpower?*, New York: Oxford University Press, 1995. Nye, Joseph "Only China Can Contain China." *The Huffington Post*, Accessed July 14, 2015. http://www.huffingtonpost.com/joseph-nye/china-contain-china_b_6845588.html.
Hillary Rodham Clinton, "America's Pacific Century", *Foreign Policy*, October 11, 2011.
Hjortdal, M., "China's Use of Cyber Warfare: Espionage Meets Strategic Deterrence", *Journal of Strategic Security*, 4 (2), 2011.
Jacques Pelkmans. 2001. European Integration: Methods and Economic Analysis. *Financial Times/Prentice Hall*, p. 3.
Jacques, M., *When China Rules The World: The End of the Western World and the Birth of a New Global Order* [*Greatly Expanded and Fully Updated*], Penguin Books Limited, 2012.
Jae-Hyung, "China's Expanding Maritime Ambitions in the Western Pacific and the Indian Ocean", *Contemporary Southeast Asia*, Vol. 24, No. 3, 2002.
Jason Dedrick, "Who Profits from Innovation in Global Value Chains? iPhones and Windmills", http://www.usitc.gov/research_and_analysis/documents/Dedrick_USITC_3-21-12_0.pdf.
Jeffrey Frankel, "China is not yet number one", 9th May, 2014, http://www.voxeu.org/article/china-not-yet-number-one.
Jérémie Cohen-Setton, "China's GDP (PPP) to surpass the United States?". 12th May, 2014, http://www.bruegel.org/nc/blog/detail/article/1328-blogs-review-chinas-gdp-ppp-to-surpass-the-united-states/.
Jian, Chen., "A Response: How to Pursue a Critical History of Mao's Foreign Policy", *The China Journal*, 49, 2003.
Joshua Cooper Ramo, The Beijing Consensus, the Foreign Policy Centre, 2004, http://fpc.org.uk/fsblob/244.pdf.
Justyna Szczudlik Tatar, "China's New Silk Road Diplomacy", PISM Policy Paper No. 34 (82), 2013, Available at: https://www.pism.pl/files/?id_plik=15818.
Kal Raustiala and Christopher Sprigman, "Fake It Till You Make It: The Good News About China's Knockoff Economy", *Foreign Affairs,* Volume 92, Number 4. Aug/Jul, 2013.
Kevin Rudd. "China under Xi Jinping: Alternative Futures for U.S.-China Relations", Match 2015, http://csis.org/files/publication/150313_rudd_speeches.pdf.
Kissinger, H., *On China*, New York: the Penguin Press, 2011.
Kuznets S., "Economic growth and income inequality", *The American economic review*, 1955.
Kynge, J., *China Shakes the World: A Titan's Rise and Troubled Future - And the Challenge for America,* Houghton Mifflin Harcourt, 2007.
Lai, David, "Coming of Chinese Hawk", *Carlisle*, Pennsylvania: Strategic Studies Institute, 2010.
Laurance, W., "Hungry dragon", *Australian Geographic*, 2012.
Mayer, M., & Wübbeke, J., "Understanding China's International Energy Strategy", *The Chinese Journal of International Politics*, Autumn 6(3), 2013.
Medeiros, Evan S., and M. Taylor Fravel, "China's New Diplomacy", *Foreign Affairs*, 82 (6), 2003.
Michael T. Klare, *Rising Powers, Shrinking Planet: The New Geopolitics of Energy*. New York: Metropolitan Books, 2008.
Myrdal, G., Myrdal Gunnar, *Economic Theory and Underdeveloped Regions*, Gerald Duckworth, 1957.
Nolan, P., *Is China Buying the World?*, Cambridge, UK; Malden, MA: Polity Press, 2012.

Ogden, D., *Dragons, Serpents, and Slayers in the Classical and Early Christian Worlds: A Sourcebook,* Oxford University Press, 2013.

Olson M., "Rapid Growth as a Destabilizing Force", *The Journal of Economic History*, 23 (04), 1963.

Overholt, William H., *China and Globalization*, Santa Monica, CA: RAND Corporation, 2005, http://www.rand.org/pubs/testimonies/CT244.html.

Paul Kennedy, *The Rise and Fall of the Great Powers: Economic Change and Military Conflict from 1500 to 2000*, New York: Random House, 1987.

Peet, Richard, *Unholy Trinity: The IMF, World Bank and WTO*, Zed Books, 2003.

Peter Navarro, *Death by China: Confronting the Dragon – A Global Call to Action*, New Jersey: Person Prentice Hall, 2011.

Pillsbury, Michael, *The Hundred-year Marathon: China's Secret Strategy to Replace America as the Global Superpower*, Henry Holt and Company, 2015. pp. 7–8.

Reuters, "China President Xi Jinping Tells Donald Trump the 2 Countries Must Cooperate", *Fortune*. November 14, 2016. http://fortune.com/2016/11/14/china-president-xi-jinping-donald-trump-cooperation/Robert.

Rhodes, R.A.W. 1996. The new governance: governing without government. *Political Studies* 44: 652–667.

Robert Wielaard, "Greece Debt Crisis: Germany Holding up European Union Bailout", *The Huffington Post*, March 19, 2010.

Shambaugh, D.L., *Tangled Titans: The United States and China*, Rowman & Littlefield, 2013.

Stephen G. Brooks and William C. Wohlforth, "The Once and Future Superpower: Why China Won't Overtake the United States", *Foreign Affairs*, Volume 95, Number 3, 2016.

Storey, I., and Yee, H., *The China Threat: Perceptions, Myths and Reality*, Routledge, 2002.

Subramanian, A., *Eclipse: Living in the Shadow of China's Economic Dominance*, Peterson Institute, 2011.

Swaine, M.D., "Perceptions of an assertive China", *China Leadership Monitor*, 32 (2), 2010.

Timperlake, E., & II, W.C.T., *Red Dragon Rising: Communist China's Military Threat to America*, Regnery Publishing, 2002.

Uckert, M.B., *China As an Economic and Military Superpower: A Dangerous Combination?*, BiblioBazaar, 2012.

Wade, Robert Hunter, "US hegemony and the World Bank: The Fight over People and Ideas", *Review of International Political Economy*, 9 (2), 2002.

Williams, David and Tom Young. 1994. Governance, the World Bank and liberal theory. *Political Studies* 42: 84–100.

Williamson, J., "What should the World Bank Think about the Washington Consensus?", T*he World Bank Research Observer*, 15 (2), 2000.

Woods, N., "The United States and the International Financial Institutions: Power and influence within the World Bank and the IMF." Foot, McFarlane and Mastanduno (Eds), US Hegemony and International Organizations, Oxford, 2003.

Zoellick, Robert B., "U.S., China and Thucydides", *The National Interest*, 2014, Accessed October 4, http://nationalinterest.org/article/us-china-thucydides-8642.

Zsolt Darvas, "Fiscal Federalism in Crisis: Some Facts and Lessons; From the US to Europe," *Forthcoming Bruegel Policy Contribution*, June 10, 2010.

Index

Y. Zhang and W. Feng, *Peaceful Development Path in China*, China Insights,
https://doi.org/10.1007/978-981-13-1439-1

MIX
Papier aus verantwortungsvollen Quellen
Paper from responsible sources
FSC® C105338

If you have any concerns about our products,
you can contact us on
ProductSafety@springernature.com

In case Publisher is established outside the EU,
the EU authorized representative is:
Springer Nature Customer Service Center GmbH
Europaplatz 3, 69115 Heidelberg, Germany

Printed by Libri Plureos GmbH
in Hamburg, Germany